Royal Canadian Air Force Headquarters (RCAF HQ)
Ottawa, Ontario

Air Staff
Canadian Space Operations Centre
Air Reserve Flight

RCAF Aerospace Warfare Centre (RAWC)
Trenton, Ontario

414 Electronic Warfare Support Squadron (at Ottawa, Ont.)
434 Operational Test and Evaluation Squadron

1 Canadian Air Division Headquarters (1 CAD HQ)
Canadian NORAD Region Headquarters (CANR HQ)
Joint Force Air Component Commander (JFACC)
Winnipeg, Manitoba

Combined Aerospace Operations Centre
Detachment 1, First Air Force (United States Air Force)
Aerospace and Telecommunications Engineering Support Squadron (ATESS) (at Trenton, Ont.)
1 Canadian Air Division Air Reserve Flight

1 Wing Kingston
(A lodger unit of Canadian Forces Base Kingston, Ont.)
Kingston, Ontario

400 Tactical Helicopter Squadron (CH-146 Griffon) (at Borden, Ont.)
403 Helicopter Operational Training Squadron (CH-146 Griffon) (at Gagetown, N.B.)
408 Tactical Helicopter Squadron (CH-146 Griffon) (at Edmonton, Alta.)
427 Special Operations Aviation Squadron (CH-146 Griffon) (at Petawawa, Ont.)
430 Tactical Helicopter Squadron (CH-146 Griffon) (at Valcartier, Que.)
438 Tactical Helicopter Squadron (CH-146 Griffon) (at Saint-Hubert, Que.)
450 Tactical Helicopter Squadron (CH-147F Chinook) (at Petawawa, Ont.)
1 Wing Air Reserve Flight

2 Wing Bagotville
(A lodger unit of Canadian Forces Base Bagotville, Que.)
Bagotville, Quebec

4 Construction Engineering Squadron (4 CES) (at Cold Lake, Alta.)
8 Air Communications and Control Squadron (8 ACCS) (at Trenton, Ont.)

3 Wing / Canadian Forces Base Bagotville
Bagotville, Quebec

425 Tactical Fighter Squadron (CF-188 Hornet)
433 Tactical Fighter Squadron (CF-188 Hornet)
439 Combat Support Squadron (CH-146 Griffon)
3 Air Maintenance Squadron
12 Radar Squadron
Forward Operating Location (FOL) (at Iqaluit, Nvt.)
3 Wing Air Reserve Flight

4 Wing / Canadian Forces Base Cold Lake
Cold Lake, Alberta

401 Tactical Fighter Squadron (CF-188 Hornet)
409 Tactical Fighter Squadron (CF-188 Hornet)
410 Tactical Fighter (Operational Training) Squadron (CF-188 Hornet)
417 Combat Support Squadron (CH-146 Griffon)
419 Tactical Fighter Training Squadron (CT-155 Hawk)
1 Air Maintenance Squadron
10 Field Technical Training Squadron
42 Radar Squadron
Forward Operating Location (FOL) (at Inuvik, N.W.T.)
Forward Operating Location (FOL) (at Yellowknife, N.W.T.)
4 Wing Air Reserve Flight

5 Wing / Canadian Forces Base Goose Bay
Goose Bay, Newfoundland and Labrador

444 Combat Support Squadron (CH-146 Griffon)
Forward Operating Location (FOL) (at Goose Bay, N.L.)
5 Wing Air Reserve Flight

8 Wing / Canadian Forces Base Trenton
Trenton, Ontario

412 Transport Squadron (CC-144 Challenger) (at Ottawa, Ont.)
424 Transport and Rescue Squadron (CH-146 Griffon, CC-130H Hercules, and CC-295*)
426 Transport Training Squadron (CC-130H/J Hercules and CC-150 Polaris)
429 Transport Squadron (CC-177 Globemaster III)
436 Transport Squadron (CC-130J Hercules)
437 Transport Squadron (CC-150 Polaris)
440 Transport Squadron (CC-138 Twin Otter) (at Yellowknife, N.W.T.)
2 Air Movements Squadron
8 Air Maintenance Squadron
8 Construction Engineering Squadron
Canadian Forces Station Alert (CFS Alert) (at Alert, Nvt.)
Multi-Engine Utility Flight (BE-350 King Air)
8 Wing Air Reserve Flight

9 Wing / Canadian Forces Base Gander
Gander, Newfoundland and Labrador

103 Search and Rescue Squadron (CH-149 Cormorant)
Air Reserve Flight Torbay (ARF Torbay) (at Torbay, N.L.)
9 Wing Air Reserve Flight

12 Wing Shearwater
(A lodger unit of Canadian Forces Base Halifax, N.S.)
Shearwater, Nova Scotia

406 Maritime Operational Training Squadron (CH-148 Cyclone)
423 Maritime Helicopter Squadron (CH-148 Cyclone)
443 Maritime Helicopter Squadron (CH-148 Cyclone) (at Patricia Bay, B.C.)
12 Air Maintenance Squadron
12 Wing Air Reserve Flight

14 Wing / Canadian Forces Base Greenwood
Greenwood, Nova Scotia

404 Long Range Patrol and Training Squadron (CP-140 Aurora)
405 Long Range Patrol Squadron (CP-140 Aurora)
413 Transport and Rescue Squadron (CH-149 Cormorant, CC-130H Hercules, and CC-295*)
415 Long Range Patrol Force Development Squadron
14 Air Maintenance Squadron
14 Construction Engineering Squadron (14 CES) (at Bridgewater, N.S.)
91 Construction Engineering Flight (91 CEF) (at Gander, N.L.)
143 Construction Engineering Flight (143 CEF) (at Lunenburg, N.S.)
144 Construction Engineering Flight (144 CEF) (at Pictou, N.S.)
192 Construction Engineering Flight (192 CEF) (at Aldergrove, B.C.)
14 Wing Air Reserve Flight

19 Wing / Canadian Forces Base Comox
Comox, British Columbia

407 Long Range Patrol Squadron (CP-140 Aurora)
418 Search and Rescue Operational Training Squadron (CC-295*)
435 Transport and Rescue Squadron (CC-130H Hercules and CC-295*) (at Winnipeg, Man.)
442 Transport and Rescue Squadron (CC-115 Buffalo, CH-149 Cormorant, and CC-295*)
19 Air Maintenance Squadron
Canadian Forces School of Search and Rescue
19 Wing Air Reserve Flight

22 Wing / Canadian Forces Base North Bay
North Bay, Ontario

Canadian Air Defence Sector Headquarters
Detachment 2, First Air Force (United States Air Force)
21 Aerospace Control and Warning Squadron
51 Aerospace Control and Warning Operational Training Squadron
22 Wing Air Reserve Flight

2 Canadian Air Division Headquarters (2 CAD HQ)
Winnipeg, Manitoba

Canadian Forces Aircrew Selection Centre (CFASC) (at Trenton, Ont.)

15 Wing / Canadian Forces Base Moose Jaw
Moose Jaw, Saskatchewan

431 Air Demonstration Squadron – "The Snowbirds" (CT-114 Tutor)
2 Canadian Forces Flying Training School (CT-155 Hawk and CT-156 Harvard II)
3 Canadian Forces Flying Training School (3 CFFTS) (CH-139 Jet Ranger, Grob-G120A, C-90B King Air, and Bell 412CF) (at Portage la Prairie, Man.)
15 Wing Air Reserve Flight

16 Wing Borden
(A lodger unit of Canadian Forces Base Borden, Ont.)
Borden, Ontario

Canadian Forces School of Aerospace Control Operations (CFSACO) (at Cornwall, Ont.)
Canadian Forces School of Aerospace Technology and Engineering
Royal Canadian Air Force Academy
16 Wing Air Reserve Flight

17 Wing / Canadian Forces Base Winnipeg
Winnipeg, Manitoba

402 Squadron (CT-142 Dash-8)
Canadian Forces School of Survival and Aeromedical Training
RCAF W/C William G. Barker VC Aerospace College
Royal Canadian Air Force Band
17 Wing Air Reserve Flight

T0366480

*The CC-295 will be phased in at these locations.

PATHWAY TO THE STARS

PATHWAY TO THE STARS

100 YEARS OF THE ROYAL CANADIAN AIR FORCE

MICHAEL HOOD AND **TOM JENKINS**

ÆVO UTP

RCAF Foundation/Fondation de l'ARC

The RCAF Foundation, a non-profit organization established in 2021, works to recognize, foster and celebrate the Royal Canadian Air Force (RCAF) through community engagement, education programs, and commemorative activities. Its goal is to inspire Canadians, particularly youth, to learn about and support this important national institution and to highlight the future of aviation, ensuring its dynamic growth and expansion.

Proceeds from this book will support the ongoing operations and programs of the RCAF Foundation, which at the time of publication include: annual scholarships for post-secondary students pursuing careers in the aviation and aerospace sector; refurbishment of historical monuments and aircraft; digital exhibitions, podcasts and campaigns highlighting stories of Canada's aviation history and future; an annual Remembrance Day ceremony and other events across Canada; and special programming for the 100th anniversary of the RCAF.

Inaugural Board of Directors: John Wright (Chair), Patrick Shea (Secretary and Treasurer), Mike Bonner, Mina Farinacci, Michael Jenkins, Kristin Long, and Gérard Poitras.

Inaugural Advisory Council: Dean Black, Bruce Bowser, Stewart Burton, David Bruce Cochrane, Aja Davis, Drew Hamblin, Penny Hicks, Kendra Kincade, Graham MacLachlan, George Nutter, Stephen Quick, Terry Slobodian, Renee van Kessel, and Tonya Yearwood.

Jeremy Diamond, *CEO*
Jennifer Blake, *Digital & Social Lead*

Learn more about the RCAF Foundation at rcaffoundation.ca and on social media @rcaf_foundation

RCAF FOUNDATION
FONDATION de l'ARC

Aevo UTP
An imprint of University of Toronto Press
Toronto Buffalo London
utorontopress.com

Library and Archives Canada Cataloguing in Publication

Title: Pathway to the stars : 100 years of the Royal Canadian Air Force / Michael Hood and Tom Jenkins.
Names: Hood, Michael (Retired lieutenant general), author. | Jenkins, Tom, 1959–, author.
Description: Includes bibliographical references.
Identifiers: Canadiana (print) 20230501141 | Canadiana (ebook) 20230501176 | ISBN 9781487547431 (hardcover) | ISBN 9781487547721 (PDF) | ISBN 9781487547714 (EPUB)
Subjects: LCSH: Canada. Royal Canadian Air Force—History. | LCSH: Canada. Royal Canadian Air Force—Pictorial works.
Classification: LCC UG635.C2 H66 2023 | DDC 358.400971—dc23

ISBN 978-1-4875-4743-1 (cloth)   ISBN 978-1-4875-4771-4 (EPUB)
                                         ISBN 978-1-4875-4772-1 (PDF)

Printed in Canada

Cover design: Michel Vrana
Cover images: (Front) A Royal Canadian Air Force CF-18 Hornet Pilot takes off for a combat training flight during Operation REASSURANCE, Air Task Force Romania, on September 28, 2020 at Mihail Kogălniceanu Air Base, Romania. Photo by S1 Zach Barr Air Task Force Romania, Department of National Defence (DND). (Front background) iStock.com/Carlos Aguilar. (Back cover, clockwise) DND, Corporal Alana Morin, Royal Canadian Air Force Public Affairs Imagery, FA03-2017-0114-171; DND, Master Corporal Johanie Maheu, 14 Wing Imaging Greenwood, GD2016-0075-31; DND, PL-16961; No. 111 Squadron RCAF Pilots: Skelly, Crowley, McLeod, Merkley, Gooding, Hicks, and Gohl in Stusiak, Alaska, July 1943, DND, PMR 76-212.

We wish to acknowledge the land on which the University of Toronto Press operates. This land is the traditional territory of the Wendat, the Anishnaabeg, the Haudenosaunee, the Métis, and the Mississaugas of the Credit First Nation.

University of Toronto Press acknowledges the financial support of the Government of Canada, the Canada Council for the Arts, and the Ontario Arts Council, an agency of the Government of Ontario, for its publishing activities.

This book is dedicated to the brave men and women of the Royal Canadian Air Force who have answered the call and put themselves in harm's way to protect and defend Canada, both at home and abroad, for the last 100 years. Your skill, daring, and determination are a great source of pride and inspiration for all Canadians.

Sic Itur ad Astra – Such is the Pathway to the Stars

CONTENTS

Opposite: Lockheed Martin F-35A.

ABOUT THE AUTHORS

Michael Hood
Lieutenant-General (Retired), CMM, CD

Mike enjoyed the great honour of Commanding the RCAF from 2015 to 2018. As RCAF Commander, he had three focus areas: people, operations, and innovation. Ensuring the well-being of the thousands of men and women serving in the RCAF remained one of the top priorities during his time in command. Initiatives to improve access to health care and childcare for RCAF families figured prominently, ensuring Air Force personnel had a strong support network at home while deployed. Being the guarantor of Canadian sovereignty meant unwavering support to RCAF continental operations, concomitantly delivering excellence on global peace and security missions. As Commander, he also championed the Air Force's first innovation strategy, which fostered key partnerships within the industry, including a permanent presence at Communitech, the innovation hub based in Waterloo, Ontario. Understanding that the future of the RCAF's success lay in its youngest and newest members, he championed initiatives like "Great ideas have no rank" and created the RCAF Vector Check, a "Dragon's Den" where anyone in the Air Force, irrespective of rank or experience, could pitch ideas straight to senior leadership.

Prior to his time in command of the RCAF, Mike held senior executive positions in acquisition, strategic planning, international security policy, and national security—where he helped shape the Government of Canada's response to numerous global security crises as Director of the Strategic Joint Staff. His early to mid-career was spent as an Air Combat Systems Officer on the CC-130 Hercules, flying tactical air mobility operations, including extensive time operating in Canada's Arctic, Europe, Africa, and the Middle East. He was also fortunate to spend a large part of his career at 8 Wing in Trenton, Ontario—the RCAF's largest base—where he commanded both 429 and 436 Transport Squadrons. He also commanded the Wing from 2007 to 2009.

Following retirement from the RCAF in 2018, Mike was an executive in the resource sector and now is a consultant, primarily in the aerospace sector. His dreams of improving his golf game following retirement remain unfortunately unfulfilled.

P. Thomas Jenkins

OC, VBO, CD, CBHOF, FCAE

Tom Jenkins has been affiliated with the Royal Canadian Air Force for more than 50 years and began his career with the RCAF as a Royal Canadian Air Cadet in CFB Trenton in 1972. He became a Squadron Warrant Officer with the Air Cadets at CRRB Hamilton and later joined the reserves first as a Corporal and then as an Officer. He received his commission in 1977 and served in CFB Cold Lake. Tom has also been the Honorary Colonel of 409 Squadron in CFB Cold Lake and the Honorary Colonel of the Royal Highland Fusiliers of Canada in Cambridge. Mr. Jenkins chaired a report on Defence Procurement for the Governement of Canada. He is currently a member of the RCAF Commanders Advisory Council.

In civilian life, Mr. Jenkins is Chair of the Board of OpenText, a Waterloo based software company listed on the NASDAQ. He previously served as Chief Executive Officer and Chief Technology Officer from 1994 to 2013. Mr. Jenkins is Chair of the World Wide Web Foundation and a Commissioner of the Tri-Lateral Commission. Mr. Jenkins has also served as a board member of Manulife Financial Corporation, Thomson Reuters Inc., and TransAlta Corporation. He was also past Chair of the Ontario Global 100 and past Canadian Co-Chair of the Atlantik Bruecke. He was the tenth Chancellor of the University of Waterloo, the Chair of the National Research Council of Canada, and a founder of Communitech, the incubator organization in Waterloo.

Mr. Jenkins received an MBA from Schulich School of Business at York University, an MASc from the University of Toronto and a BEng & Mgt from McMaster University. Mr. Jenkins has received honorary doctorates from six universities. He is a member of the Waterloo Region Entrepreneur Hall of Fame, a Companion of the Canadian Business Hall of Fame and recipient of the Ontario Entrepreneur of the Year Award, the McMaster Engineering L.W. Shemilt Distinguished Alumni Award, and the Schulich School of Business Outstanding Executive Leadership Award. He is a Fellow of the Canadian Academy of Engineering. Mr. Jenkins was awarded the Canadian Forces Decoration, the Queen's Diamond Jubilee Medal, and the Cross of the Order of Merit of the Federal Republic of Germany. Mr. Jenkins is an Officer of the Order of Canada.

Tom loves to hike mountains with his family and tries his best to go to a new range every year.

FOREWORD

April 1, 2024 marks the 100th anniversary of a richly storied organization: the Royal Canadian Air Force or RCAF.

We are pleased to take you on a remarkable journey spanning 100 years of the RCAF—the people, the aircraft, and the operations. *Pathway to the Stars: 100 Years of the Royal Canadian Air Force* is a story about courage, innovation, loyalty, honour, and sacrifice, but mostly, it describes a history created by some of Canada's most visionary and courageous problem solvers.

It is also a book of firsts. The RCAF contributed many advances in aviation over the past 100 years, from helping to invent the G-suit to developing the first helicopter landing system on a naval ship, to designing the first flight safety organization to investigate crashes.

It is a story about Canada and its place in the world over the past century. From humble beginnings at the birth of the first heavier-than-air flight, to global humanitarian assistance, to endeavours that reached beyond the limits of the earth itself.

The RCAF's story unfolds at a time of great tragedy. In the midst of the First World War, a small group of Canadians within the British Empire began to experiment with a new form of combat: dogfighting. These pilots were similar to medieval knights that jousted in another era. Names such as Barker and Bishop would become known as legends in this nascent group of Canadian aviators.

From these auspicious beginnings, the RCAF was formally created by royal decree in 1924 and would soon come into its own during another great conflict, the Second World War. During this war, Canada contributed well beyond its weight in support of combat operations globally through the creation, implementation, and operation of a massive air training organization for the entire British Commonwealth. The endeavour helped to secure peace for the Allies and left a legacy of aviation that exists to this day. At the end of this war, Canada would have the fourth-largest air force in the world, setting the stage for the RCAF's key role in the postwar period, the creation of NATO and NORAD, and throughout the duration of the Cold War.

Aircrew and groundcrew of 433 Squadron in front of their Halifax bomber "Pride of the Porcupines."

The history of the RCAF is best described as a unique combination of people and technology that were shaped by global events. Whether it was fighting in the air in a Hurricane in the Battle of Britain, or delivering disaster relief around the globe, or leading search and rescue operations in Canada's arctic, the missions required of the RCAF have challenged the people of Canada to create aircraft, machines, and other technologies to persevere and succeed.

In story after story, you will find the consistent "can do" nature of the RCAF that exists to this very day. There is a consistency in the actions of the people of the RCAF that transcends the skill and requirements for the job; this is something distinct about who they are and what drove them to succeed. This is the essence of the Canadian spirit.

The people of the RCAF are innovators, fiercely breaking barriers, glass ceilings, and records. They never quit but went about their business in a very Canadian way: with a quiet confidence, understated courage, and a calm demeanour. Through their actions and contributions they emboldened the "providence of now," advancing both the RCAF and the aviation industry in Canada forward through the decades, regardless of the situation and events.

When a country called for help during war or peace, the RCAF answered and delivered on the mission.

The RCAF leaned on Canadian industry and resources to help, whether it was an indigenously designed and produced Fleet Finch biplane used in the British Commonwealth Air Training Plan or encouraging the first ever female pararescue nurses to join search and rescue, the RCAF got the job done where and when it was needed.

Pathway to the Stars: 100 Years of the Royal Canadian Air Force also explores the future trajectory of the RCAF. As the world looks beyond the earth into space, the RCAF will play an increasing role in developing new technologies and capabilities to project Canadian interests and ensure Canadian sovereignty, whether it be in the high Arctic, along our coastlines, or in the heart of Canada.

The RCAF is an organization with a proud tradition of problem solvers at every level, from administration to engineering to aerospace and beyond. The characteristics that drove the achievements embodied in this book will continue to serve the RCAF and Canada with excellence into the next hundred years.

Lieutenant-General Eric Kenny

CMM, MSC, MSM, CD

Commander of the Royal Canadian Air Force

ACKNOWLEDGEMENTS

Contributors

We would like to thank the following people for their time, energy, and efforts in telling the stories of the Royal Canadian Air Force: Chris Albinson, John Albinson, Bethany Aitchison, Christine Aquino, Larry Ashley, Christine Balasch, David J. Bercuson, Dave Birrell, Jennifer Blake, Martin Breton, Lloyd Campbell, Scott Clancy, James Craik, Louis Cuppens, Al DeQuetteville, Andre Deschamps, Steven P. Deschamps, Jeremy Diamond, S.E. (Steven) Dieter, Shayne Elder, Marg Emery, Philip Engstad, Rick Findley, Billie Flynn, D.W. Forbes, David Fraser, Ryan Goldsworthy, Andrew Gregory, Erin Gregory, Ronda Hicks (Slaunwhite), David Huddleston, Len Husband, Shannyn Johnson, Paul Johnston, Emily Jolliffe, Mireille Khouri, Christopher Kitzan, Karl Kjarsgaard, Peter Krayer, Janet LaCroix, Denis Langlois, Tom Lawson, Steven Leclair, Emily Lindahl, Lloyd Lovatt, David W. Lowthian, Shawn MacNeil, Jadene Mah, Paul Manson, Christian Martel, Richard Mayne, Karen McCrimmon, Mouhab Meshreki, Al Mickeloff, Robert Mitchell, Stephanie Muloin, Erin Napier, Danielle Nasrallah, Tammy Negraeff, Keith C. Ogilvie, Paul Ormsby, Fred Paradie, Bruno Paulhus, Prakash Patnaik, Walt Pirie, William Radiff, John Roeterink, David Rohrer, Susan Scarborough, Harold Skaarup, Kirk Shaw, Tom Slater, Deborah Slaunwhite, Don Slaunwhite, Michael W. Slaunwhite, Patricia Slaunwhite, Ron Slaunwhite, Brad St. Croix, Iain Stewart, Nancy Tremblay, Anu A. Vashisht, Randall Wakelam, Kevin Windsor, John Wright, Ibrahim Yimer, Fred Zeggil, and Matthijs Zwaal.

A sincere thank you to The Right Honourable David Johnston, PC, CC, CMM, COM, CD, FRSC, FRCPSC, Governor General of Canada, 2010–2017, for his collaboration on Chapter 8, "Reflecting on the Impact of the RCAF: Canada and the World."

Thanks to Elizabeth Chestney-Hanson, editor, Brandon Radic for layout and design, and Joe Dwyer for image collection and project management.

We would also like to thank the Royal Canadian Air Force, the Royal Canadian Air Force Association, and the following organizations for all their assistance: the Billy Bishop Museum, the Bomber Command Museum, the Canadian Aviation and Space Museum, the Canadian Forces Museum of Aerospace Defence, the Canadian Space Agency, the Canadian Warplane Heritage Museum, Library and Archives Canada, the National Air Force Museum of Canada, the National Research Council of Canada, the Royal Canadian Military Institute, and the Royal Aviation Museum of Western Canada.

CHAPTER 1
THE ORIGIN OF THE RCAF
The First World War through to 1938

Opposite: 1928 propeller swinging class.

THE ORIGIN OF THE RCAF
THE FIRST WORLD WAR THROUGH TO 1938

Over the past 100 years, the history of the Royal Canadian Air Force (RCAF) has been inextricably linked to the rise of aviation in Canada. Aviation took off in Canada—literally—with the first powered, heavier-than-air flight made in the British Empire. In 1909, five years after the Wright brothers' famed flight in Kitty Hawk, North Carolina, Douglas McCurdy flew the Silver Dart over a frozen lake in Baddeck, Nova Scotia. The plane was designed and built by Alexander Graham Bell and his Aerial Experiment Association. Based on its success, McCurdy and his partner F.W. "Casey" Baldwin formed the Canadian Aerodrome Company and pitched the aircraft to Canada's Department of Militia and Defence. They were invited to fly the Silver Dart in military trials at Camp Petawawa. The plane failed to captivate the Canadian Army after a number of crashes. The government's interest in military aviation would not be rekindled until the First World War.

When Canada entered the First World War on August 4, 1914, air defence was not considered an important capability for the military. However, after noticing that some European countries were using aircraft during the war, Canada's Minister of Militia and Defence, Sir Sam Hughes, authorized the creation of the Canadian Aviation Corps (CAC). The absurdly small unit, made up of two officers and one mechanic, would accompany the Canadian Expeditionary Force (CEF) overseas. It was given $5,000 to outfit itself with an aircraft. In October 1914, the CAC purchased a Burgess-Dunne biplane, Canada's first official military aircraft, and shipped it to England. Neither the CAC nor its aircraft saw battle, and the CAC was disbanded in 1915.

During the First World War, Canadian pilots served with either the British Royal Flying Corps (RFC) or its Royal Naval Air Service (RNAS). In 1916, the RFC set up airfields in Canada to recruit and train pilots in airspace far from the conflict. Thousands trained and many graduates went on to become Canadian aces, amazing the world with their courage, prowess, and precision in air combat. While Billy Bishop (with 72 victories) and William Barker (with 50 victories) are perhaps the most famous, Canada produced an impressive total of 82 aces (each with 10 or more victories), including Roy Brown, Donald MacLaren, Frederick McCall, Wilfrid "Wop" May, and Naval Pilot

Raymond Collishaw—who won 60 victories as the second highest scoring Canadian ace in the First World War. Alongside the pilots, the expertise of Canadian groundcrews was also recognized as an important element of success. A total of 22,812 Canadians served with the British air services in war and 1,563 sacrificed their lives.

In September 1918, the Royal Canadian Navy (RCN) formed the Royal Canadian Naval Air Service (RCNAS), responsible for Anti-Submarine Warfare (ASW). That same year, the British Ministry created two Canadian air squadrons, one fighter and one bomber. A newly formed Canadian Air Force (CAF) took control of the squadrons under the command of Lieutenant-Colonel Billy Bishop in England. Both naval and air arms were short-lived, however, when Canadian forces demobilized after the First World War.

Back at home in Canada, the government realized it needed a policy to regulate a growing aviation industry. In 1919, an Air Board was established under the guidance of civil servant John Armistead Wilson to manage civil aviation and defence. Wilson, a long-time advocate of the value of air power to industry and defence, served as Civilian Secretary of the Air Board from 1920 to 1923. The CAF was re-established in Canada using surplus British aircraft leftover from the war. In 1923, the Air Board merged with the Department of Militia and Defence and the Department of the Naval Service to form Canada's Department of National Defence (DND). The CAF was placed under command of a director who reported to the Chief of the General Staff for both military and civil aviation. Around this time, all scientific research and development (R&D) in Canada fell under the National Research Council of Canada (NRC). As pioneers of aeronautical R&D, the NRC worked closely with the DND, and later the RCAF, to advance aerospace innovation and defence.

On April 1, 1924, the CAF was officially renamed the Royal Canadian Air Force, with the prefix "Royal" approved by King George V. Throughout the 1920s, the RCAF participated in civil air operations, working for the government to complete aerial mapping and surveys, conduct forest and fishery patrols, and deliver mail, medicine, food, and other critical supplies to remote settlements. Called "bush pilots in uniform," RCAF airmen pioneered the exploration of Canada. Pilots like Wop May, Punch Dickins, Roy Brown, Doc Oaks, Jack Moar, and others flew thousands of miles across Northern Canada in planes made by the early aviation giants Avro, Curtiss, Junkers, Vickers, Boeing, de Havilland, Fairchild, Lockheed, and Noorduyn. For those who enlisted in the RCAF, very little military training was completed during this time of peace. When the Great Depression hit in the 1930s, the Canadian government reduced the RCAF by one-fifth and cut its budget in half.

As the economy rebuilt in Canada, the government invested in aerial defence and increased funding for the RCAF. The Air Force grew steadily, cementing its status as a separate arm of Canada's defence when its organizational structure changed in 1938 with the Senior Air Officer reporting directly to the Minister of National Defence. The RCAF now shared equal standing with the RCN and the Canadian Army. Although the creation of Western and Eastern Air Commands helped to establish air power at home in Canada, the Second World War would require the RCAF to expand and invest in every aspect of air defence to rise to the challenge.

Alexander Graham Bell and the members of the Aerial Experiment Association.

The Silver Dart on Bras d'Or Lake in Baddeck, Nova Scotia.

Silver Dart Airplane: The Birth of Aviation in Canada

The flight of the Silver Dart on February 23, 1909 marked the birth of aviation in Canada. The aircraft was the first powered, heavier-than-air machine to fly over Canadian soil—or more accurately, to fly over Canadian ice. After being towed onto a frozen Bras d'Or Lake in Baddeck, Nova Scotia, by a horse-drawn sleigh and helped along by volunteers on skates, the Silver Dart caught some air. It flew at 65 km/h for a stretch of 800 m (about 40 mph for 2,400 ft). This first flight is commemorated every February 23 as Canada's National Aviation Day. What is lesser known about the Silver Dart is that it flew the first military flight trials ever flown in Canada, setting the RCAF on its path to reach through adversity to the stars.

The Silver Dart was one of five planes designed and built by Aerial Experiment Association (AEA). Four years after the Wright brothers completed their famous flight, Alexander Graham Bell founded the AEA. He was joined by engineers Casey Baldwin and J.A.D. "Douglas" McCurdy,

American motorcycle racer Glenn Curtiss, and U.S. Army Lieutenant Thomas Selfridge, with their endeavours funded by Bell's wife, Mabel. The Silver Dart was constructed out of steel tubing, wood, bamboo, friction tape, and wire, and named for the silver rubberized fabric used to cover the airplane. It was a hefty plane with a wingspan of 49 ft, weighing roughly 800 lb or 363 kg. Canadian aviation pioneer McCurdy piloted the Silver Dart on that first successful flight in 1909.

In March of the same year, the Canadian Army took an interest in the aircraft for military purposes and the Silver Dart was shipped to what is now Canadian Forces Base (CFB) Petawawa in Ontario. The first airplane hangar in Canada was built to accommodate the Silver Dart and another plane called the Baddeck I. Here, the Silver Dart would fly over 200 times before being damaged beyond repair during a landing. When the First World War broke out in 1914, J.A.D. McCurdy recommended the formation of a

Canadian Air Force to Colonel Sam Hughes, Canada's Minister of Militia and Defence. To which Hughes replied, "...*the aeroplane is an invention of the devil and will never play any part in the defence of the nation, my boy!*"

In 1958, Lionel McCaffrey of the RCAF proposed rebuilding a replica of the Silver Dart on the 50th anniversary of its first flight. The replica was built at No. 6 Repair Depot, RCAF, at Trenton and shipped to Baddeck on February 5, 1959. Wing Commander Paul A. Hartman flew the Silver Dart over Baddeck Bay on its anniversary, but the plane crashed due to high winds (Hartman fortunately wasn't injured). The Silver Dart was repaired for the opening of the Aviation and Space Museum in Ottawa in October 1960, where it remains on display today.

Alexander Graham Bell and the members of the Aerial Experiment Association.

"We breathed an atmosphere of aviation from morning till night and almost from night to morning"
– Alexander Graham Bell, 1908

The Silver Dart flying above Bras d'Or Lake in Baddeck, Nova Scotia.

Billy Bishop: Ace of Aces

Air Marshal William Avery Bishop, VC, CB, DSO & Bar, MC, DFC, ED

"It was the mud," Billy Bishop claimed, *"that made me take to flying..."*

One rainy day in England in 1915, Bishop was checking on some horses as a Cavalry Officer in the 7th Canadian Mounted Rifles during the First World War. Mired up to his knees in mud, Billy heard the distinct sound of an airplane overhead. It landed in a nearby field, with the pilot seeking and securing directions, then the trim little biplane took off. *"When I turned to slog my way back through the mud, my mind was made up,"* Bishop later wrote. He would meet his enemy in the sky.

Shortly afterwards, Lieutenant William Avery "Billy" Bishop applied for a transfer. Two months later, he became a Royal Flying Corps observer, setting his career on a trajectory to become Canada's top flying ace, a world-famous aerial duellist, and a founding father of Canadian aviation.

When Bishop earned his wings in November 1915, the average lifespan of a First World War fighter pilot was 11 days. In spite of these odds (and being sent back to flight school), Bishop persevered, flying with such abandon that he was admired as fearless by many and considered reckless by some. According to legend, he returned from one combat mission with 210 bullet holes in his plane.

Bishop's aerial strategy was the surprise attack. He won victory after victory, earning the nickname "Hell's Handmaiden" from his enemies. A skilled sharpshooter, Billy attributed his sharp eye and steady hand to a youthful pastime of hunting small game in the Ontario bush. After downing 22 planes, Bishop became flight leader of 60 Squadron based out of Filescamp Farm, France. Dogfights dominated the skies over the Western Front, and Billy met the notorious rival Manfred von Richthofen, the Red Baron himself, in a skirmish though neither was victorious.

During the Battle of Vimy Ridge in 1917, Bishop shot down 12 planes and was given the Military Cross and a promotion to Captain. In June of the same year, Bishop flew his Nieuport 17 across enemy lines to attack a German airfield. He was awarded the Victoria Cross for the daring solo attack, the first Canadian pilot to receive such distinction (to read the citation, see Appendix 2: RCAF Victoria Cross Recipients). One year later, after downing five Pfalz scouts in five minutes, Bishop earned the Distinguished Flying Cross for "unrelenting valour." By the end of the war, Bishop was credited with destroying 72 enemy aircraft and promoted to Lieutenant-Colonel. The era of the flying ace had arrived. As "ace of aces," Billy Bishop would serve as a role model for generations to come.

As Lieutenant-Colonel George A. Drew wrote in *Canada's Fighting Airmen*, *"It is true that Richthofen and Fonck exceeded his total by a few machines (Richthofen, the German, brought down 80 and Fonck, the French ace, brought down 75), but in the short period of his active service during 1918, Major Bishop proved himself beyond question the most brilliant aerial duellist the world has known."*

William Avery "Billy" Bishop in the cockpit of his Nieuport 17 fighter.

"On the edge of destiny, you must test your strength"

– William A. "Billy" Bishop

At the close of the First World War, Lieutenant-Colonel Bishop was Commanding Officer of the CAF, which consisted of two squadrons—one fighter and one bomber administered by No. 1 Wing CAF (Bishop is listed with other RCAF Commanders and Command Chiefs in Appendix 1). In 1924, the CAF was granted a royal title by King George V and renamed the Royal Canadian Air Force.

When the Second World War began, Canada became the training centre for the British Commonwealth Air Training Plan. As Air Director of Recruiting for the RCAF, Bishop played a vital role in this program, campaigning tirelessly for Canada's war effort and inspiring many to serve. In 1974, Billy Bishop was inducted into Canada's Aviation Hall of Fame for helping to establish the RCAF at home and advancing postwar civil aviation abroad.

Captain Billy Bishop with his Nieuport 17, 60 Squadron RFC, France, 1918.

Nieuport 17: Captured and Copied by the Enemy

The Nieuport 17 was another classic fighter of the First World War. Produced by the French firm the Société Anonyme des Établissement Nieuport, the plane reached the French front in 1916. Six Royal Flying Corps squadrons and eight Royal Naval Air Service squadrons used the Nieuport 17—the most famous of the Nieuport designs. This model of the "sesquiplane" featured different sized wings to combine a monoplane's drag with the stability of a biplane. A more powerful 110 horsepower Le Rhône rotary engine gave the Nieuport 17 excellent manoeuvrability and a faster climbing rate. The inclusion of innovative Alkan-Hamy synchronization gear permitted a Vickers gun mounted on the fuselage to fire through the Nieuport's propeller arc. Superior to many other warplanes, Nieuport 17s were adopted by the Dutch, Belgian, Russian, and Italian air forces. Germany was so impressed with the Nieuport 17, they captured one and built their own model. It was a favourite of many Canadian aces, including Arthur Roy Brown and Billy Bishop, the latter of whom was awarded a Victoria Cross for outstanding service while flying the plane.

William Barker: The Hero's Hero

Wing Commander William George Barker, VC, DSO & Bar, MC & Two Bars

Major William G. Barker.

Billy Bishop called him the greatest pilot who ever lived. During the First World War, William Barker shot down 50 enemy planes, was decorated 12 times for bravery, and was even immortalized in Hemingway's short story "The Snows of Kilimanjaro." Despite being the most decorated Canadian in history, William Barker remains Canada's unsung hero of the skies.

What drove a farm boy from Dauphin, Manitoba, to become a fighter pilot? Growing up, William George "Billy" Barker was an exceptional shot. Like Bishop, Barker served with the Canadian Mounted Rifles Regiment before deciding to become a pilot. He made his first solo flight after only 55 minutes of dual instruction and received his wings in 1917. After clocking over 500 operational hours of flying, Barker became known as a gifted aerial tactician.

In dogfights, Barker was ruthless, calculating, and inventive. For his Christmas Day attack on a German airfield, Hemingway fictionalized Barker as "a bloody murderous bastard," but he was much more than a cold-hearted warrior. Loved and admired by his men, Barker embodied the qualities of a military leader: a keen sense of self-sacrifice, the push to excel, and an audacity balanced by prudence. Barker once lost two wingmen on a mission and then vowed to take better care of his men. After that, no pilot he led into combat or plane he escorted was ever shot down.

For outstanding service, Barker was awarded the Distinguished Service Order and Bar, the Military Cross and two Bars, two Italian Silver Medals for Military Valour, and the French Croix de Guerre. He earned the Victoria Cross for fighting alone against a large formation of German Fokkers (for the full citation, see Appendix 2: RCAF Victoria Cross Recipients). Barker nearly died in the battle, sustaining injuries in both legs and a shattered elbow that left him a one-armed pilot. While recovering in London in 1919, Barker met Billy Bishop. After the war, the two men returned to Canada and formed a business partnership, Bishop-Barker Aeroplanes Limited.

Barker achieved many remarkable postwar firsts. When the aviation industry was in its infancy, he set up airports, was the first pilot to fly international mail between Toronto and New York, and flew the first commercial cargo between the United States and Canada. In 1919, he led an aerial demonstration at the Canadian National Exhibition in Toronto, flying in formation for the first time in Canada in front of a non-military audience.

In 1922, Bishop-Barker Aeroplanes ceased operations and Barker rejoined the CAF. He served as Wing Commander (see Appendix 1) and then, as Acting Director, the highest ranking position in the CAF, and later became Liaison Officer for the RCAF in England. He is credited with introducing parachutes into the RCAF, developing aerial strategic tactics, and creating Canada's first aerobatic team.

After leaving the RCAF, Barker became the first President of the Toronto Maple Leafs. For the remainder of his life, he would struggle with his wartime injuries and adapting to civilian life. William Barker died at age 35 when he lost control of his Fairchild KR-21 biplane during a demonstration flight for the RCAF. His funeral was the largest state event in Toronto's history,

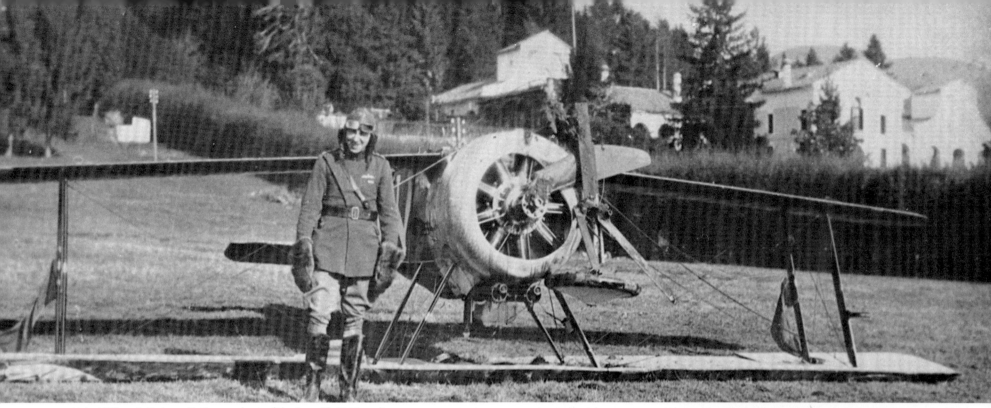

Major William G. Barker with the wreckage of the Sopwith F.1 "Camel" aircraft from 28 Squadron RFC.

with 50,000 civilians and 2,000 in an honour guard attending. Sadly, Barker's untimely death caused many of his accomplishments to fade from memory. His slip into obscurity ended in 2011 when a plaque was placed on his tomb in Toronto's Mount Pleasant Cemetery, recognizing Barker as the "most decorated war hero in the history of Canada, the British Empire, and the Commonwealth of Nations." In 1974, William Barker was inducted into Canada's Aviation Hall of Fame.

Major William Avery "Billy" Bishop and Lieutenant-Colonel William G. Barker in front of a German Fokker D.VII.

John Armistead Wilson (centre) accepts the prestigious Trans-Canada (McKee) Trophy in Ottawa in 1944.

Members of No. 1 Squadron Canadian Air Force at Shoreham, United Kingdom, 1919.

The Birth of the RCAF: Establishing Air Power in Canada

The pride Canadian aircrews brought home after the First World War translated into the desire to have a national air force in Canada. In 1919, the Canadian government established an Air Board of seven members to control commercial and civil aviation. The Board was also responsible for air defence, which led to the organization and administration of the Canadian Air Force (CAF) on February 18, 1920.

Despite the newly formed CAF, Canada was war-weary and its government leery about making investments in air defence. It was a widely held view at the time that "Canada would never need an air service." But the Secretary of the Air Board, John Armistead Wilson, had other ideas. At the core of his "airmindedness" was the belief that in a sparsely populated and vast country like Canada, the Air Force would only survive if it were tied to civilian aviation and the aerospace industry. Considered by many to be the father of civil aviation in Canada, Wilson argued that, in order to remain relevant during peacetime, the CAF needed to perform civilian functions. And so, the "bush pilots in uniform" flew on forest fire and maritime patrols, delivered mail, medical, and other supplies, and contributed to geological surveys and the aerial mapping of Canada.

At its inception, the CAF was given 1,340 officers and 3,905 Non-Commissioned Members (NCMs) and operated out of Camp Borden, Ontario. Named after Sir Frederick William Borden, Canada's former Minister of Militia, Camp Borden is considered to be the birthplace of the RCAF. The site was selected for a military aerodrome by the Royal Flying Corps (RFC) during the First World War. Camp Borden became the CAF's training centre in 1920, with the Air Board offering a 28-day flying course to any officer who had served in the RFC or Royal Naval Air Service (RNAS) during the war. The British government donated 114 aircraft, required equipment, and even hangars to the base. Taking over seaplane docks at Dartmouth and Sydney, the Air Board established new CAF bases in Vancouver, British Columbia, Morely, Alberta, and Roberval, Quebec, with 24 Curtiss Flying Boats donated by the United States.

In 1923, the Department of Militia and Defence, the Department of Naval

Service, and the Air Board merged to form the Department of National Defence (DND) in Canada. The CAF, which had mostly been small and non-permanent, became responsible for all flying operations in Canada. The prefix "Royal" was added on approval from King George V and its organization made official on April 1, 1924. The RCAF continued to oversee civil flying until a Civil Aviation Branch of the DND was created in 1927, later becoming the Department of Transport.

The newly established RCAF was to be led by a director who reported to the Chief of the General Staff. It consisted of three parts: a permanent Active Air Force, an Auxiliary (part-time) Air Force, and a Reserve (non-active). On the day of its inception, a modest Active Air Force was 68 officers and 307 NCMs strong. The RCAF modelled its organization on the RAF, having a similar insignia, ensign, and badges, and adopting the Latin motto: *Per Ardua Ad Astra* which translates to "through adversity to the stars."

Another champion of air power in Canada was A.G.L. McNaughton, Chief of the General Staff of the Canadian Army in 1929. Notably, McNaughton was also an electrical engineer who served as President of the National Research Council of Canada from 1935 to 1939 and later became Canada's Minister of National Defence in 1944. McNaughton was aware of the importance of air defence, especially at home with its response to threats on Canadian coasts. In 1932, he launched a draft plan for the RCAF with its primary role as coastal defence and its secondary as an expeditionary force overseas. Prime Minister William Lyon Mackenzie King echoed McNaughton's approach in his 1937 admission of protection "in a mad world" on the sea and in the air. That same year, the RCAF was given primary responsibility for the defence of Canada. With this came new investments for the RCAF, namely a tripled share of the defence budget.

In 1938, the Second World War was looming and Canada's air power was about be thrust into action. Having established a peacetime professionalism and permanency, the RCAF would have to transform itself into a modern military power. This required building up its air strength quickly —a daunting task for some 4,061 personnel and 270 military aircraft, many of which were obsolete. All available resources were about to be called on to step up to the colossal task that lay ahead.

A restored Sopwith Camel from the Canada Aviation and Space Museum collection.

Sopwith Camel: The Red Baron's Nemesis

The Sopwith Camel is one of the most legendary fighter planes of the First World War. Many Canadian aces flew the plane, including Roy Brown, who was flying one when he shot down the infamous Red Baron, Manfred von Richthofen. Canadian ace Alexander Shook was the first pilot to destroy an enemy aircraft in a Sopwith Camel, and Donald MacLaren scored 54 victories in the plane, more than any other ace that flew the Camel.

Nicknamed for its distinctive hump—a housing for two mounted Vickers machine guns—the biplane was introduced to the Western Front in 1917. At the time, the Camel was considered state of the art. A single rotary engine, guns, fuel tank, and cockpit were packed into the front 2.1 m (7 ft) of the aircraft, making the plane highly manoeuvrable for skilled pilots but deadly in the hands of a novice. Despite its tendency to spin, the Sopwith Camel was a superb fighter. Its pilots downed 1,294 enemy aircraft, more than any other Allied aircraft in the First World War. After the war, in 1924, several Camels were sent to the RCAF at Camp Borden. The following year, the RCAF purchased seven more "navalized" models to be used for parts and in training. The Sopwith Camel is featured in Appendix 3: List of Aircraft (Current and Historical).

Canadian Vickers "Vedette" II flying boat G-CYYD of the RCAF.

Vickers Vedette

The Canadian Vickers Vedette was the first commercially mass-produced aircraft designed and manufactured in Canada. Canadian Vickers, a boat building company in Montreal, built the first Vedette in 1924. Another 60 were built in five different versions.

The flying boat was initially purchased by the RCAF for forestry survey and fire protection. Built specifically to cope with the harsh Canadian climate, the amphibious aircraft completed many civil operations in Canada, including taking photographs as part of a photographic survey of unmapped Canada.

The Vickers Vedette was instrumental in the creation of topographical maps of Canada, many of which are still in use today.

NRC and the RCAF: Defining a New Age in Aerospace Defence

The development of Canada's aerospace industry is a success story with a rich history. After the First World War, the National Research Council of Canada (NRC) was put in charge of scientific Research and Development (R&D) in Canada. The synergy between the NRC and a fledgling RCAF sparked early and was based on a shared, passionate desire to advance R&D in aviation. With their combined projects testing the limits of what aeronautics could achieve, the two organizations defined a new age in aerospace defence.

Collaboration between the RCAF and the NRC predates the formation of the RCAF itself. At the request of the Air Board, the NRC set up an Associate Air Research Committee which held its first meeting on February 7, 1920. The function of the committee (which evolved into today's Aerospace Research Centre at the NRC) was to advise on all matters related to aeronautical R&D. From the outset, the RCAF was the NRC's primary client. At a time when the Department of National Defence (DND) managed civil aviation, the Chief Aeronautical Engineer of the DND, E.W. Stedman, ensured that issues raised by the RCAF were promptly addressed in NRC laboratories.

The NRC pioneered aeronautical research in 1929 with the construction of wind tunnels, engine test facilities, and a structures laboratory. In the following decade, innumerable NRC projects were undertaken for the DND with the close cooperation of the RCAF. Initial research tested the development of propeller de-icing systems and the performance of skis on aircraft. Engine, fuel, and lubrication problems specific to aircraft in Canadian weather were also investigated. Thousands of aircraft instruments were dismantled, tested, and overhauled in the NRC's former Instruments Laboratory—the only one of its kind in Canada. Models of RCAF aircraft were built and tested in the NRC's innovative wind tunnel, along with models of new aircraft designed by Canadian companies, to optimize aircraft performance and safety.

In 1940, the DND authorized an Experimental Flight Centre at Rockcliffe led by Stedman. Consisting of four to five planes plus staff and aircrew,

The RCAF's Canadair North Star "Rockcliffe Ice Wagon," an icing research aircraft.

the committee was a joint RCAF and NRC endeavour with three members representing each organization. As aircraft began to fly longer routes at higher altitudes, the NRC and RCAF commenced a joint icing research program, outfitting a Canadair North Star aircraft, nicknamed the "Rockcliffe Ice Wagon," for de-icing equipment trials. De-icing equipment was fixed onto its nose and "Shark's Fin," which was mounted on the plane's fuselage to collect research. The plane travelled overseas to demonstrate the innovative electro-thermal method of de-icing and was observed by more than 500 researchers.

At the outbreak of the Second World War, military research was allocated to the NRC. Flight research transferred from Rockcliffe to an air station at Arnprior, Ontario, under full control of the NRC. The RCAF continued to provide aircraft, pilots, and maintenance to assist with NRC's aeronautical research. As warplanes became larger and more powerful, they required vigorous testing and development. In 1942, the NRC initiated a study on the balancing of aircraft controls using an RCAF Harvard II trainer in the wind tunnel.

Throughout the war, the NRC remained dedicated to keeping the RCAF's planes in the sky and its British Commonwealth Training Plan (BCATP) running smoothly. Specifically, the NRC addressed the issue of ground looping of training aircraft for the BCATP to prevent accidents, tested the effect of gun turrets and floats on aircraft, and validated the serviceability of alternate parts when others were in short supply. Though a postwar NRC would work more for government departments, its relationship with the RCAF would endure for over a century, producing critical research and ingenious innovations to ensure that RCAF aircrew and planes were airworthy and defence capable.

Pioneers of the North: Interwar Mapping and Exploration in Canada

Bush flying began in earnest after the First World War when a flood of pilots returned to Canada. Many had caught the flying bug and wanted to continue working as pilots. The northern frontier of Canada was a challenge waiting to be overcome. Bush pilots heeded the call of the wild, flying in surplus aircraft leftover from the war to the most remote and unhospitable parts of Canada.

During the interwar years, the RCAF became part of a survey program that would open Northern Canada and revolutionize map making. Between the 1920s and 1930s, bush pilots photographed a quarter of a million miles of Canada's uncharted regions in Vickers Vedette flying boats and Fairchild and Bellanca seaplanes (see insets on pages 12, 15, and 16). Rugged terrain could be photographed from the air in a fraction of the time it would have taken to cover by boat, dog team, or on horseback. The flights were dangerous; there were no airfields, weather forecasts, navigational aids, or accessible repair services. A new breed of pilot had to master the subarctic temperatures, rough landings in unknown terrain, and rickety planes that weren't suited to Canada's harsh climate.

In 1921, the Air Board conducted its first survey. A flying boat covered 1,502 km² (580 mi²) of Northern Ontario using vertical photography. The technique, in which one camera took a fan of three exposures covering 180° in front of the aircraft, was slow and inaccurate. This method, called vertical photography, was soon replaced by the tri-camera method, which involved three cameras taking pictures from a single mount at the back of a plane. It is still in use today.

Based on the successful 1921 Air Board survey, in 1924 the RCAF became responsible for aerial photography in Canada's photographic survey program. The development of equipment was given to the National Research Council of Canada (NRC) and map making to the Department of the Interior. Through the years, the close relationship between the RCAF

Aircrew with a North American Mitchell II aircraft of No. 13 (Photographic) Squadron, RCAF Station Rockcliffe, Ontario, Canada, July 4, 1944.

and the NRC was critical to the success of Canada's survey program, still considered one of the best in the world. Aerial surveys were an important part of RCAF operations and provided training that formed the foundation of the British Commonwealth Air Training Program. With the outbreak of war in 1939, aerial photography for mapping purposes was put on hold but the partnership between the NRC and the RCAF would continue to grow into a critical component, helping the RCAF establish air power during the Second World War.

In 1945, the RCAF revitalized the program with a focus on Canada's Arctic North. Three B-25 Mitchell bombers were retrofitted with special cameras developed by the NRC. These planes were based at No. 22 Photo Wing, Rockcliffe, Ontario, the former Air Board base that housed one of the world's leading air photo laboratories. Rockville was home to 413 and 414 Squadrons, along with numerous aircraft for photographic and supply operations.

The Second World War gave the RCAF innovative new equipment, radar, and veteran pilots eager to participate in one of the greatest aerial surveys undertaken by a country. Mitchell, Canso, Norseman, Anson, Dakota, and Lancaster aircraft were equipped with cameras. Some were outfitted with instruments developed by the NRC for SHORAN-controlled photography (see inset on page 16). By 1947, the RCAF had surveyed 337,000 km² (130,000 mi²) of Arctic territory. In 1948, all of Baffin Island was photographed, along with large areas of Labrador, Ungava, the Northwest Territories, and Yukon. RCAF operations expanded with the addition of 408 Squadron at Rockcliffe. By 1953, only 14,600 km (5,648 mi²) on North Ellesmere Island remained to be surveyed.

At the close of the 1950s, most of the Canadian North had been surveyed. In just a decade, the RCAF had completed one of the most ambitious aerial mapping programs ever undertaken. Canada's North was opened up to the rest of the country while securing it sovereignty in the Arctic. Today, commercial companies conduct the aerial surveys that the RCAF used to, with the Air Force playing their part by providing protection, transport, search and rescue, and survival training when required.

Shown is a multi-camera installation in an RCAF Bellanca Pacemaker.

Bellanca

The reliable Bellanca Pacemaker was used for transport as a bush plane and built by Bellanca Aircraft Corporation in the United States in the late 1920s and early 1930s. The Pacemaker was known for its reliability and its load-bearing capacity. The RCAF purchased six Bellanca CH-300s built by Canadian Vickers Ltd., in Montreal to be used for aerial photography and as bush planes. In total, the RCAF operated 13 Pacemakers for mapping and aerial photography. The development of aircraft, equipment, and aerial photographic methods continued throughout the 1920s and 1930s.

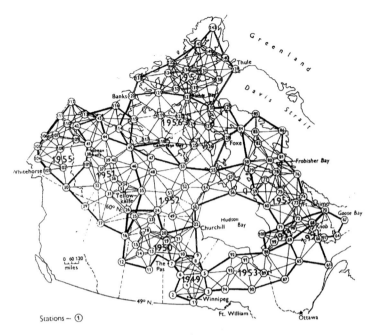

Areas covered by SHORAN Trilateration from 1949 to 1957.

SHORAN: Short Range Aid to Navigation

SHORAN was a system of airborne radar equipment and ground radar beacons developed to guide Allied aircraft to more precise bombing locations. The RCAF determined that SHORAN could also be used to measure the accuracy of aerial photography for mapping purposes. This method was tested and evaluated by the NRC, along with the Department of Mines and Technical Surveys, the Dominion Meteorological Service, and the RCAF's 413 Squadron. SHORAN-equipped Lancasters and Mitchells improved the RCAF's mapping program considerably. Transmitting airborne radar pulses to a pair of ground stations, they measured the time differences between return pulses. An aircraft's exact position relative to the ground stations could then be determined, enabling aerial photographs to be mapped against ground locations.

Fairchild 71-C from airbrushed original.

Fairchild 71-C

The Fairchild 71-C was a popular bush plane produced by the American Fairchild company, which also happened to make cameras for aerial photography. The high-wing monoplane passenger and cargo aircraft was later built in Canada by Fairchild Aircraft Ltd. for both military and civilian use. The aircraft offered an enclosed cabin, carried a large payload, and had the versatility to operate on wheels, skis, or floats. Deemed an all-season bush plane, it was used by the RCAF and the RCMP. In 1935, renowned Canadian bush pilot C.H. "Punch" Dickens flew the Fairchild on an epic 13,500 km (8,400 miles) survey mission of the Northwest Territories.

Groundcrew of the Aerial Survey Squadron prepare a B-25 Mitchell for flight.

NRC Innovation: Accuracy in Aerial Photography

After the First World War, with small budgets and foreign threats far away, the function of the RCAF was mostly focused on air mapping and courier services. Prior to this, early surveyors used observation towers and high points such as mountaintops. Maps took years to make and were often incomplete due to inaccessible areas of the country. In 1920, an experimental flight in Canada combined photography with surveying and a revolutionary solution was in the making. The National Research Council of Canada (NRC) launched the Associate Committee on Survey Research with a photographic subcommittee. Heading up the committee's work, the NRC's L.E. Howlett brought together physics, metrology, optics, and radar to design and produce exacting instruments for aerial photography.

The committee researched problems related to north country aircraft operations and aerial surveying, such as the effects of drag on aerial photography,

recording conditions while a picture was being taken, and the stability of the aircraft used for aerial survey. Based on this research, camera instruments and related aeronautics improved.

Using flight altitude to determine which camera lens to use and its settings helped pilots and surveyors take clearer pictures. The NRC's wind tunnel refined the three-camera system, enabling more precise aerial identification and both the adjustment and measurement of camera angles. NRC innovations in engineering and aerial photography, along with evolving surveying methods, helped the RCAF safely and more accurately map Canada's most remote, northern regions.

CHAPTER 2
THE CRUCIBLE OF WAR
The RCAF and the Second World War 1939–1945

Opposite: No. 111 Squadron RCAF Pilots in Stusiak, Alaska, July 1943.

THE CRUCIBLE OF WAR
THE RCAF AND
THE SECOND WORLD WAR
1939–1945

Mary Rainville and her brother-in-law Phil Rainville.

Germany invaded Poland in September 1939 and the world went to war. Britain declared war on Germany on September 3, 1939, and Canada followed soon after, declaring war one week later. The RCAF would play a key role in the ultimate Allied victory over Germany, supporting three of its largest missions: the British Commonwealth Air Training Plan (BCATP), home defence, and overseas operations.

Three months after the outbreak of war, in December 1939, a group of men gathered in Prime Minister Mackenzie King's office for a momentous occasion. On behalf of Canada, Britain, Australia, and New Zealand, they would sign an agreement to train aircrew in Canada under the BCATP. Described by U.S. President Roosevelt as "the aerodrome of democracy," the highly successful training program was one of the RCAF's greatest contributions to the war.

Of the more than 131,533 pilots and aircrew that trained in Canada under the BCATP, almost 73,000 were Canadian and served as part of the Home War Establishment in Canada. Fifteen RCAF squadrons had been formed in October 1939, with 12 designated for homeland defence and three for overseas service.

Located on both coasts of Canada, these commands broadened into 37 squadrons responsible for protecting Allied shipping routes and Canadian coasts from enemy attack. In the Battle of the Atlantic, which lasted as long as the war itself, Canadian maritime patrol bombers found themselves battling German U-boats along the East Coast and supporting the U.S. defence during the Aleutian Islands Campaign. Twenty types of aircraft were in service at this point, with many such as the "Fleet Finch" enlisted for training. Although the RCAF would begin the war with just 29 fighter and bomber aircraft, this list would soon grow to include the ever popular Supermarine Spitfire, the Handley Page Halifax Bomber, the Hawker Hurricane, and the Avro Lancaster.

The Overseas War Establishment arm of the RCAF served in missions abroad. The first three RCAF squadrons were sent to England during the first six months of 1940. No. 1 (Fighter) Squadron arrived in time to participate in the epic Battle of Britain—the first battle won solely by air power and the RCAF's first opportunity to demonstrate its combat capabilities. Squadron Leader Ernest Archibald McNab was

Commanding Officer of No. 1 Squadron when it landed in England, soon to be renamed 401 Fighter Squadron as part of the new designation of all RCAF squadrons in a "400 series."

Over 100 Canadians flew in the Battle of Britain, including Keith "Skeets" Ogilvie, who survived with five victories only to later be shot down and taken as a prisoner of war (POW) by the Germans. Detained in Stalag Luft III in March 1944, Ogilvie was part of "The Great Escape," when 76 Allied prisoners escaped the Luftwaffe-run POW camp.

The RCAF's overseas contingent established a strong and respected presence in British-run Fighter, Bomber, Coastal, and Transport Commands. While 48 RCAF squadrons served in theatres of war ranging from Europe to the Far East, thousands of Canadians served abroad in RAF organizations that they had joined prior to the war. In 1942, five RCAF bomber squadrons served with Bomber Command. Distinguished RCAF Officer Reginald "Reg" Lane of 35 Squadron flew as "Master Bomber" with Bomber Command's No. 8 Group, refining bombing techniques with the legendary Pathfinder Squadron. In 1942, all Canadians serving in the RAF were transferred into 11 newly formed RCAF bomber squadrons, which became No. 6 Group of Bomber Command. By the end of 1944, No. 6 Group was suffering the lowest losses of any Bomber Command group and had the highest rate of accuracy in bombing its targets.

Along with the Battle of Britain, the RCAF conducted overseas operations in Egypt, Italy, Sicily, Malta, Ceylon, India, and Burma in roles such as night fighter, reconnaissance, anti-shipping, anti-submarine, strategic bombing, fighter-bomber, and transport. High-scoring Canadian aces included George "Buzz" Beurling and James "Stocky" Edwards, while Leonard Birchall, also known as the "Saviour of Ceylon," surveilled the seas in a 413 Squadron Catalina. Two RCAF squadrons, 435 and 436, flew C-47 Dakotas across the Himalayas—a passage called the "Burma Hump"—on dangerous missions to supply Allied forces in the jungle.

Back in Canada, the RCAF became the first Canadian military to actively recruit women, forming the Canadian Women's Auxiliary Air Force on July 2, 1941, which later became the Women's Division (WD) of the RCAF. Wilhelmina "Willa" Walker, who earned the highest Air Force rank for women at the time, was one of thousands of Canadian women who volunteered to serve. Many were part of the 6,000 RCAF radar specialists, whose expertise and operations were a determining factor in Germany's defeat. With the motto, "We Serve that Men May Fly," their sacrifice cemented them a place in Canadian history. Another notable woman, Elsie MacGill, was a visionary in the war effort at home. The first woman to earn a master's degree in aeronautical engineering, MacGill became Chief Aeronautical Engineer of Canadian Car and Foundry, where she headed the Canadian production of a record number of Hawker Hurricane fighter planes for the Second World War.

As the RCAF expanded, it diversified. At the outbreak of the Second World War, government regulations dictated that RCAF recruiting practices enlist only people of "pure European descent." Many recruiting officers ignored this policy and allowed visible minorities to join, such as the Carty brothers. For Canada's Indigenous Peoples—First Nations, Inuit, and Métis—the experience was similar. Despite regulations that barred Indigenous Peoples from receiving commissions, 29 First Nations members were assigned air service from 1942 to 1943, including Officer Willard John Bolduc and RCAF Combat Pilot Jack Beaver.

The RCAF changed their recruiting policies in March 1942 to better reflect a diverse Canadian society, welcoming visible minorities to enlist as both pilots and aircrew. A total of 49 Black Canadians served with the RCAF during the Second World War. As the first Canadian-born Black combat pilot in the RCAF, Allan Bundy changed cultural attitudes towards visible minorities in the military. Along with fellow airmen E.V. Watts, Gerald Bell, the Carty brothers, and Tarrance Freeman, Bundy overcame racial biases as a respected member of one of Canada's most valued squadrons, proving that bravery and skill triumph over race or religion. Today, the RCAF is proud of its inclusive policies, which embody its belief in a diverse military as a strategic advantage and that Canada's multicultural population is one of the country's greatest strengths.

By late 1944, the RCAF reached its peak as the fourth-largest Allied Air Force with over 215,000 personnel, including 17,000 members of the WD. Contributing to this, the Air Cadet League of Canada had been established with 135 squadrons and 10,000 cadets. By the end of the war, more than 18,000 members of the RCAF had given their lives in the service of their country. The RCAF memorial at the BCATP Museum, Canada's first national RCAF memorial, commemorates their great sacrifice, listing each by name and age.

A group of pilot trainees inspect a Fleet Finch at No. 7 Elementary Flying Training School in Windsor, Ontario.

Fleet Finch: The Husky, Trusty Trainer

In 1940, the RCAF purchased its first Fleet Finch (16B) from Fleet Aircraft of Canada Ltd. in Fort Erie, Ontario. During the Second World War, the RCAF would acquire over 600 more Fleet Finches to be used as primary trainers in the British Commonwealth Air Training Plan at sites across Canada. The popular biplane replaced the earlier Model 7 Fawn and was used in parallel with the de Havilland Tiger Moth.

The feisty bright yellow biplane was a rugged, versatile aircraft that was relatively easy to fly, earning it the nickname "the husky, trusty trainer." After a sliding cover was introduced to protect pilots from severe Canadian weather, the Kinner-powered trainer was put to the test by both novice pilots and instructors alike. One problem identified early on was that pilots could accidentally fly the plane into an inverted flat spin, a position that was hard to manoeuvre out of, which was later remedied by a redesign of the aircraft's tail. According to Spencer Dunmore's book *Wings for Glory*, a total of 48 Finches were destroyed in training, while 92 were returned to the manufacturer and 648 repairs were completed onsite at RCAF bases.

Able to "fly loops all day long," the Fleet Finch remained a mainstay of the RCAF until 1947 when they were replaced by the Fairchild PT-26 Cornell. The trainer had served its purpose, improving flying standards and providing training for thousands of pilots in support of the war effort.

RCAF recruiting poster in 1939.

Opposite: RCAF aerodrome sign of the British Commonwealth Air Training Plan.

ROYAL CANADIAN AIR FORCE

Service Flying Training School

BRITISH COMMONWEALTH AIR TRAINING PLAN

BCATP airmen study a map before take-off in their Avro Anson on a training flight from RCAF Station Hagersville, May 1943.

British Commonwealth Air Training Plan: The Aerodrome of Democracy

U.S. President Franklin Roosevelt called Canada the world's "aerodrome of democracy" during the Second World War. And for no small measure; one of our greatest contributions to Allied victory was the British Commonwealth Air Training Plan (BCATP). The goal of the program was to provide facilities and training for aircrews from the Commonwealth, an endeavour for which Canada was ideally suited, being an ocean away from the hostilities in Europe with land and blue skies to spare.

To say that the BCATP was an enormous undertaking would be an understatement. In 1939, the RCAF consisted of 4,000 personnel, less than 12 designated airfields, and only enough facilities to train a few hundred aircrews and groundcrews annually. The expectation now was that it would train thousands. Hundreds of thousands, in fact.

By war's end, over 131,000 pilots, navigators, wireless operators, air gunners, flight engineers, and aircrew men and women had been trained for the Allied war effort. In Canada, schools and airfields were set up in 231 locations—many the precursor to facilities still in existence today in places like Chatham, New Brunswick, Picton, Ontario, Dauphin, Manitoba, and Moose Jaw, Saskatchewan. Over 7,000 hangars, barracks, and drill halls were built, with enough concrete used for the runways to pave a six-metre or twenty-foot-wide highway from Ottawa to Vancouver. As "Chubby" Power, the Canadian Minister of National Defence for Air, said to the House of Commons in 1942, *"Wherever the British forces are attacking, there you will find graduates of our air training plans."*

Vickers Supermarine Spitfire Mk. V of the RCAF during high altitude tests, RCAF Station Rockcliffe.

The Spitfire: A Symbol of Allied Perseverance

With its sleek lines and elliptical wings, the Spitfire is a symbol of Allied perseverance in the darkest hours of the Second World War. The fighter rose to fame during the Battle of Britain, playing an integral role in the defeat of the German Air Force, the formidable Luftwaffe. Enemy raids over the southeastern coast of England and London were led by bombers with Messerschmitt escorts. The nimble "Spits" would appear from nowhere (thanks to Britain's sophisticated radar system), draw the Messerschmitts away into dogfights, and Hurricanes would zoom in to attack the bombers.

Throughout the Second World War, 14 RCAF squadrons flew Spitfires. Many Canadians flew Spitfires in RAF squadrons, including top flying ace George "Buzz" Beurling. Eleven RCAF Spitfire squadrons provided air cover for the D-Day landings in June 1944 and for the Allied advance across Europe in 1945. Interestingly, the first Spitfire that arrived in Canada was used to test the "G-suit" invented by members of the National Research Council of Canada in 1940.

Spitfires were loved by their pilots, many of whom trained in Canada as part of the BCATP. The fighter plane evolved from a legacy of racing airframes designed by R.J. Mitchell and built by Supermarine Aviation Works, a subsidiary of Vickers-Armstrong. Outfitted with a Rolls-Royce Merlin engine, the Spitfire was the fastest military aircraft in the world at the time with a maximum speed of 550 km/h (or 342 mph).

For a span of 11 years, over 20,000 variants of the fighter were built, including the Seafire which was adapted to fly from aircraft carriers. They remained in service well into the 1950s and around 70 Spitfires are airworthy today. One such aircraft is the Y2-K, restored by members of the Comox Air Force Museum on Vancouver Island, along with Michael Potter in Ottawa. The plane pays homage to Arnold Roseland, a Canadian who flew 442 Squadron's Y2-K Spitfire on more than 65 missions before being shot down and killed over France in 1944.

The RCAF in the Battle of Britain: The Canadian "Few"

"Never in the field of human conflict was so much owed by so many to so few..." – Sir Winston Churchill, British Prime Minister, 1940

In the summer of 1940, the Allied Forces endured their darkest hour of the Second World War. France had just fallen, Germany occupied most of Western Europe, and Hitler was preparing for a full-scale invasion of Great Britain, code-named "Operation Sea Lion." To reach British soil, however, Germany needed supremacy in the skies. And so the Battle of Britain began, the first war waged between nations in the skies.

In July 1940, the Luftwaffe initiated a string of raids that would last for months, dropping bombs on British ports, radar stations, and airfields. These culminated through the summer in large-scale attacks known as the "Blitz" of London and other British cities. Finally, on September 15, Germany launched an all-out aerial attack on England to finally defeat the Allies. Despite being outnumbered three planes to one, Allied pilots scrambled their Hurricanes and Spitfires to meet the onslaught. More than a thousand planes fought over southern England and, by the end of the day, Germany had lost over 60 aircraft. A demoralized Luftwaffe turned around and limped home. Although air raids would continue for the next month, the threat of invasion was over. The Allies had won the Battle of Britain and Operation Sea Lion was shelved.

The lionized "few" in Churchill's famous speech refer to 3,000 British and Allied pilots who fought in the Battle of Britain. This included over 100 Canadians, 23 of whom paid the supreme sacrifice. Many of these Canadians flew as part of RAF squadrons. Flying with the RAF's No. 1 Squadron, Flight Lieutenant Mark "Hilly" Brown won 15 victories during the Battle of France and Battle of Britain. Another Canadian ace, Keith "Skeets" Ogilvie, who would later take part in The Great Escape from Stalag Luft III, fought with RAF's 609 Squadron. Countless more Canadians (somewhere in the thousands) would serve as groundcrew and support staff.

The RAF also formed a designated Canadian unit, 242 Squadron, in October 1939. Twelve Canadians flew with 242 Squadron. During the Battle of Britain, they were led by Squadron Leader Douglas Bader, the

Two pilots race to their awaiting Hurricanes.

No. 242 "Canadian" Squadron, from left to right: Pilot Officer Denis Crowley-Milling, Flying Officer Hugh Tamblyn (Canadian), Flight Lieutenant Percival "Stan" Turner (Canadian), Sergeant Joseph Ernest Saville, Pilot Officer Norman Neil Campbell (Canadian), Pilot Officer William Lidstone McKnight (Canadian), Squadron Leader Douglas Bader, the Squadron's Commanding Officer, Flight Lieutenant George Eric Ball, Pilot Officer Michael Giles Homer, and Flying Officer Marvin Kitchener "Ben" Brown (Canadian).

respected RAF fighter pilot who lost both legs in a plane crash in 1931 yet returned to fly with rudimentary prosthetics. Canadians in 242 Squadron included aces Stan Turner of Toronto (with 15 victories) and Willie McKnight of Calgary (with 10 confirmed victories). Until the arrival in the United Kingdom of the RCAF's No. 1 Squadron, 242 Squadron would be the largest unit of Canadians in the RAF.

The Canadian government sent No. 1 Squadron to England on June 8, 1940. Arriving in Britain with 27 officers and 314 groundcrew, it was redesignated as 401 Squadron to avoid confusion with RAF's No. 1 Squadron. The squadron engaged with enemies in late August, surprising a formation of German bombers over England. Three enemy planes were shot down and four were damaged in this "baptism by fire" for the RCAF. By mid-October, 401 Squadron had downed 31 enemy aircraft and damaged 43 more, losing three pilots and 16 Hurricanes. Commanding Officer, Squadron Leader Ernie McNab, scored the RCAF's first aerial victory of the war. Squadron members Hartland de Montarville Molson and Arthur Nesbitt went on to command Wings in Canada, the Aleutians, and Europe. Built on such a legacy, 401 Squadron remains an active tactical fighter squadron today based at 4 Wing in Cold Lake, Alberta.

All told, Canadian pilots would account for 194 Luftwaffe losses during the Battle of Britain. Back home, young men and women flocked to join the RCAF, inspired by heroic Canadians who flew Spitfires and Hurricanes overseas. Graduates from the BCATP joined the next wave of pilots and crews to serve, later demonstrating the same courage and sacrifice as the Canadians who fought in the Battle of Britain. By the end of the war, the RCAF had become the fourth-largest air force in the world.

A 401 Squadron RCAF pilot and his Spitfire watch his friends set course to tangle with the enemy.

Elizabeth "Elsie" MacGill: Queen of the Hurricanes

Elizabeth "Elsie" MacGill.

Who was the Queen of the Hurricanes? The short answer is Elsie Gregory MacGill. The longer and more impressive answer is that she was the first woman engineer in Canada, earning two degrees—one in electrical engineering and a master's in aeronautical engineering. MacGill was also the first woman to design a plane, the first woman chief of aeronautical engineering at an aircraft company, and the first person to mass-produce the Hawker Hurricane fighter planes during the Second World War—hence the title.

As the only woman in a field dominated by men, there wasn't a lot that held Elsie back, including a polio diagnosis in 1929. Confined to a wheelchair and told she may never walk again, a determined MacGill taught herself to walk using two metal canes. She went on to finish her postgraduate studies at the Massachusetts Institute of Technology and returned to Canada to work as an assistant aeronautical engineer at Fairchild Aircraft Ltd. Here, Elsie worked on a number of aircraft designs and formed professional relationships with the aeronautical staff at the National Research Council of Canada (NRC).

It was her job as chief aeronautical engineer at Canadian Car and Foundry (Can Car) in what is now Thunder Bay, Ontario, that would change Elsie's life and the aviation industry in profound ways. One of the projects she worked on was the design, construction, and testing of the Maple Leaf II Trainer. The first aircraft flew in 1939 with MacGill as a passenger. Although the Maple Leaf II never went into production, it was recognized as the first aircraft designed by a woman.

Opportunity soon replaced MacGill's disappointment at the Maple Leaf II being abandoned. After the Second World War began, Can Car was selected by the RAF and the RCAF to manufacture Hawker Hurricane fighters. Elsie was put in charge of its mass production, streamlining operations to build over a thousand aircraft in a short period of time. It was a massive undertaking but the 35-year-old—one of Canada's top aeronautical engineers at the time—set to work retooling the Can Car plant into an airplane assembly line.

The first mass-produced Hurricane flew in January 1940, with modifications designed by MacGill to equip the fighter for cold weather flying. By 1943, Can Car had produced more than 1,400 Hurricanes and its workforce had grown to 4,500, with more than half being women. Having perfected the mass production of aircraft, Elsie became a war hero. In 1942, her story was celebrated in the *American True Comics* series dubbed "Queen of the Hurricanes."

MacGill was a firm believer that technology could create a better world. Her passions for engineering and feminism drove Elsie to succeed throughout her life. She became an outspoken advocate for women's rights as the National President of the Canadian Federation of Business and Professional Women's Clubs from 1962 to 1964. She was also a member of the Royal Commission on the Status of Women in Canada from 1967 to 1970. During her career, Elsie was accepted into the Engineering Institute of Canada as its first woman. MacGill was inducted into Canada's Aviation Hall of Fame and the Canadian Science and Engineering Hall of Fame. Other awards include the Gzowski Medal, the Award for Meritorious Contribution to Engineering, and the Society of Women Engineers with its Achievement Award, and she was invested into the Order of Canada.

The Hawker Hurricane.

The Hurricane: Guts over Glory

The Hawker Hurricane was the workhorse of the Second World War. It fought alongside the plucky Spitfire in the Battle of Britain, inflicting 60 per cent of the losses sustained by the Luftwaffe. Some argue that while the Hurricane contributed significantly to an Allied victory, the Spitfire got all the glory.

The Hurricane played a pivotal role in the Second World War, serving the RAF, Royal Navy, RCAF, and the Soviet Air Force. The single-seat monoplane was designed by Chief Designer Sydney Camm at Hawker Aircraft in the early 1930s. Its enclosed cockpits and retractable landing gears were unorthodox at the time; pilots were used to flying biplanes with open cockpits and fixed wheels. A highly adaptable plane that could carry a diverse load of weapons, the Hurricane became the most versatile fighter plane in the war. More than 24 versions of the aircraft were developed, including bomber-interceptors, fighter-bombers, ground support aircraft, fighters, and a model designed for the navy known as the Sea Hurricane.

In response to potential air attacks over Canada from the east, the RCAF established an air defence network. It received its first Hurricanes at Dartmouth Station with No. 1 Squadron, later renamed 401 Squadron. After transferring to England, this squadron flew Hurricanes in the Battle of Britain. Other Hurricanes were flown in overseas operations by RCAF 402 and 417 Squadrons. Ten squadrons flew Hurricanes in operations in Canada for training and coastal patrols. In 1940, the Can Car began Canadian production of the airframe under the leadership of the facility's chief engineer, Elsie MacGill—also known as the "Queen of the Hurricanes." A total of 1,451 Hurricanes were built in Canada with most shipped overseas to Britain. By the end of 1944, over 14,000 Hurricanes were produced in both Britain and Canada. Dozens of Hurricanes survive today as museum pieces but less than 20 are considered airworthy.

Pilot Officer Allan Selwyn Bundy.

Allan Bundy: Soaring Beyond Racial Bias
Pilot Officer Allan Selwyn Bundy

The man who broke the colour barrier in the RCAF, Allan Selwyn Bundy, was born in Dartmouth, Nova Scotia, where much of Canada's Black population resided. Serving his country was in Allan Bundy's blood. Both his grandfather and father, each named William Henry Bundy, served in the First World War in Canada's No. 2 Construction Battalion (the all-Black unit). Allan's younger brothers carried on the military tradition with Carl enlisting for the RCAF in 1943, and Milton joining the Royal Canadian Air Cadets.

Although Bundy studied to become a doctor, when the Second World War began, he decided to enlist as a pilot with the RCAF instead. But it was 1939 and Black Canadians weren't permitted to serve in the more "prestigious" roles of pilots or as aircrew; they could only enrol for general duties as a cook, clerk, mess person, or driver. Determined to become a pilot, Bundy passed on general duties and, after he was conscripted, he insisted that he be given a chance to fly with the RCAF. The RCAF reconsidered their biased recruiting policies, and on March 31, 1942, visible minorities were permitted to enlist as both pilots and aircrew.

Bundy was assigned first to No. 5 Manning Depot in Lachine, Quebec, and then to No. 9 Elementary Flying Training School in St. Catharines, Ontario, for pilot training. He flew solo in the Tiger Moth and moved on to Harvards at No. 14 Service Flying Training School in Aylmer, Ontario. On September 3, 1943, Bundy received his wings as a Pilot Officer, a top graduate in his class. Following his commission, Bundy spent nine weeks training at the General Reconnaissance School in Summerside, Prince Edward Island. In December 1943, Bundy was posted to the United Kingdom and stationed with 404 Squadron, known as the "Buffaloes" because of the insignia on their badge.

The primary mission of the 404 Squadron was 404 Squadron's primary mission was to defend against German U-boats, and the Buffaloes sank more submarines than any other Allied squadron, flying the rugged Bristol Beaufighter and the de Havilland Mosquito. Armed with rockets, torpedoes, and bombs, these twin-engine aircraft packed a deadly punch. They were not easy to fly and required a Navigator as part of their strike crew, who doubled as a Radar Operator.

Though Bundy was an excellent pilot, initially nobody would fly with him because of the colour of his skin until Sergeant Elwood "Lefty" Wright stepped up to be his Navigator. Deployed on their first mission in 1944, Bundy and Wright sank two enemy ships off Norway and went on to complete 42 successful combat missions together. When the Second World War ended, 404 Squadron was disbanded and in 1945, Bundy concluded his military service with the RCAF and returned to Canada to live in Toronto.

Three-quarter view of a Bristol Beaufighteron, October 19, 1941.

Leading Aircraftman Allan Bundy receives his wings.

Bristol Beaufighter in flight.

The Bristol Beaufighter: A Multi-Role "Beau"

The Bristol Type 156 Beaufighter, affectionately known as "Beau," was a multi-role aircraft built in Britain during the Second World War. It replaced the Bristol Beaufort as a torpedo bomber against Axis shipping and was used in later operations as a maritime strike and ground attack aircraft. The Beaufighter first flew with the RAF during the Battle of Britain. An excellent night fighter, due to its size, the Beau could carry heavy armament and air-to-air radar without sacrificing performance. Four RCAF squadrons flew Beaufighters during the Second World War.

James "Stocky" Edwards: Rising through the Ranks to Knighthood

Lieutenant-Colonel James Francis Edwards, CM, DFC, DFM, CD; Knight of the French Legion of Honour

James "Stocky" Edwards is Canada's highest scoring ace in the Western Desert Campaign of the Second World War. By the end of the war, he had flown a record 373 combat missions and shot down 20 enemy aircraft (with probable kills increasing this to 30). Stocky's illustrious career describes a rise through the ranks of the RCAF to Wing Commander, a post he held for 20 years.

When war broke out in 1939, there were two things that Edwards knew he wanted to be—a pilot and a leader. Later in life, Stocky would say he was driven to achieve both by his desire to save lives. In 1940, Edwards joined the RCAF with two of his buddies. Just 19 at the time, James passed on a scholarship to Gonzaga University, Spokane, and a tryout with the Chicago Blackhawks to enlist. He received his pilot's wings in 1941.

Stocky was posted to 94 Squadron RAF in North Africa as a Flight Sergeant in 1942. Flying a Kittyhawk on his first mission, Stocky downed his first enemy Messerschmitt. Within a year, he had scored six combat victories, was commissioned as a Pilot Officer, and had been awarded both the Distinguished Flying Medal and the Distinguished Flying Cross.

It was with 270 Squadron RAF as a Flight Commander, during the Western Desert Campaign, that Stocky shot down the bulk of his victories, earning respect for his bravery, deadeye shot, and flying skills. His desert campaign tally in 1943 was 11 destroyed, eight probables, and five damaged. That year, Stocky led his squadron to victory in the desert, helping the Allies drive the Axis forces into a full retreat off the continent. Stocky then traded his Kittyhawk for a Spitfire VII in the Italian Campaign, serving with 417 Squadron and the 92 Squadron RAF. Edwards turned 23 on D-Day and was promoted to Wing Commander.

After the war, Stocky remained in the RCAF, serving as Officer Commanding of the of RCAF Station Centralia and then as Commander of the first RCAF Sabre Squadron, 430 Squadron, in North Bay, Ontario. In 1952, Stocky was posted to France to fly Sabres with Canada's North Atlantic Treaty Organization forces. Three years later, he served at the Air Defence Headquarters of the United States Air Force at Colorado Spring before flying CF-100 jets in Cold Lake, Alberta.

Over the course of his amazing career, Stocky admits to never feeling fear. It was subdued by a profound sense of duty as a Canadian to defend his country. But Edwards knew he couldn't do it alone. As he schooled himself to be a senior officer, Stocky became a vital leader, inspiring his pilots in his remarkable progression from Flight Sergeant to Wing Commander. Famed RCAF pilot Syd Burrows nominated Stocky for knighthood, recognizing Edwards as a "legend." On the 70th anniversary of D-Day, the day he turned 93, Stocky Edwards was knighted by the French government.

In 1972, after 32 distinguished years of service, Edwards retired. In 2009, he was named one of the 100 most influential Canadians in aviation. Stocky Edwards was also an Order of Canada recipient and a Canadian Aviation Hall of Fame inductee.

James "Stocky" Edwards in 1943, aged 21, at Castel Benito aerodrome near Tripoli.

Wing Commander James "Stocky" Edwards, 430 Squadron, Operation Leap Frog II, 1952.

Pilot Officer R.D. Guest of Montreal and his Kittyhawk.

Kittyhawk: Frontline Service throughout the War

The Curtiss Kittyhawk was a single-engine, single-seat fighter and bomber manufactured by Curtiss-Wright Corporation from 1939 to 1944. Despite its mediocre performance—a lack of power at high altitudes, for example—13,750 were built and the fighter plane was used extensively by Allied forces during the Second World War, appearing in theatres in North Africa, the Pacific, the Middle East, Southeast Asia, the Soviet Union, Alaska, and Italy. The RCAF operated seven squadrons of Kittyhawks in both Canada and Alaska. It was No. 112 Squadron RAF in North Africa that gave the Kittyhawk its distinctive, bared shark's teeth markings. The Kittyhawk is featured in Appendix 3: List of Aircraft (Current and Historical).

George "Buzz" Beurling: The Falcon of Malta

Flight Lieutenant George Frederick Beurling, DSO, DFC, DFM & Bar

"There are not two ways about it, he was a wonderful pilot and an even better shot." – James Harry "Ginger" Lacey, one of the top scoring RAF fighter pilots of the Second World War.

George Frederick "Buzz" Beurling was the most successful Canadian flying ace in the Second World War. He earned the nickname "The Falcon of Malta," based on his keen eye for spotting and attacking enemy planes over the Mediterranean Sea. Beurling downed a record 28 Axis aircraft in just 14 days over the besieged island of Malta in 1942.

As a young boy, Buzz Beurling was obsessed with flying. He spent hours helping out at the Cartierville airfield near his home and built model airplanes to sell in exchange for flying lessons. At the age of 12, George took his first flying instructions and was piloting solo by 1938. He left school at 15 and in 1939, flew for a cargo company in Gravenhurst, Ontario, as a licensed pilot. When the Second World War broke out, George wanted to sign up as a fighter pilot. Ironically, the RCAF turned away the boy who would become Canada's top combat pilot, telling him to finish high school first.

An undeterred Beurling sailed for England to join the RAF. After forgetting his birth certificate and crossing the Atlantic a second time, Beurling was accepted. He received his wings in September 1941 and flew a Spitfire in the all-Canadian RAF 242 Squadron. When Buzz Beurling was posted to the 249 Squadron, based on the Island of Malta, his fate as a legend was sealed.

Fighter pilots played a critical role in the defence of Malta. Their mission was to defend against enemy attacks on supplies en route to North Africa by both air and sea. Luftwaffe bombers and fighters hammered away at the island where conditions were deteriorating—until Buzz Beurling arrived. Known by his squadron mates as "Screwball," Beurling destroyed 28 enemy aircraft on Malta, boosting his squadron's wins to 300, the best record of any fighter squadron in the world. Beurling's combat technique involved anticipating enemy manoeuvres and firing to where the plane was flying, a skill known as "deflection shooting."

Beurling was awarded his first Distinguished Flying Medal (DFM) for shooting down four planes in one day. That same year, he won a second DFM for destroying nine enemy aircraft, bringing his total victories to 17. He was commissioned as a Pilot Officer and awarded the Distinguished Flying Cross. During his last mission in Malta in 1942, Beurling was shot down. He was rescued at sea, and after recovering in England, received the Distinguished Service Order. Beurling returned to Canada to sell war bonds but yearned to be back in the skies, engaged in combat. "I would give ten years of my life to live over again those six months I had in Malta in 1942," he once said, adding, "...combat, it's the only thing I can do well; it's the only thing I ever did that I really liked."

In 1943, Beurling transferred to the RCAF. Despite having disciplinary issues with his commander, the controversial but charismatic Beurling was promoted to Flight Lieutenant. He transferred to 126 Wing Headquaters and then to 412 Squadron. In 1944, with 31 victories and now a squadron leader, Beurling

Flight Lieutenant George Frederick Beurling.

Buzz Beurling marking kills on his Spitfire, Malta 1942.

was honourably discharged from the RCAF. He signed up for the Israeli War of Independence but was killed on May 20, 1948, when the Noorduyn Norseman he was ferrying to Israel crashed. Buzz Beurling was inducted into Canada's Aviation Hall of Fame in 1974.

Statue of Buzz Beurling at the Canadian Warplane Heritage Museum.

King George VI, his wife Queen Elizabeth, and their daughter, Queen Elizabeth II (then Princess Elizabeth), are escorted by Air Vice-Marshal Anderson, Air Marshal Breadner, and Air Commodore McBurney, as they inspect 419 Squadron RCAF.

Did You Know… "Canadianization" Was a Thing?

During the Second World War, the RCAF overseas wasn't distinct from the RAF; Canadian personnel trained in the British Commonwealth Air Training Plan were posted into the RAF where they were needed most, and this was often on British squadrons. Though the RCAF sent full squadrons, these were assigned as units within the RAF under British command. As the war progressed, a policy of "Canadianization" was pursued—consolidating RCAF personnel into Canadian squadrons and grouping these into Canadian-led units. No. 6 Bomber Group was a success in the Canadianization of RCAF squadrons overseas.

No. 6 (Bomber) Group: Surpassed by None

"One day... it will be recorded that when human society stood at the crossroads and civilization itself was under siege, the Royal Canadian Air Force was there to fill the breach and help give humanity the victory. And all those who had a part in it will have left to posterity a legacy of honour, of courage, and of valour that time can never despoil." – Father J.P. Lardie at the 1985 dedication of the RCAF Memorial at Middleton St. George, the wartime base of the RCAF's 419 Squadron, 420 Squadron, and 428 Squadron.

Hundreds of Canadians served with Bomber Command in the RAF during the Second World War. While No. 6 (Bomber) Group was originally an RAF organization, in October 1942, the Group 6 designation was transferred in its entirety to the RCAF to establish a consolidated presence in Canadian overseas forces.

No. 6 Group was initially made up of eight squadrons and headquartered at Allerton Hall, a mansion in North Yorkshire, England nicknamed "Castle Dismal." Operations officially began on the night of January 3, 1943, when six Vickers Wellingtons from 427 Squadron dropped mines in the North Sea, near the Frisian Isles. Although the Group suffered heavy losses at first, after additional training and experience on dangerous missions, performance significantly improved. At the height of its strength, No. 6 Group was made up of 15 squadrons: 405, 408, 415, 419, 420, 424, the mostly French-Canadian 425, 426, 427, 428, 429, 431, 432, 433, and 434, flying from bases at Linton, East Moor, Tholthorpe, Leeming, Skipton, Middleton St. George, and Croft.

The squadrons of No. 6 Group flew Vickers Wellington, Handley Page Halifax, and Avro Lancaster bombers. Operations included raids on U-boat bases in Lorient and Saint-Nazaire, France, and night bombing raids on Germany. Over the course of one month, No. 6 Group RCAF flew 3,740 operational sorties and dropped 13,274 tonnes of bombs—more than the Luftwaffe dropped on London during the entire war. In 1945, eight of No. 6 Group's Squadrons (405, 408, 419, 420, 425, 428, 431, and 434) were assigned to "Tiger Force" and sent to the South Pacific to join in the war against the Japanese.

By the end of the Second World War, No. 6 Group had completed 40,833 operational sorties, dropped 126,122 tonnes of bombs and mines, and destroyed 116 enemy aircraft. Many paid the ultimate price, as an estimated 814 aircraft failed to return to base and 4,277 aircrew lost their lives.

No. 6 Group represents the outstanding capabilities and contributions of the RCAF. Its aircrew faced overwhelming odds each time they climbed into a bomber. Out of every 100 pilots who flew for Bomber Command, 45 would be killed. Despite these odds, No. 6 Group earned a reputation as being among the very best. Air Chief Marshal Sir Arthur Harris paid the group tribute, saying, "You leave this country, after all you have done, with a reputation that is equal to any and surpassed by none. We in Bomber Command have always regarded our Canadian Group and Canadian crews outside the Group as among the very best."

Aircrew walking to their No. 6 Group RCAF Handley Page Halifax Bomber in October 1944.

Aircrew and groundcrew of No. 428 (Ghost) Squadron, RCAF, with Avro Lancaster B Mk. X aircraft KB760, which flew the squadron's 2,000th sortie, a raid on Bremen, Germany.

A Halifax Bomber from 405 Squadron, RCAF.

The Handley Page Halifax Bomber: The Warhorse of Bomber Command

Designed by Handley Page, Ltd., the Handley Page Halifax was a British heavy bomber used in the Second World War. The four-engine, mid-winged heavy bomber began its service with the RAF's Bomber Command in March 1941. Thirty-four squadrons flew the Halifax, affectionately known as "the Halibag" or "Hali" in some 75,500 sorties over Europe and the Middle East between 1941 and 1945.

The Halifax participated in some of the earliest Pathfinder operations in 1942 and was the first plane to be outfitted with the H2S, a ground scanning radar system used for blind bombing. Along with Bomber Command, Halis were used by nine squadrons in Coastal Command for anti-submarine and shipping patrols. Powerful and stable—especially after being fitted with Bristol Hercules 14-cylinder engines (the Halifax Mk. III)—Halifaxes were converted to serve in various roles, including as glider tug, towing the General Aircraft Hamilcar glider, a military glider used to transport tanks and other heavy cargo. Halis were also used on special operations to drop supplies, troops, and agents for the resistance in occupied Europe.

Notably, every bomber squadron in the RCAF would fly the Halifax for part of, if not the entire, war. The aircraft could withstand severe punishment and still return home. One Halifax aircraft named "Friday the Thirteenth" survived 128 sorties. The Halifax was well-respected by Canadian aircrew with over 6,000 built before production ceased at war's end.

First Canadian-built Avro Lancaster, a KB700 named the "Ruhr Express."

The Avro Lancaster B Mk. X bomber was built by Victory Aircraft Ltd. in Malton, Ontario, and is now flown by the Canadian Warplane Heritage Museum in Hamilton, Ontario.

Avro Lancaster: The Heaviest Payload

Manufactured as a contemporary of the Handley Page Halifax and the Short Stirling, the Avro Lancaster was the most famous Allied bomber of the Second World War. The four-engine heavy bomber first flew in 1942, and soon became a favourite with Bomber Command in air raids over Europe.

Based on the earlier, largely unsuccessful Avro Manchester bomber, Avro upgraded the Lancaster by replacing two Rolls Royce Vulture engines with four Rolls Royce Merlin engines, proven in both Hurricanes and Spitfires. The upgrade was a success and the reliable "Lanc" went on to carry the 12,000 lb "Tallboy" and 22,000 lb "Grand Slam" bombs—the largest payload of any bomber in the war.

In 1942, it was decided that the bomber should be produced in Canada by Victory Aircraft Ltd. in Malton, Ontario. Avro Lancaster B Mk. I, built in the United Kingdom, was flown to Canada to serve as the prototype.

One year later, the first Canadian-built Lancaster Mk. X, also known as the "Ruhr Express," made its journey back to England.

The Lancaster proved its mettle in precise bombing raids on the Ruhr Dams in Operation Chastise, 1943, by 617 Squadron RAF ("the Dambusters"), and with the sinking of the German battleship, *Tirpitz*, in 1944. The bomber delivered 608,612 long tons (618,378,000 kg) of bombs in 156,000 operational sorties. Thousands of Canadians served on RCAF and RAF Lancaster squadrons in England, including Pilot Officer Andrew Charles Mynarski, who was awarded a posthumous Victoria Cross for bravery during an attack on Cambrai, France (for the citation, see Appendix 2). By late 1944, No. 6 Group RCAF operated 13 squadrons of Lancasters. After the war, Canadian-built Lancasters served in various roles, including Arctic reconnaissance, maritime patrol, photo survey, search and rescue, and navigator training.

Reg Lane: Canada's Legendary Pathfinder

Lieutenant-General Reginald John Lane, CMM, DSO, DFC, CD

Reg Lane began his remarkable RCAF wartime career as a bomber pilot with the RAF's 35 Squadron in 1941. Graduating as a pilot from No. 10 Flying Training School in Canada, he completed 187 hours of bomber training in Berkshire, England, and flew his first raid on Berlin as second pilot in a Halifax Bomber. By July 1942, Lane had completed 23 dangerous operations as a bomber pilot, including the historic "Thousand Bomber Raids" over Cologne and Essen, along with daylight raids on Brest and attacks on the German battleship, *Tirpitz*, in Norway. After his first tour and at just 22 years of age, Reg was awarded the Distinguished Flying Cross (DFC) for "unshakeable determination to reach his targets, and his coolness under fire."

At the close of Lane's first tour, 35 Squadron was chosen to join the Pathfinder Force in Bomber Command's No. 8 Group. Operating as an elite unit under the command of Australian bomber pilot, D.C.T. Bennett, the Pathfinders were a target-marking squadron that used sophisticated navigational technology and techniques for more precise bombing, especially during night raids. After 18 months of operations, Reg was awarded the Distinguished Service Order (DSO) for successful raids on Berlin, Stuttgart, and Munich. By this time, he had gained the reputation as a brilliant bomber pilot. Amid much fanfare, Reg returned to Canada in 1943 to fly the first Canadian-built Avro Lancaster, called the "Ruhr Express," back across the North Atlantic to England.

For his third tour of operations, Lane joined the RCAF's 405 Pathfinder Squadron, the only Canadian squadron that was part of the Pathfinder Force. In 1944, Lane became Commander of 405 Squadron. In this role, he perfected "Master Bomber" techniques, circling the target, sometimes for as long as 45 minutes, directing hundreds of bomber planes while under heavy attack. Reg was awarded his second DFC for outstanding bravery and leadership in 1944. He flew his 65th and last operation just before D-Day in a raid of Caen, France. The Pathfinder Force would go on to fly a staggering 50,490 sorties against an estimated 3,440 targets at great cost. At least 3,727 members perished. Lane was later Mentioned in Dispatches for meritorious action in the face of the enemy.

After the war ended, Lane remained in the service and returned to RCAF Headquarters as Director Air Plans and Programmes. He was promoted to Chief of Plans and Intelligence in 1958, when the North American Air Defense Command (NORAD) agreement was signed. From 1961 to 1965, Reg served as Air Officer Commanding Air Transport Command in Trenton, Ontario. He set up Air Command Units at bases across Canada, oversaw critical overseas air transport missions, and was responsible for integrating the Lockheed CC-130 Hercules into RCAF service. Lane then became Air Vice Marshal and Air Officer Commanding No. 1 Air Division in 1966 when CF-104 Starfighters replaced Sabres to counter the Soviet threat. After completing his tour with No. 1 Air Division, Lane returned to Canada as Deputy Commander, Mobile Command in St. Hubert, Quebec, with tactical fighter aircraft, transport, and helicopters under his operational control.

Reg was promoted to Lieutenant-General and made

Reginald John Lane as a young RCAF pilot with his Distinguished Flying Cross.

Canadian Pathfinder Reg Lane with crew and Lancaster KB700 in September 1943.

Deputy Commander NORAD at its headquarters in Colorado Springs in 1972. Post-NORAD, Reg was appointed Officer of the Legion of Merit in the United States. After 35 years of service, he retired from the RCAF in 1974 and was inducted into Canada's Aviation Hall of Fame in 2000.

A flypast of 12 CF-104 Starfighters honouring Reg Lane.

An all-Canadian crew from 419 Squadron, RCAF, in front of their Vickers Wellington Mk. 1C bomber.

Vickers Wellington: Anything but "Wimpy"

Affectionately called the "Wimpy" (after Popeye's hamburger-loving friend in the cartoons), the Vickers Wellington was Bomber Command's first principal night bomber and the most mass-produced bomber of the Second World War. In fact, the Wellington flew in the very first raid a day after war was declared, and later played a role in establishing the Pathfinder Master Bomber techniques.

Slow and sturdy, the Wellington was a twin-engine medium bomber with a geodesic airframe that made it tough enough to withstand battle and still fly home. The bomber was armed with twin machine guns in the nose and tail turrets and could carry a 2,041 kg (4,500 lb) bomb load. Along with the twin-engine Whitley and Hampden, the Wellington dominated the skies until four-engine heavy bombers like the Halifax and Lancaster became available in 1942.

A total of 11,461 Wellingtons were built. The bombers flew 47,409 missions, dropping 41,823 tonnes of bombs on the enemy. Eleven RCAF bomber squadrons flew the aircraft with Bomber Command from 1941 until 1944. A further two RCAF squadrons, 407 and 415, flew Wellingtons on Coastal Command missions, with 407 Squadron sinking four U-boats. As the war progressed, many Canadian squadrons converted from the Wellington to fly Halifaxes and Lancasters—all of which appear in Appendix 3: List of Aircraft (Current and Historical).

The Battle of the Atlantic: The Longest Battle

The Battle of the Atlantic lasted six years, almost as long as the Second World War itself. Considered to be as strategically important as the Battle of Britain, it was a struggle for control of the shipping lanes in the North Atlantic Ocean. England needed supplies to continue fighting. Germany put its stealthy U-boat submarines into action to destroy the shipping convoys carrying goods to Europe. The official battle began when a German submarine torpedoed the SS *Athenia*, a passenger ship on its way to Montreal with 1,400 passengers and crew aboard. The boat sank, killing 112 people, including four Canadians.

Convoys of ships sailing across the Atlantic received air protection from the RAF's Coastal Command, which included seven RCAF squadrons. Coastal Command defended supply lines in the Battle of the Atlantic, as well as in the Mediterranean, Middle East, and African theatres. Bases were located in England, Iceland, Gibraltar, the Soviet Union, and West and North Africa. RCAF 404, 407, and 415 Squadrons took part in attacks against German ships along the coasts of northwestern Europe. In 1941, 413 Squadron was formed and equipped with Consolidated Catalina flying boats, one of the best aircraft for anti-submarine warfare at the time.

The prowling German submarine "wolf packs" were elusive. Advances in sonar technology enabled navies to effectively target and sink them. The Consolidated B-24 Liberator aircraft equipped the RCAF's Coastal Command with the ability to fly long-range patrols over the "Atlantic Gap," where U-boats waited to ambush convoys, previously out of range of aerial support. This was crucial to the Allies winning the Battle of the Atlantic.

The Allies defeated the German navy. By the end of the war, Coastal Command was credited for destroying over 200 U-boats, with the RCAF sinking 19 of those. Victory came at a price, however, as German U-boats sank 2,900 Allied ships. More than 70,000 Allied seamen and airmen lost their lives, including 4,400 Canadians. Many civilians also lost their lives.

The giant four-motor Liberator (No. AM92) was ferried across the Atlantic to Britain from Eastern Canadian bases.

The Kraut Line: Bobby Bauer, Woody Dumart, and Milt Schmidt.

The Kraut Line: Carrying the Bruins—and the Allies—to Victory

Three Boston Bruins hockey players played on one of the most powerful forward lines in NHL history: The Kraut Line. They were left wing Woody Dumart, centre Milt Schmidt, and right winger Bobby Bauer. The three led the Bruins to Stanley Cup victories in 1939 and 1941 and finished in the top three consecutive spots in NHL scoring in 1939–1940. But the Kraut Line would go down in history for more than setting stellar hockey records.

It was no ordinary game when the Boston Bruins faced off against the Montreal Canadiens at Boston Gardens on February 10, 1942. This was the last game the Kraut Line would play before serving overseas in the Second World War. All three had traded their Bruins uniforms for the dignified blue of the RCAF.

The line led the Bruins to a decisive 8–1 victory, picking up three of the goals and eight assists. At the end of the game, the home crowd roared in applause. Canadiens players, together with some Bruins, hoisted the Kraut Line onto their shoulders in a celebratory send-off, skating them around the rink while devoted Bruins fans sang "Auld Lang Syne." General Manager Art Ross called the Kraut Line "the most loyal and courageous players in the Bruins' history."

Once enlisted, the three men played for the Ottawa RCAF team that won the Allen Cup in 1942. Bauer returned to Canada early because of poor health, but Schmidt and Dumart served overseas for the entire war. The Kraut Line reunited with the Bruins in 1946, and Schmidt eventually coached the team. For them, nothing would top the memorable farewell they received from their opponents, who put aside a humiliating defeat to honour a higher cause.

Squadron Leader Alfred Keith "Skeets" Ogilvie.

Keith "Skeets" Ogilvie: The Great Escape
Squadron Leader Alfred Keith Ogilvie, DFC

An adventurer at heart, Keith "Skeets" Ogilvie always wanted to fly. He got his wish when he was accepted into the RAF at a recruiting office in Ottawa. A few days later, Keith sailed for England and an incredible future as one of Canada's most celebrated fighter pilots.

Ogilvie initially trained at Hatfield, where in a defining moment he soloed just sixteen days after his first full day of instruction. "On the first circuit I bounced her and scurried across the 'drome like a startled deer. The second landing was no hell but at least I got her down," Skeets wrote in his diary. "Today I am a pilot." Thirteen months later, he would fly his first sortie in the Second World War.

By July 1940, Ogilvie had graduated as a multi-engine instructor from Central Flying School at Upavon. In August, recognized as a talented pilot, he was posted to 609 Squadron in Fighter Command, flying Spitfires. He became one of the 100 or so Canadian pilots who fought in the Battle of Britain.

Skeets was eventually credited with six confirmed victories and the damage of several enemy aircraft. On September 15, 1940 when a staggering 1,500 aircraft filled the skies above Britain, Ogilvie was credited with shooting down a German Dornier 215 bomber. The plane dropped its bombload near Buckingham Palace with minimal damage and Ogilvie became known as the "savior of Buckingham Palace." Unbeknownst to either pilot, it was later reported that Sergeant Ray Holmes of 504 Squadron also contributed to downing the aircraft, which crashed into Victoria Railway Station.

In 1941, Flying Officer Keith Ogilvie was awarded the Distinguished Flying Cross (DFC) for displaying "great keenness and determination to seek and destroy the enemy." But his remarkable story didn't end with the Battle of Britain. That same month, while escorting a squadron of Stirlings in a raid on Lille, France, Skeets was shot down. Severely injured, he parachuted from his burning Spitfire and landed in occupied France. Soon after, he was arrested by a German patrol.

Ogilvie recovered from his injuries and was sent to Stalag Luft III, a German prison camp for downed Allied aircrew in Sagan, Germany (now Poland). Here, his contribution to Roger Bushell's elaborate plan to free more than 100 fellow prisoners of war in what became known as The Great Escape was the "collection"—by whatever means—of materials and documents vital to the success of the operation. Over a period of months, prisoners used whatever they could to dig three tunnels called "Tom," "Dick," and "Harry." On March 25, 1944, 76 men escaped through the 122 m-long "Harry." Ogilvie was one of the last to clear the tunnel before it was discovered. He was recaptured two days later.

Of the 76 escapees, 73 were recaptured with 50 of them shot in retribution on Hitler's orders. Ogilvie was transferred to the Gestapo prison in Gorlitz, then Czechoslovakia, where he was interrogated and kept in appalling conditions with his fellow escapees. Promoted to Flight Lieutenant while in captivity, Ogilvie was freed by a British unit in May 1945. The Great Escape was made into a motion picture

Opposite: 609 Squadron in 1941, Skeets is in the bottom row, third from the right.

celebrating Allied perseverance and heroism. Ogilvie demonstrated charisma and the indelible spirit of a survivor. These qualities, along with Ogilvie's exploits, have made him an RCAF legend.

Alfred Keith Ogilvie returned to Canada, transferred to the RCAF, and became Squadron Leader at RCAF stations Centralia, Rockliffe, and Downsview. He retired in April 1962 and was a member of the RCAF Prisoner of War Association. Ogilvie passed away in Ottawa in 1998.

This aircraft flown by Flying Officer J. Duguid is on its way over Burma to drop supplies to Allied troops who have been surrounded by the Japanese, No. 62 Squadron.

435 and 436 Squadrons: Flying the Burma Hump

Crossing the remote Himalayas is not an easy flight on the best of days. The likelihood of monsoon winds and near-zero visibility, along with very poor (if any) navigation tools, make the passage nothing short of treacherous. Yet the RCAF made this crossing—known as the Burma Hump—tens of thousands of times during the Second World War. Two squadrons, specifically 435 "Chinthe" and 436 "Elephant," made the legendary long-distance supply missions to isolated Allied forces in the jungle.

In 1944, the Allies started the Burma Campaign to push the Japanese forces out of eastern India and Burma, a largely unsung theatre of the Second World War. Air was the only way in, as there were no roads or airfields. RCAF squadrons flew C-47 Dakotas over the Hump from bases in India. Each plane carried 7,000 lb of critical supplies—ammunition, barbwire, rations, tobacco, beer, troops, and even donkeys. Pilots made three or four passes to unload their parachute drops. The loadmasters, then called "Kickers," literally kicked the supplies out of the plane's small cargo door.

The pace of transport over the Burma Hump was gruelling but the constant resupply paid off. Allied victory in the Burma Campaign demoralized the Japanese army. 435 and 436 Squadrons contributed to this win, transporting entire divisions to the front and unloading supplies under threat of enemy fire—a testament to the grit, bravery, and skill of RCAF groundcrew and pilots. By the end of the campaign, 435 Squadron flew nearly 30,000 operational hours to deliver over 27,000 tonnes of cargo and 15,000 passengers and wounded. 436 Squadron flew almost 32,000 operational hours—sometimes up to 70 sorties a day—delivering almost 29,000 tonnes of cargo and more than 12,500 passengers and wounded.

Adopting the emblem, "Canucks Unlimited," 436 Squadron was behind the "Bricks Away" incident when RCAF Kicker, Art Adams, suggested the transport drop their load of bricks on a Japanese fighter plane on a beach—the only instance during the war when bricks were used as a bomb. Approximately 500 Canadians died in the Burma Campaign, with many others injured or captured. Those who completed operations in Burma received the Burma Star medal for their service.

Both 435 Transport and Rescue and 436 Transport Squadrons continue to shoulder heavy loads as tactical airlifters for the Canadian Armed Forces today, participating in every major airlift operation over the past 66 years, including Iraq, Afghanistan, and Libya.

A C-47 of 436 Squadron "Canucks Unlimited" in RCAF wartime colours, now flown by the Canadian Warplane Heritage Museum in Hamilton, Ontario.

In honour of the "kickers" who dispatched loads from C-47s with their boots in the Second World War, this trophy is today awarded to 436 Squadron's top Loadmaster annually.

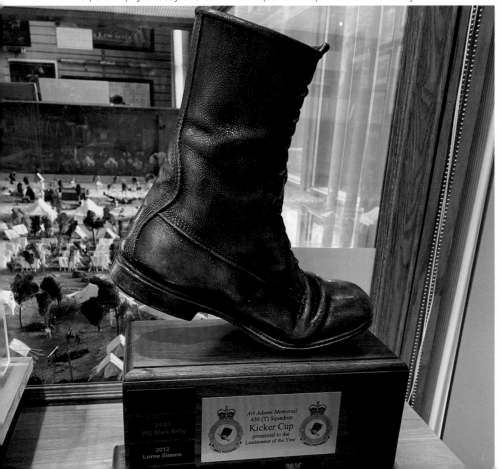

The C-47 Dakota.

The C-47 Dakota: "Dak" of All Trades

The Douglas C-47 Skytrain or Dakota is a military transport aircraft that was developed based on the civilian Douglas DC-3 airliner. Specific modifications were made to customize the C-47, including a cargo door, hoist attachment, strengthened floor, a shortened tail cone, and an astrodome in the cabin roof. During the Second World War, the C-47 was used to transport troops, cargo, and wounded. The RCAF acquired its first Dakota in March 1943, having 169 at its peak.

Designated "Dakota" or C-47 by the RAF and RCAF, the aircraft was also known as the Skytrain, Skytrooper, DAK, and Goonie Bird, along with different designations (DC-3, C-47, C-53, R4D). The transport was highly adaptable, serving a wide variety of roles in both the RCAF and the Canadian Armed Forces including training for navigation, radio and radar, along with target towing, transport, and search and rescue duties. Of the nearly 13,000 DC-3s built, many are still in service today, more than 75 years after its first flight.

Pilot Officer Tarrance Freeman (at far right) poses with his Lancaster crew during the war. After being commissioned with the RCAF, Freeman was stationed overseas as a Navigator with 105 Squadron.

Lincoln Alexander and fellow members of a 1943 course at No. 7 Air Observer School, Manitoba. Lincoln retired from the RCAF as a Corporal serving as a wireless operator in the British Commonwealth Air Training Plan in Portage la Prairie, Manitoba, during the Second World War.

Diversity as a Mandate

Before the Second World War, Canada's policy mirrored that of England's: applicants to the military needed to be British subjects and of "pure European descent." And while some visible minorities were accepted into more menial trades, in March 1942, the RCAF took the lead in Canada's military and eliminated all restrictive regulations, allowing any Canadian to serve in any Air Force role, including aircrew and groundcrew. During this period of transition, trailblazing RCAF members such as Tarrance H. Freeman, Gerald "Gerry" Bell, Lincoln Alexander, Ed Lee, Jean Lee, Eric Victor Watts, Jean Suey Zee, Gurmael "George" Singh Aulak, Charlie Chow, and Jack Beaver overcame racial bias to serve their country with honour and distinction.

Ed Lee was a member of the groundcrew for 404 Squadron, serving as an aero engine fitter mechanic when Allan Bundy flew with the Squadron.

As part of the Women's Division, Jean Lee trained in Toronto and was stationed at the RCAF Depot, Eastern Air Command, at Rockcliffe, Ontario, for the duration of the Second World War.

The G-suit: Putting the Squeeze on the G-force

The advanced aerodynamics of the Second World War fighter jets meant that pilots could fly their planes higher and faster than ever before. But this presented certain problems. Specifically, the rapid acceleration of high-speed manoeuvres subjected pilots to significant gravitational (G) force. As a result, their hearts couldn't pump enough blood to their brains and they risked experiencing light-headedness, fatigue, nausea, or even passing out.

To put this in perspective, one "G" is the force that gravity exerts on a person on Earth. As a passenger on a commercial airplane, you might experience one-and-a-half Gs. Fighter pilots can experience up to nine Gs accelerating out of a dive.

In 1941, Allied air forces needed a solution to this problem. Dr. Wilbur Franks, from the University of Toronto, led the NRC's Associate Committee on Aviation Medical Research. He took over this position after his mentor, Sir Frederick Banting, passed away. Franks began to experiment with flight suits. He outfitted them with bladders, which inflated when the pilot experienced an increase in G force. This applied pressure to the stomach and legs, preventing blood from rushing away from the brain and forcing it to circulate normally—thereby reducing the probability of blackouts. Later designs replaced water with air pressure.

The first Franks Flying Suit was tested in Canada using a Spitfire on loan from the RAF. G-suits were used by the British military during operations in North Africa in 1942. Franks Mark I suits were worn by RAF Hurricane and Spitfire pilots, and the Franks Mark II suits were used by both RCAF and United States Air Force pilots.

Rocket science? Almost. The pressure suits astronauts wear today are basic iterations of Franks' design. Both pilots and astronauts can withstand significantly higher G-loads thanks to resistance training and G-suits. In fact, G-suits are actually anti-G suits because they counter the effects of G-force on the human body.

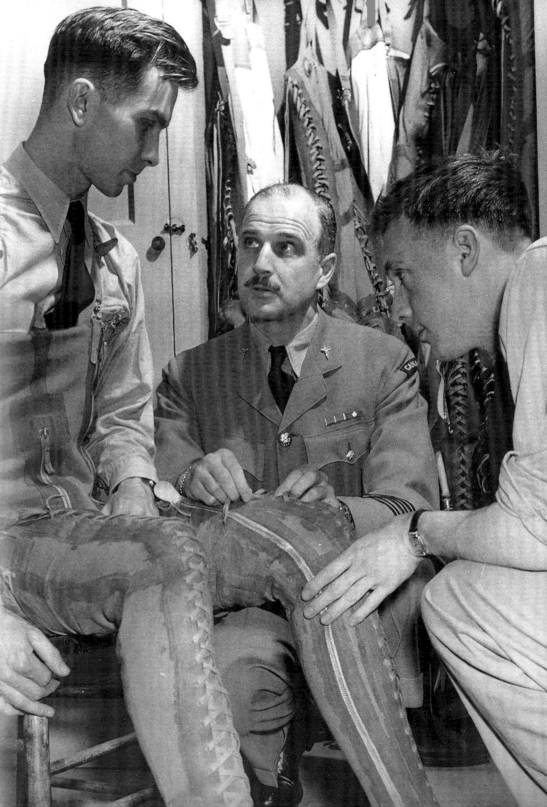

The anti-gravity suit invented by Wilbur Franks—one of the many projects undertaken by the NRC to protect the RCAF and other aircrew during the Second World War.

Willard Bolduc: Indigenous Officer and Decorated War Hero

Flying Officer Willard John Bolduc, DFC

Flying Officer Willard John Bolduc.

Willard John Bolduc was the son of Barbara, an Ojibway (Ojibwe) from Hearst, Ontario, and Joseph, a Cree from Sherbrooke, Quebec. Bolduc had big shoes to fill: his father fought with the Canadian Expeditionary Force during the First World War and served in Europe with No. 1 Construction Battalion. In August 1918, Joseph transferred to 1st Bridging Company and was posted to Egypt the next month, where he unfortunately died of malaria.

Upholding a family tradition of military service, Bolduc enlisted with the RCAF in June 1941 in North Bay, Ontario, and was assigned general duties. He was sent to a Manning Depot to learn the basics, which included two hours of physical training a day and instruction in drills. After three weeks, Bolduc was posted to No. 5 Squadron, Bomber Reconnaissance in Dartmouth, Nova Scotia. He was then posted to No. 116 Squadron for aircraft duty on anti-submarine missions on the East Coast of Canada.

Having proved his mettle, Bolduc was reassigned from general duties to aircrew in 1942. He trained as a gunner with the BCATP at No. 9 Bombing and Gunnery School in Mont-Joli, Quebec. He graduated, was promoted to Sergeant, and left for England to train with the RAF. When Bolduc's training was complete, he joined Bomber Command in No. 15 Squadron. As rear gunner for this squadron, Bolduc participated in bombing missions over Europe during the Second World War, flying in the intrepid Lancaster.

Thousands of air gunners were killed in action. Located at the end of the fuselage in a cramped space with little legroom, the rear air gunner was exposed to the most extreme movements of the plane. In the underbelly of the bomber, they were often the easy target of an attacking plane.

Bolduc was awarded the Distinguished Flying Cross (DFC) for his bravery on operational sorties and gunfire accuracy on two occasions in 1943. Once over Cologne, when his aircraft was attacked by an enemy and again, over Nuremburg, when they were attacked by a Junkers 88. Willard John Bolduc was honoured for his "keenness and devotion to duty." He received his DFC from King George VI in 1944 and was promoted to Flying Officer. After completing his operational tour of duty, which was typically 30 combat missions, Bolduc returned to Canada a hero. In March 1945, Willard John Bolduc was released from military service.

Flight Sergeant Nick Leone, rear gunner of the "Ruhr Express," the first Canadian-built Lancaster to go out on operations against Germany from Britain.

Left to right: Flight Sergeant Adolphus Carty, Flight Sergeant William Carty, Leading Aircraftman Clyde Carty, Aircraftman Second Class Donald Carty, and Pilot Officer Gerald Carty.

The Carty Brothers: The RCAF—A Family Affair

For the Carty brothers, the RCAF was a family affair. Their father, Albert Carty, and his three brothers-in-law served in the First World War with the No. 2 Construction Battalion. Keeping the family tradition of service strong, five brothers from the Saint John, New Brunswick Carty family became airmen in the RCAF.

Flight Sergeant Adolphus Carty, the eldest, was an airframe mechanic and his brother, Flight Sergeant William Carty, was an aeronautical inspector. Both men served with No. 118 Coastal Artillery Co-operation Squadron, an auxiliary squadron, in the war. Leading Aircraftman Clyde Carty was an RCAF firefighter while his brother, Leading Aircraftman Donald Carty, was an equipment assistant. Their younger brother, Gerald "Gerry" Carty, enlisted at age 18 and went on to become one of the youngest commissioned Officers in the RCAF.

After receiving the highest mark in his class on the written exam, Gerry was promoted to Flight Lieutenant at age 19. During the Second World War, he completed a total of 35 missions over enemy-occupied territory, flying in Wellington and Lancaster bombers at a time when Black-Canadian bomber pilots were rare. As an aircrew member of Bomber Command, Gerry had one of the most dangerous jobs during the war. He was wounded when his four-engine bomber was struck and crash landed in France. Carty was rescued by members of the French Resistance and recovered in Britain.

On returning to Canada, Gerry received the first electronic technician certification issued in New Brunswick. He remained involved with aviation, founding the Fredericton Flying Club and serving as its President, establishing Air Acadia, an air charter service with a small fleet of aircraft, and serving as an instructor and Commanding Officer of the Fredericton No. 333 Air Cadet Squadron.

All five Carty brothers survived the war and returned home decorated airmen. After the war, younger brothers, Robert and Malcolm, joined the Army and Air Cadets respectively. At the time of writing this book, seven Carty family members were serving with the Canadian Armed Forces.

Leonard Birchall: The Saviour of Ceylon

Brigadier-General Leonard Joseph Birchall, CM, OBE, DFC, OOnt, CD

Air Commodore Leonard J. Birchall, May 30, 1961.

Air Commodore Leonard Birchall embodies all the best qualities of an RCAF leader: exceptional aviation skills, a heightened sense of duty, and courage in the face of overwhelming odds. What he is best known for, however, is his outstanding "gallantry and devotion" to his men as fellow prisoners of war (POWs) during the Second World War.

Raised in St. Catharines, Ontario, Leonard "Len" Birchall graduated from the Royal Military College in 1937 and was commissioned into the RCAF. Posted with No. 5 Squadron in Dartmouth, Nova Scotia, he flew early anti-submarine combat patrols in Stranraer flying boats. In 1941, Birchall was selected to serve on 413 Squadron in the Shetland Islands. He became Squadron Leader and Deputy Commander of the flying-boat squadron, leading anti-submarine patrols in the Consolidated Catalina long-range amphibious aircraft.

In April 1942, Len's unit was dispatched to Ceylon (today's Sri Lanka) to support reconnaissance activities in the Indian Ocean. Two days after arriving, Birchall and his eight-man crew were conducting a patrol south of Ceylon when they spotted an Imperial Japanese Navy fleet. Birchall's crew radioed the fleet's speed, course, and composition to the Royal Navy's Eastern Fleet headquarters, successfully warning the British. Seconds later, Birchall's Catalina was shot down by a Japanese "Zero" fighter from the carrier *Hiryū*.

The Allied forces averted a surprise attack on Ceylon, inflicting substantial losses on the Japanese force. For his heroic action, Birchall was dubbed the "Saviour of Ceylon" by Sir Winston Churchill and later awarded the Distinguished Flying Cross. This wouldn't happen for years, however, as he and five of his surviving crew, including Canadian Warrant Officer G.C. Onyette, would be pulled from the ocean and sent to Japan as POWs.

Birchall spent the remainder of the war—three years and four months—as a senior officer in Japanese POW camps. The many indignities he suffered, including starvation, torture, forced labour, pestilence, and being beaten on behalf of his men, only served to strengthen Birchall's resolve. He fought to improve POW living standards, ultimately reducing the fatality rate in the camps from 30 per cent to less than two per cent. For his commitment to his men, Birchall earned their trust and became one of the RCAF's most well-respected leaders. In Len's own words: "Your leadership is judged not by your rank but by whether your men feel you have the knowledge, training, and character that they will obey you unquestioningly, and that they can trust you with their lives."

After the Japanese surrendered, Birchall's 22 diaries detailing his POW experience were used as evidence at Japanese war crime trials. Before returning to Canada, Birchall was awarded the Order of the British Empire (OBE) for his efforts at POW camps because "...he continually displayed the utmost concern for the

413 Squadron in front of Birchall's Catalina, March 1942.

Supermarine Stranraer taxiing out for take off at Bella Bella on July 20, 1942.

The Supermarine Stranraer

The Supermarine Stranraer was a flying boat built during the 1930s for the RAF by the British Supermarine Aviation Works. In the early 1940s, the Canadian Vickers company in Montreal, Quebec, manufactured 40 Stranraers to be used in anti-submarine and coastal defence by the RCAF. As aircraft became more advanced, the affectionately named "Strannies" were increasingly used for training duties. Postwar, they remained in regular service, patrolling Canadian East and West Coasts, until 1946.

welfare of fellow prisoners with complete disregard for his own safety. His consistent gallantry and glowing devotion to his men were in keeping with the finest traditions of the service."

Postwar, Birchall returned to active duty in the RCAF, reaching the rank of Air Commodore and holding the post of Commandant of the Royal Military College. He was also the long-time Honorary Colonel of his beloved 413 Squadron. Before his death, Birchall was awarded a fifth clasp to his Canadian Forces Decoration (CD) for 62 years of loyal service, the only other recipient of five clasps being Queen Elizabeth The Queen Mother.

Wilhelmina "Willa" Walker: Fighting for Gender Equality

Wing Officer Wilhelmina Walker, MBE

RCAF Wing Officer Wilhelmina Walker.

In 1941, war was exclusively a man's domain. But that didn't stop Wilhelmina "Willa" Walker from becoming one of the first Canadian women to hold the Women's Division rank of Wing Officer in the RCAF, the equivalent of a Lieutenant-Colonel today.

During the Second World War, Canadian women insisted on making more significant contributions to the war effort. Willa Walker was part of this wave. At the age of 28, she signed up for the Canadian Women's Auxiliary Air Force (CWAAF) and was one of the first 150 applicants selected. Willa graduated top of her class, winning the Brookes Medal and becoming Staff Officer at No. 1 Training Command, Toronto. In this role, Willa led the integration of women officers into the flying training schools in the British Commonwealth Air Training Plan.

In 1942, the CWAAF was renamed to the RCAF Women's Division (WD) and Willa was promoted to Commanding Officer. Known as "The Wing" among her ranks, Willa set up WD training depots across Canada, visiting 33 air bases in 1943, from Winnipeg to Vancouver Island to promote women in uniform. While recruiting for the WD, Willa advocated equal opportunity for women, telling parents, "You would consider it the right thing for your sons to do, and you should also feel that it is the only right course for your daughters."

At every training depot she visited, Willa was shut out of mess halls that were exclusively for male officers.

Taking matters into her own hands, a frustrated Willa sat outside the window of an Officers' Mess in sub-zero degree weather, eating in her car in plain view of her colleagues. Her steely determination paid off and Willa shamed her fellow officers into letting her in. Willa Walker had effectively broken the glass ceiling.

Initially, RCAF WD members received two-thirds the pay of their male counterparts and only nine roles were available to women. By 1943, pay was increased to four-fifths and women's duties expanded to include 69 trades, including mechanic, parachute rigger, intelligence officer, instructor, weather observer, pharmacist, wireless operator, and service police—all roles typically held by men.

Over 17,000 women served with the WD before it disbanded in 1946. As a high-ranking officer, Willa paved the way for women to enrol in the RCAF again in 1951, and to later be accepted as both military pilots (1980) and fighter pilots (1988). For her achievements, Willa was named a Member of the Order of the British Empire in 1944. For 100 years, women have contributed to Canada's rich military history and for over 20 years, they have been fully integrated in all occupations and roles. It is thanks to Willa Walker's courage, dedication, and professionalism that women continue to enrol in the RCAF today.

Douglas "Digby" aircraft 751 of the RCAF equipped with experimental radar equipment at Rockcliffe, Ontario, on October 1, 1941.

Did You Know... 6,000 RCAF Radar Technicians Helped Turn the Tide of War?

Radar was introduced in the late 1930s and played a decisive role in winning both the Battle of Britain and the Second World War. In October 1940, when a critical shortage of technical personnel needed to operate radar was identified, Canada stepped up and provided the Allies with trained radar mechanics and officers. By 1944, one-third of RAF personnel working on radars were RCAF members. In total, approximately 6,000 RCAF personnel were radar specialists during the Second World War.

Left: RCAF Women's Division members Mary Rainville, Eddie Brokeshire, Dot Handly, and Margaret (Peggy) Jewell in front of Nelson's Monument.

Kaden Lac (front) and his best friend William Youn (rear) from 637 Arrow Squadron in Burnaby, British Columbia, prepare for take off in Glider 10 at Pitt Meadows.

Royal Canadian Air Cadets of 530 "Havoc" Squadron graduate in Waterloo, Ontario.

Royal Canadian Air Cadets: To Learn. To Serve. To Advance.

Initiated to recruit young pilots for the Second World War, the Royal Canadian Air Cadets have come a long way since 1940, when the Minister of National Defence for Air, Charles G. Power, called for a country-wide voluntary organization to sponsor this movement. The non-profit Air Cadet League of Canada was established to partner with the RCAF and promote the program. Membership has grown steadily from 135 squadrons and 10,000 cadets in 1942 to over 450 squadrons and 28,600 Air Cadets today. An estimated one million young Canadians have participated in the program. Interestingly, many private pilots in Canada are ex-Air Cadets, and over half of all commercial pilots in the country began their careers as an Air Cadet.

While its primary purpose was a military one, the program's vision has expanded. In 1975, women were invited to enrol in the Royal Canadian Air Cadets. Moving beyond the basics of aviation and aeronautics, instruction is now offered in good citizenship, leadership, survival and first aid, health and fitness, drills, ceremonies, music, and public speaking. Central to the program are gliding and flying courses. Cadets who are 16 and qualify can apply to take pilot training as a summer course to become a glider or power aircraft pilot.

The motto of the Royal Canadian Air Cadets is "To learn. To serve. To Advance." The world-class program encourages Canadians between the ages of 12 and 18 to explore skills and experiences that will give them a strong foundation for the future, regardless of whether or not they join the Canadian military. Today, Air Cadets can be found in over 1,200 cadets corps and squadrons in more than 800 communities in Canada, including at 22 Cadet Training Centres and 59 flying sites across the country. Technical courses are available for various aviation-related trades, including air traffic control and the operation of instruments and mechanics of an aircraft. Aerospace and related technologies courses are also available. Cadets design model rockets and can participate in simulated living conditions in space.

In 2021, the Air Cadet League of Canada celebrated its 80th anniversary. Over the past eight decades, the organization has continued to support squadrons in communities across Canada, enhancing the development of confident, knowledgeable, and capable youth to take leadership roles in improving their communities, Canada, and the world.

Opposite: These Air Cadets of the 120th Runnymede Lions Air Cadet Squadron are listening intently as Cadet Flying Officer K.W. Fenton helps them along with their first aid classes on February 17, 1943.

CHAPTER 3
THE COLD WAR DETERRENT FORCE
1946–1991

Opposite: Four Mk. 5 Sabre jet aircraft from Tactical Flight at RCAF Station Chatham, New Brunswick, are seen in a stepped up formation Echelon Port. The four aircraft are participating in the International Air Display, Toronto, Ontario.

THE COLD WAR DETERRENT FORCE
1946–1991

During the Cold War, the RCAF was Canada's front-line of defence both at home and abroad. Although tensions between the Eastern Soviet Bloc and Western Allies never escalated to an all-out "hot" war, it always was very "warm" and Canada and the RCAF played an important role as a deterrent. Over the course of the Cold War, the RCAF's contribution formed the backbone of the North Atlantic Treaty Organization (NATO), while both North American Aerospace Defense Command (NORAD) and United Nations (UN) operations placed significant demand on Canada's airmen and airwomen. The early postwar years became known as the "Golden Age of the RCAF," and was a time of tremendous growth for Canada's Air Force. To meet increasing need for a global air defence, the RCAF expanded from 12,000 postwar personnel and five squadrons to 50,000 personnel and 41 squadrons, carrying out missions in regions around the world.

After the Second World War, the RCAF focused on nation building and establishing Search and Rescue (SAR) as a capability. The RCAF continued the aerial photography and surveys it began after the First World War, using floatplanes, Lancasters and, later, Mosquitos, to help map the most remote parts of Canada. In 1947, the RCAF acquired its first military helicopters, Sikorsky H-5s, to use for training and Search and Rescue (SAR). The vulnerability of Canada's northern border was becoming apparent and the RCAF took part in military expeditions to the high Arctic, establishing the most northern base in the world, Canadian Forces Station Alert.

In 1949, Canada was a founder of NATO to counter Russia and the Warsaw Pact. Few Canadians are aware of the extent of Canada's commitment to NATO in the 1950s. For the first time in history, Canada stationed its forces abroad during peacetime, and the RCAF sent thousands of world-class fighter pilots, aircrew, and groundcrew to Europe. Four wings, totalling 12 squadrons of Sabre jets, collectively designated No. 1 Air Division, were established at bases in France and West Germany. RCAF pilots, fighter planes, and staff crossed the Atlantic in the epic mission, "Operation LEAP FROG." The legendary swept-wing Sabre Jet built by Canadair, along with its skilled pilots and aircrew, is considered to be one of the greatest stories of Canada's contribution to defence during the Cold War.

A CH-124 Sea King helicopter from HMCS *Winnipeg*.

While the RCAF was building up its presence in Europe, the skies over North America needed to be protected from the threat of Soviet bombers. NORAD was established in 1958, pairing the RCAF with the United States Air Force (USAF) in one of the most enduring defence partnerships of all time. NORAD coordinated fighter interceptors and an early warning system of radar lines: the Pinetree Line at the 50th parallel; the Mid-Canada Line through Hudson Bay; and the Distant Early Warning Line at the northern perimeter of the continent. Maritime squadrons monitored the coastal approaches to Canada with long-range patrols conducted by Argus, Neptune, and, later, Aurora aircraft.

The Canadian Navy played a crucial role in the Cold War with its Anti-Submarine Warfare (ASW), working closely with allies to patrol and monitor the North Atlantic and Pacific Oceans for Soviet submarine activity. Canada invested in new technology and continually modernized its fleets of ships and aircraft to better detect and counter Soviet submarines. This included equipping its destroyers with Sea Kings, leading to the invention of the Beartrap, an innovative haul-down device that enabled helicopters to land safely on the deck of warships in the punishing waves of the North Atlantic.

The Korean War was yet another critical operation that the RCAF supported. The UN Security Council was quick to condemn the invasion of South Korea by the North Korean People's Army in 1950, and in June of the same year, U.S. President Truman ordered USAF and naval support of South Korea. The RCAF was heavily involved in the transport of troops and supplies, and 426 Squadron was vital to the airbridge from North America in support of UN operations in Korea. In addition, 22 RCAF fighter pilots flew on exchange duty on F-86 Sabres with the USAF. RCAF Squadron Leader Joseph A.O. "Omer" Lévesque and Flight Lieutenant E.A. "Ernie" Glover both scored air-to-air victories in the Korean War.

As Soviet technology progressed, the threat to North American cities grew and it became clear that Canada needed a supersonic interceptor. The RCAF and the Canadian aviation industry began design of a new Canadian fighter interceptor, the Avro CF-105 Arrow. Highly advanced for its time, the Arrow's Iroquois engines were tested in the National Research Council of Canada's (NRC) Aerospace Research Centre. Unfortunately, the Avro Arrow never made it past the flight test stage. The changing threat from Soviet long-range bombers to Intercontinental Ballistic Missiles, coupled with budgetary difficulties, saw the program scrapped in 1959 in favour of the BOMARC nuclear-tipped anti-aircraft missiles.

In the 1960s, the RCAF introduced nuclear weapons and its European Sabre squadrons converted to the CF-104 Starfighter in the nuclear strike and reconnaissance roles. At home, CF-101 Voodoos armed with nuclear warheads replaced the CF-100 Canuck, and Canada established two BOMARC missile sites. Canada's northern proximity to the Soviet Union made it ideal for gathering Soviet intelligence through closely monitored radio signals. The most ideal location was Alert in the Northwest Territories, which also happens to be the most northern inhabited settlement in the world. In 1958, Alert became a signals intelligence unit under the command of the Canadian Army, first as the Alert Wireless Station and then as Canadian Forces Station Alert. The RCAF's C-119 Flying Boxcar was instrumental in establishing the base in Alert and routinely supported Operation BOXTOP to help maintain Canada's presence in the North.

In the later stages of the Cold War, financial restraint reduced the size of Canada's military forces. The possible use of nuclear weapons was controversial in Canada and, by 1983, the last of the nuclear-equipped systems were retired. Although the Golden Age of the RCAF in the 1950s was over, Canada's Air Force had left an indelible mark as a world-class deterrent force, consistently "punching above its weight." In the fifties, RCAF Sabre pilots famously excelled at NATO's Guynemer Trophy competition for air-to-air gunnery, and later Starfighter pilots distinguished themselves by winning NATO Tactical Weapons Meets. In 1969, the two Canadian CF-104 reconnaissance squadrons came first and second in the NATO Royal Flush competition. Meanwhile back in NORAD, Canadian aircrews often led in the William Tell gunnery competition held by the USAF, flying first in the CF-101 and then the CF-18. Learning the difficult lessons from fatal aircraft accidents, the RCAF put flight safety protocols in place and developed a program respected around the world. By the close of the Cold War, 4 Wing at Baden–Soellingen in Germany, was the epitome of a "full-up combat round" air force base. With three squadrons of CF-18s (discussed in Chapter 4), fully capable of all-weather air defence and ground attack, CFB Baden–Soellingen maintained the proud legacy of the RCAF as a truly formidable fighting machine.

The RCAF Flyers: Bringing Home Olympic Gold

Hockey is inseparable from the Canadian identity and it only follows that the top of the podium for Olympic hockey is our rightful place. Did you know that in the 1948 Winter Olympics, a humble team from the RCAF brought the Gold Medal home for Canada?

It all started when A. Gardner "Sandy" Watson, a Senior Medical Officer at RCAF Headquarters in Ottawa, discovered that Canada wouldn't compete in the 1948 Winter Olympics because it didn't meet the guidelines for an amateur hockey team. A die-hard hockey fan, Watson persuaded his superiors that the Ottawa-based RCAF Flyers—then at the bottom of their league—could meet the amateur eligibility requirements to compete in the Olympic Games in St. Moritz, Switzerland. Air Marshal Wilf Curtis agreed and the rest, as they say, is history.

The original 13-member team was cobbled together from bases across Canada. After losing a string of exhibition games, the team of "Misfits" was panned by the media. Their losing streak led to some last-minute players being added right up until the team sailed from New York for Europe on the *Queen Elizabeth*. Once they arrived in Switzerland, however, the team gelled. And despite being pelted with snowballs, the team played with poise and professionalism, personifying the Air Force adage of "max flex"—that anything could be accomplished in the line of duty. Even winning Olympic Gold.

According to the Canadian Olympic Hall of Fame, "the Flyers reeled off six straight victories before registering a scoreless tie with heavily-favoured Czechoslovakia." The 22-year-old goaltender, Murray Dowey, finished the tournament with five shutouts in eight games. The RCAF team returned home with the Gold Medal and a hero's welcome. In 2008, the RCAF Flyers were inducted into the Canadian Olympic Hall of Fame.

Members of the RCAF Flyers, winners of the ice hockey gold medal, on the winners' podium at the 1948 Winter Olympic Games in St. Moritz, Switzerland.

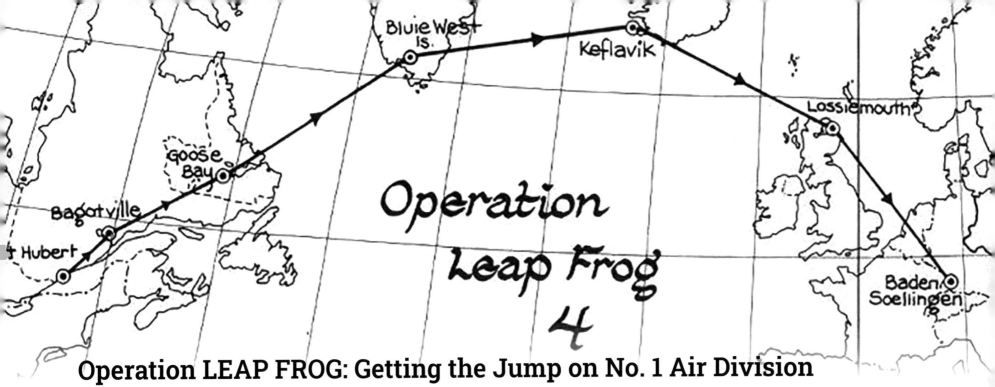

Operation LEAP FROG: Getting the Jump on No. 1 Air Division

During the Cold War, the RCAF committed four wings to protect NATO and then the real work began. The mission, "Operation LEAP FROG," relocated 12 squadrons from Canada to bases in Western Europe to equip and staff 1 Canadian Air Division. The planes followed a North Atlantic ferry route developed by the RAF during the Second World War. Departing from Goose Bay, or Gander, Newfoundland, they flew to Greenland, Iceland, and then on to Scotland, England, France, and Germany. All 12 RCAF squadrons flew F-86 Sabres. Due to range limitations, the Sabres couldn't fly direct and had to "LEAP FROG" from island to island en route—hence the name of the mission.

Operation LEAP FROG was completed in four legs. Leap Frog I commenced in May 1952 with 439 and 441 Squadrons landing in June to form 1 Wing. In September 1952, Leap Frog II saw 416, 421, and 430 Squadrons fly to Grostenquin, France as 2 Wing. In the third operation, Leap Frog III, 413, 427, and 434 Squadrons crossed in March 1953, becoming 3 Wing at Zweibrücken, Germany. The last operation relocated 414, 422, and 444 Squadrons to Baden-Soellingen, Germany as 4 Wing. Arriving in September 1953, this last crossing was completed in a record eight days, four hours, and 40 minutes.

Operation LEAP FROG was a huge undertaking, and part of the delivery of some 800 planes overseas to support NATO. Strong leadership, fair weather, a bit of luck, and teams of 100 individuals for each crossing made Operation LEAP FROG a success. The USAF supervised the crossing of Allied planes with help from RAF liaison staff. Air Defence Command and Air Force Headquarters, along with Air Material Command, Training Command, and Maritime Command, coordinated logistical and rescue facilities. In all, the air forces of three countries came together to help outfit 1 Canadian Air Division in Europe.

Canadair Sabres with No. 2 Wing at Grostenquin, France. Two squadrons have landed and people wait for the third to arrive.

Syd "Cyclops" Burrows: Surviving a Bird Strike

Lieutenant-Colonel Sydney Edward Burrows AFC, MSM, CD

Flight Lieutenant Syd Burrows and his F-86 Sabre.

"We were a formidable force," said Syd Burrows about his Sabre days with 1 Canadian Air Division in Europe. *"The Russians were threatening all the time—like they are today."* – From *Times Colonist*, September 13, 2014, A4.

Lieutenant-Colonel Syd Burrows was one of the daring young RCAF pilots stationed in Europe during the Cold War. His story is one of bravery and trial by perseverance. Syd Burrows joined the RAF in 1951, just after Canada made its commitment to the North Atlantic Treaty Organization in the fight against communism. Syd earned his wings in 1952, and was posted to 3 Wing at Zweibrücken, Germany. To get there, he led a team of four Sabres across the Atlantic in the now famous Operation Leap Frog III. When Syd wasn't flying an operational mission just outside the Iron Curtain, he flew with the Fireballs aerobatic team at the base.

RCAF pilots flew 300 Sabres in 12 squadrons as part of 1 Canadian Air Division. Though they never saw combat, 100 pilots died in accidents in Europe. Burrows escaped this fate but suffered a near fatal bird strike. September 13, 1954 started out like any other day. Burrows was flying a routine exercise as part of a four aircraft flight from 434 Squadron in Baden–Soellingen, en route to simulate an air attack on Zweibrücken. Approximately 32 km (20 miles) from 4 Wing, a hawk crashed into the canopy of Burrows' Sabre, shattering the plane's perspex canopy. It exploded in Syd's face and blinded his left eye. After radioing Mayday, Syd tore off his helmet, cutting off further communications, and cleared the blood from his right eye.

By positioning his exposed head in the slipstream, Syd realized he could keep the blood flow away from his good eye. Barely conscious, Flying Officer Burrows was flanked by a wingman for the trip back to 4 Wing. Although he was losing blood, suffering from intense pain, in shock, and almost completely blinded, Syd managed to land his Sabre. He then taxied it clear of the runway, enabling the remainder of the formation to land. Instead of parachuting to safety and losing his aircraft, Burrows demonstrated extreme bravery and devotion to duty in flying his Sabre back to base under duress.

Burrows was awarded the Air Force Cross (AFC) for his cool reaction and courage displayed during the accident and earned the call sign "Cyclops." Syd jokes that he received the AFC for his "feat of recovering an expensive aircraft." After the incident, Syd was graded as monocular and transferred to Flying Control duties. Grounded for 12 years, he lobbied and regained flying category on both the T-33 and Dakota Navigational Training aircraft. Burrows went on to become Commander of 440 (Rescue) Squadron in 1968. In 1971, he transferred to 424 Squadron Detachment and served with the United Nations forces in Srinagar, Kashmir, flying the Twin Otter. Syd ended his career as the Base Operations Officer at Comox and retired in September 1982. In 2004, Syd Burrows was awarded a Minister of Veterans Affairs Commendation for leading the creation of *In the Service of Canada: The Seventh Book of Remembrance*, a commemoration to CF who have lost their lives on duty.

No. 1 Fighter Wing: Luffenham Base Sign.

No. 1 Air Division: CF-101 Voodoo with Genie Rocket.

No. 1 Air Division: Establishing the RCAF's Nuclear Period

With the very real threat of the Soviet Bloc to European security, NATO centralized its air power into Allied Air Forces Central Europe, head-quartered in France. The RCAF played a pivotal role in NATO's collective defence with the formation of No. 1 Air Division, deploying 12 squadrons and 300 fighters, building airfields and infrastructure, staffing each base, and training thousands of NATO aircrew. No. 1 Air Division consisted of four bases, two in France and two in West Germany. Originally at each base, three squadrons flew the Canadair F-86 Sabre, and in 1957, one Sabre squadron at each base was replaced with an Avro CF-100 all-weather fighter squadron. Then, in 1962, the CF-104 Starfighter was introduced as the Air Division's operational fighter, employed in the nuclear tactical strike role, with conditional access to U.S. nuclear weapons. Several years later two of the strike squadrons were replaced with CF-104s in the tactical reconnaissance role. Before deploying to Europe, CF-104 pilots trained at Cold Lake, Alberta, where they enrolled in intensive ground school courses on nuclear aircraft systems and delivery. They put in 80 hours of flying and all members, including groundcrew, were screened for security clearance. In Canada, CF-101 Voodoo squadrons carrying AIR-2 Genie nuclear-armed air-to-air rockets replaced the CF-100. Prepared to launch in 15 minutes, the CF-101 was Canada's primary means of air defence at Canadian air bases until it was replaced by the CF-18 Hornet. All nuclear weapons were on loan to the RCAF and could only be authorized for launch by the President of the United States. In 1969, Prime Minister Pierre Trudeau withdrew Canada from the nuclear role.

Most Canadians never knew about the RCAF's nuclear period. Although it was short and controversial, it is an important part of Canada's history. Our fighter forces in Europe had to make sweeping operational changes to accommodate it, moving from the day fighter Sabre and CF-100 roles to low-level nuclear weapon delivery, day or night, in all types of weather. The squadrons were able to accomplish this transition through effective leadership and the skill and ingenuity of its personnel. As part of this new role, the RCAF created a low-level radar bombing method using contoured maps that was adopted around the world.

Canadair Sabre F-86 Mk. 5 of 414 Squadron RCAF, 1954.

F-86 Sabre, Mk. 6: Made (Better) in Canada

The silver, sleek F-86 Sabre lanced through the air at supersonic speeds as the RCAF's frontline fighter in the early days of the Cold War. Based on the design of a German swept-wing fighter captured during the Second World War, the original Sabres were produced by North American Aviation in the United States in the late 1940s. When the RCAF commissioned the plane, Canadair rebuilt the Sabre under licence, making the historical additions of larger wings for improved manoeuvrability and an Avro Orenda turbojet engine. It was the Canadian version, the Mk. 6, that would leave its unforgettable "mark" as the best Sabre ever built.

Throughout the 1950s, Canadair produced more than 1,800 Sabres in six variants. Most of these were used by the 12 RCAF Squadrons of 1 Canadian Air Division in Europe. The RAF, Luftwaffe, Pakistan Air Force,

and USAF purchased the later, superior, Canadian-made models. Armed with six 0.50 cal (12.7 mm) machine guns, Sabres battled Soviet MiGs in the Korean War with an impressive 6–1 kill record and were also used in the Indo-Pakistani War of 1971.

Some Orenda-powered Sabres became famous for feats other than fighting. The RCAF's precision aerobatic team, the Golden Hawks, flew in Mk. 5s and Mk. 6s in the five seasons they performed. The first F-86 produced in Canada was immediately given to the NRC for the investigation of issues related to operating an aircraft at high Mach speeds. In 1953, Jacqueline Cochran set speed records in the Sabre and became the first woman to break the sound barrier.

The Sikorsky H-5 Dragonfly.

The Sikorsky H-5 Dragonfly: Canada's First Military Helicopter

The Sikorsky R-4 (also called the "Hoverfly") was the first mass-produced helicopter in the world. With its single rotor, the two-seat helicopter was a wonder of vertical flight. It could fly straight up or down, sideways, forwards, or backward, hover in the air, and fly lower than planes could—which made it ideal for observation during the Second World War. The addition of a hoist significantly advanced the machine's utility. In 1946, the four-seat Sikorsky S-51 H-5 Dragonfly took to the skies. Foreseeing that the helicopter would become indispensable to SAR over the most remote and roughest terrain in Canada, the RCAF purchased seven H-5s in 1947.

RCAF pilots learned how to fly and maintain the helicopters, observing how the H-5 performed in the harsh Canadian climate. A dedicated groundcrew and technicians kept the machines fuelled and flying.

"The S-51 was a brand new beast to me, [and was] very difficult to fly, especially in the back seat... It could be very unstable, and one had to be on the controls all the time. The S-51 was underpowered with a lot of vibration. I credit a lot of the early success with the helicopter to all the maintenance people that worked on them." – Flying Officer Bob Heaslip

The first H-5 was stationed in RCAF Station Trenton, Ontario, and the second at 103 Rescue Unit on the East Coast of Canada. Five days after arriving at 103, the H-5 went out on its first rescue mission to help a Navy Seafire fighter that went down near Dartmouth, Nova Scotia. This would mark the first of countless rescue missions flown by an RCAF helicopter. The Sikorsky H-5 served the RCAF with distinction for 18 years, introducing rotary wing operations into SAR in Canada. You can visit the H-5 Dragonfly 9601 at the National Air Force Museum of Canada in Trenton, Ontario.

Walt Pirie: The Sabre Pilots of 1 Canadian Air Division

Colonel Walter Pirie, CD

Canadians who flew the Canadair F-86 Sabres during the Cold War were some of the best fighter pilots in Europe. Walt Pirie, one of these Sabre "Jockeys," joined the RCAF in 1959 at age 17. Two years later, after completing pilot training in the "Chipmunk," Harvard, T-33 Silver Star, and Sabre, Walt was sent to Zweibrücken, Germany to fly with 1 Canadian Air Division.

It was an exciting time for the 19-year-old but not without risk. "We flew as a deterrence to the Soviet Warsaw Pact. I was honoured to be part of one of the largest post–Second World War RCAF forces ever assembled, with four wings, headquarters, and the Yellow Jack radar squadron. We had a formidable presence in Europe."

Pirie joined the renowned 427 "Lion" Squadron, which flew with No. 6 Group in Bomber Command during the Second World War. The squadron was reactivated as a fighter squadron based in St. Hubert, Quebec and deployed to Germany in 1953. Walt made lifelong friends at 427, noting with a smile that "we considered ourselves the best of the 12 Sabre squadrons, but so did all of the others."

Designated "Interceptor Day Fighter," 427 Squadron practised interceptions and participated in NATO-wide exercises. "We would fly in two-plane or four-plane formations at high altitudes, above the clouds, looking for planes to bounce." Sabre squadrons were kept on five-minute "Zulu Alerts." At a moment's notice, fully armed planes were scrambled with five minutes to get airborne. Walt's squadron was "always airborne in under three minutes. Sometimes it was an exercise, other times, an airliner or Soviet fighter had strayed into the buffer zone between the Warsaw Pact and NATO."

The F-86 Sabre Mk. 6 holds a special place in Pirie's heart. He says it was often referred to as the "Spitfire of the Jet Age," because "climbing into the cockpit felt like putting the plane on." High seating in the cockpit allowed for 360 degree visibility and, "the swept wing gave very good references to fly in close and still be safe. It was a great formation airplane." Europe was in awe of the Sabre, not based on the Canadair design alone, but also because of how Canadian pilots flew them. They consistently outflew their rival NATO forces, as proven by four consecutive wins of the Guynemer Trophy. Pirie attributes this to the BCATP and Training Command that "taught great airmanship and encouraged largely unstructured thinking and decision-making, thus allowing skilled pilots to excel."

In 1962, 427 Fighter Squadron became 427 Strike/Attack Squadron and was re-equipped with CF-104 Starfighters. Pirie transitioned from air-to-air fighting to low-level flying at supersonic speeds and went on to fly the CF-104 for 14 years. In 1976, he was a member of Canada's winning team in the Fourth Allied Tactical Air Force (4ATAF) Tactical Weapons Meet. Pirie returned to Cold Lake as a Starfighter instructor before serving as Deputy Ops Officer and Wing Flight Safety Officer in Germany from 1981 to 1986.

In 1986, Walt was posted to 4ATAF Headquarters in Heidelberg, Germany. That same year, he returned

Walt Pirie in a CF-104.

to Canada to serve as an Air Command Staff Officer at National Defence Headquarters in Ottawa. From then on, Pirie held a number of "very interesting, influential RCAF jobs" in Ottawa until 1997. After spending 38 years in uniform and another six consulting for the RCAF, Walt has never looked back. He maintains a strong connection to his fellow Sabre pilots, organizing reunions as National Chairman of the Sabre Pilots Association of the Air Division Squadrons. Pirie is proud of his career and appreciates the opportunities the RCAF gave him and his family. "I was part of the RCAF's Golden Age when we flew leading-edge fighter jets and defending against a global nuclear war was a priority."

Type 80 radar in Metz, France, run by 1 Canadian Air Division.

Yellow Jack Squadron: The Best Radar in the Cold War

Based at headquarters in Metz, France, 1 Canadian Air Division had its own radar squadron called "Yellow Jack." Using state-of-the-art, British long-range radar, they were one of the only units in Europe able to pick up targets at high altitudes. As well as identifying aircraft, the squadron used radar for aircraft recovery to get squadrons and aircrew back to base in severe weather. The Yellow Jack Squadron was staffed by the best controllers from RCAF Pinetree Stations, part of the Pinetree Line located on the 50th parallel. Installed as part of the early warning capability of a network of NATO radars, Yellow Jack provided radar control for 1 Canadian Air Division, the RCAF, and other NATO aircraft.

Two munitions and weapons technicians de-arm a Sabre aircraft after an air-to-air gunnery exercise. From left to right: Leading Aircraftman Roy Mann and Leading Aircraftman Art Murphy.

The Korean War: 2,200 Combat Missions and 1,500 Airlift Flights

Sitting in his Canadian-built Sabre "Rufus" fighter aircraft, Flight Lieutenant Ernie Glover greets Sergeant Allan Reveley, a Canadian who joined the USAF directly from Canada.

The Korean War broke out in June 1950 when the North Korean army invaded South Korea. To prevent a third world war, the UN intervened and appointed the United States to lead the defence of South Korea. Canada joined forces with the United States and other UN countries to protect the Republic of Korea (South Korea) against North Korean and Chinese advances south of the 38th parallel.

Over three years of combat, the RCAF contributed a sizable number of airmen and airwomen to the Korean war effort. Approximately 800 people served with 426 Transport Squadron at RCAF Station Lachine, Quebec, as part of the USAF Military Air Transport Service. The squadron flew 599 trans-Pacific flights in Canadair North Stars, delivering 3,000 tonnes of supplies and 13,000 personnel to nearby Japan.

Although there wasn't any direct squadron-level participation in the Korean War, 22 RCAF fighter pilots flew Sabres with the USAF's 4 and 51 Wings. Each Fighter Interceptor Wing had three fighter squadrons and Canadians served on all six. RCAF pilots flew 50 combat missions or served for six months. After being assigned to a squadron, pilots were given a short introductory flying program called "Clobber College," and then went directly into combat.

In November 1950, the first RCAF combatant, Flight Lieutenant Omer Lévesque, flew to Korea on a one-year exchange duty with the USAF. Also on the flight was Flying Officer Joan Fitzgerald, the first RCAF flight nurse to serve in the war. The RCAF flight nurses program ran from November 1950 to March 1955 and involved 40 nurses who served in pairs. At the time, they participated in 250 medical evacuation flights in the Pacific and many more throughout Canada.

The RCAF fighter pilots who flew with the USAF destroyed nine MiGs with two probable kills and ten damaged planes. They were awarded eight Distinguished Flying Crosses and 10 U.S. Air Medals. Flight Lieutenant Ernest Glover was the only RCAF pilot to be awarded the Commonwealth Distinguished Service Cross. A Second World War veteran, Glover shot down three MiGs in two days, and six in total. Other RCAF Flight Lieutenants who downed one MiG each were Claude LaFrance, Omer Lévesque, Larry Spurr, and Squadron Leader John MacKay.

The RCAF played a critical role in helping the UN maintain air supremacy during the Korean War, completing more than 2,200 combat missions and more than 1,500 round-trip airlift flights over three years of war. They were part of the more than 26,000 Canadians who served on land, at sea, and in the air during the conflict. Often called "The Forgotten War," Korea was Canada's third-bloodiest overseas conflict, and, sadly, 516 Canadians gave the ultimate sacrifice with 1,200 wounded.

Omer Lévesque: From Spitfires to Sabres—Canada's Distinguished Flying Ace

Flight Lieutenant Joseph Auguste Omer Lévesque, DFC

After ten years of flying in both the Second World War and Korean War, Canadian fighter pilot Omer Lévesque scored the fifth victory over Korea that would win him the designation of flying ace.

Born in Montreal, Quebec, Joseph Auguste Omer Lévesque joined the RCAF in 1940. He graduated in 1941 and travelled overseas to fight in the Second World War. Luck would be on Omer's side, as only two of the nine pilots in his graduating class would survive the war.

Assigned to No. 55 Operational Training Unit in Scotland, Lévesque flew the Hawker Hurricane before joining the RCAF's 401 "Ram" Squadron in England to fly Spitfires. He was one of the first pilots to shoot down the new German Focke-Wulf 190 and downed three more enemy planes before being shot down himself in 1942. Lévesque was escorting a British air attack on German battleships *Gneisenau*, *Prinz Eugen*, and *Scharnhorst*, when his Spit caught flak from the ships and he was forced to ditch in the English Channel. Picked up by Germans, Omer spent the rest of the war in Stalag Luft III, the prisoner of war (POW) camp from which 76 men escaped in 1944, inspiring the movie, *The Great Escape*. In another lucky twist, Omer didn't participate in the escape and wasn't one of the 50 POWs who were recaptured and executed.

After the war, Omer returned to Canada. He flew C-47 Dakotas in Canada's North. Lévesque then transferred to 410 "Cougar" Squadron in Quebec, flying the de Havilland Vampire and performing as one of the Blue Devils aerobatic team at air shows in 1949.

Lévesque was a Flight Lieutenant when the Korean War broke out. He was posted to the USAF's 334 Interceptor Squadron in Korea flying the F-86 Sabre. Lévesque was the first Canadian to fly air combat missions in the Korean War. In March of the same year, Omer escorted B-29 Bombers as they attacked bridges over the Yalu River, a section of the sky called "MiG Alley." Lévesque was attacked by a North Korean MiG and engaged in a corkscrewing dogfight that spiralled down from 40,000 to 17,000 ft. Omer won the battle, destroying his fifth enemy aircraft, and returned to base an ace.

Lévesque was awarded the U.S. Air Medal for flying 20 missions in five days. By the end of his tour, Lévesque had participated in 71 missions over Korea and was awarded the American Distinguished Flying Cross. He remained in the RCAF, completing a stint at NORAD before retiring in 1965 and was inducted into the Quebec Air and Space Hall of Fame in 2002.

Flight Lieutenant Omer Lévesque.

An RCAF Canadair North Star C-5 flying near Ottawa, Ontario, on September 25, 1951.

Tom Lawson: A Legacy of Gratitude

General Thomas James Lawson, CMM, CD

General Thomas James Lawson.

As part of a family that spans four generations in the RCAF, General Tom Lawson looks back on his 40-year military career with a deep appreciation. Lawson's grandfather flew Sopwith Camels in the First World War with the RFC, and his father flew Spitfires and Mustangs in the Second World War. Tom remembers them exchanging stories during Sunday visits.

Flying was ingrained in Lawson's DNA. At 16, he learned to fly Cessna 150s on an airfield north of Toronto, paying for lessons with money earned on a paper route and teaching guitar. Tom enrolled at the Royal Military College of Canada straight out of high school and studied electrical engineering. After a year of training in Moose Jaw, Lawson earned his RCAF pilot's wings in September 1980. "One of the proudest moments of my life was having my father pin my wings onto my uniform."

Another year of training to be a fighter pilot landed Tom his first operational posting overseas in Baden–Soellingen, Germany. According to Lawson, "I cut my teeth flying CF-104 Starfighters during the Cold War." Baden–Soellingen was one of four bases established by the RCAF for NATO's air defence in the 1950s. By the time Lawson arrived, the Starfighter had transitioned from a nuclear strike role to conventional weapons delivery.

Lawson never engaged in combat but prepared diligently for the possibility: "Canadians had a reputation for getting the job done in very tough conditions. We flew out of the foggy Rhine River valley, with the Black Forest mountains on one side and the Vosges on the other. We became accustomed to taking off in horrible weather and picking our way through the stratus clouds and mountain peaks." Low-level flying at high speeds in such conditions contributed to a significant number of Starfighter crashes, especially prior to Lawson's posting in Germany.

The Starfighter fleet was retired in 1986. Thirty years later, Tom Lawson retired himself, the last Starfighter pilot still in RCAF uniform. Of all the planes he's flown—including the Canadair CF-5, CF-18 Hornet, CC-144 Challenger, CC-150 Airbus, and the King Air 200—the CF-104 Starfighter stands out as his favourite. For Lawson, the legacy of the Starfighter embodies the "can-do" attitude of Canadian pilots that stretches back through the world wars to our early bush pilots. "Canada is a vast country and our pilots had to be resilient, flying in hazardous weather and landing in subarctic temperatures to refuel. An absolute determination drove them to support the logging and mining industries, ferry supplies and mail to remote locations, and help to develop Northern Canada. The mindset, 'if it can be done, we'll get it done,' is a common thread of every RCAF story."

The same drive is epitomized by Lawson's son, Ben, who routinely flies the RCAF's CC-130J Hercules to places like CFS Alert in Nunavut to deliver critical supplies. His youngest son, Jack, an Air Combat Systems Officer, commands missions on Sea King and Cyclone helicopters. The RCAF has brought Lawson's life full circle. Its legacy "rolls forward generation after generation, through the lessons we take from

Left: George Lawson, Tom Lawson's father.

Middle: Norman Moran, his grandfather.

Right: Tom receiving his wings from his father George.

those who flew before us." Some of the pilots who trained Lawson in Moose Jaw were instructed by his father's colleagues from the Second World War.

The RCAF invokes an overriding sentiment for Tom Lawson: "I feel a profound gratitude listening to my boys tell their stories today in the tradition of my grandfather and father sharing theirs. We owe a lot to those who serve. The RCAF does an exceptional job and will continue to deliver outstanding Canadian defence and security for another hundred years."

Tom Lawson pinning wings on his sons Ben (left) and Jack (right).

Avro Canada CF-100 Canuck.

Avro Canada CF-100 Canuck: Conceived, Designed, and Built in Canada

While the RCAF called the CF-100 Canuck, after the Curtis JN-4 Canuck trainer of the First World War, the name never really stuck. The twin-engine, all-weather interceptor was more often referred to as the "Clunk" based on the noise its retracting landing gear made or "the Lead Sled" due to its heavy controls. The two-seater, all-weather fighter interceptor was designed and built by Avro Canada Limited specifically for the RCAF. It boasted an excellent climb rate, first-rate fire control and radar systems, and powerful twin Orenda engines. The Canuck served in RCAF defence roles with NATO throughout the Cold War. It also completed missions for NORAD to intercept Soviet long-range bombers that might attack over the Arctic. After serving with the RCAF, CF-100s were fitted with electronic countermeasures equipment or as target tugs for training. The last CF-100 retired in September 1981. The Canuck is listed, along with the Voodoo, in Appendix 3: List of Aircraft (Current and Historical).

McDonnell CF-101 Voodoo.

McDonnell CF-101 Voodoo: Armed with Nuclear Power

After the cancellation of the Avro Arrow in February 1959, Canada needed an interceptor to arm against the threat of Soviet bombers. Enter (at Mach speeds) the interceptor, the CF-101 Voodoo. Based on an American jet fighter designed and built by McDonnell Aircraft Corporation, the CF-101B dual seater was fitted with the Pratt and Whitney engines and distinctive large afterburners. In June 1961, the RCAF purchased 66 CF-101B Voodoos to be used for ground attack, reconnaissance, and all-weather interception and training. Though many Canadians didn't know it at the time, the Voodoo was armed with the Genie nuclear missile before carrying the falcon missile. The strike fighter flew at speeds of Mach 1.72 (1,825 km/h or 1,134 mph). Serviceability for the aging aircraft became an issue in the 1970s, and in 1980, the CF-Hornet was selected to replace the Voodoo. After 24 years of service the CF-101 Voodoo was phased out in 1984, with its last flight made in April 1987.

The C-119 Flying Boxcar: Expanding Canada's Presence in the North

As a military transport aircraft, the Fairchild C-119 "Flying Boxcar" gained its nickname based on its twin-boom design and a 14,000 kg/30,000 lb payload (or ability to carry 62 troops or 35 stretchers). Throughout the 1950s and 1960s, the RCAF used Flying Boxcars to transport troops, for medevac, and to airdrop supplies overseas in UN peacekeeping missions and to military bases, weather stations, and radar sites across the Canadian Arctic.

During the Cold War, the Soviet threat required an air defence base close to the North Pole. When NORAD was formed in 1958, the 41 Distant Early Warning Line sites were completed and Frobisher Bay became a base for U.S. Strategic Air Command. With this continued American presence, it was decided that the RCAF should play a greater role in establishing air supremacy in the North. The only problem was that their Dakotas and North Stars couldn't transport heavy payloads to Arctic bases. This changed in 1950 when the RCAF took command at the Resolute Bay and Frobisher Bay bases and purchased 32 C-119 Flying Boxcars, with the first arriving in 1952.

Both 435 and 436 Squadrons in Air Transport Command were equipped with C-119s. Well-known for their daring Allied supply drops in Burma (Myanmar) during the Second World War, the two squadrons re-established their reputation by making dangerous supply runs to Arctic bases. This included hauling construction materials to the new Alert Wireless Station. Construction workers barely had time to level

The C-119 Flying Boxcar.

crude runways for the hefty Flying Boxcars bringing in supplies of oil, food, and equipment. Conditions were hazardous with blizzards, blowing snow, and subarctic temperatures. Occurring in the spring and fall, these resupply missions were the original Operation BOXTOP flights, the name derived from the Flying Boxcars ("box") that flew their missions at the "top" of the world.

The RCAF has been operating in the Canadian Arctic since its formation in 1924. From mapping Canada's remote regions to NORAD operations in the Cold War and the establishment of CFB Alert, the Flying Boxcar's resupply of Arctic bases and outposts helped to cement Canada's air sovereignty. In 1960 the first CC-130 Hercules was delivered as the RCAF's new all purpose heavy transport for airlift missions. The Flying Boxcar's RCAF career ended officially in 1967.

Fairchild C-119F Flying Boxcar (Serial No. 22110), loading paratroopers for a cold winter drop.

CF-104 Starfighter from the Aerospace Engineering Test Establishment carrying a full load of bombs.

The CF-104 Starfighter: From Nuclear-Strike to Reconnaissance Role

Long and slender with a T-tail, it's no wonder that the CF-104 Starfighter was called the "Missile with a man in it." Thanks to its Orenda J79-OEL-7 turbojet engine and 15,800 lb of thrust, the Starfighter could fly Mach 2.2 or over 2,695 km/h. The sleek aircraft excelled at flying high speeds at low altitudes, under the Russian radar—just what the RCAF needed at the time in its role with NATO.

During the Cold War, the RCAF commissioned a replacement for the Canadair F-86 Sabres to counter the Russian threat. Built by Canadair (Bombardier), the CF-104 Starfighter entered Canadian service in March 1962. Eight RCAF squadrons were stationed in Europe in the tactical nuclear strike and reconnaissance role. Originally designed as interceptors, Starfighters were armed with B28, B43, and B57 nuclear weapons and carried a reconnaissance camera pod. In the early 1970s, the RCAF shifted its NATO role to ground attack and outfitted the Starfighters with conventional weapons like the Canadian-designed CRV-7 rocket pods, British BL755 cluster bombs, Mk. 82 Snakeye "iron" bombs.

Several squadrons transitioned to flying the CF-104 in a tactical reconnaissance role, a move prompted by French President de Gaulle's refusal to allow non-French nuclear weapons in France. RCAF 439 and 441 Squadrons stationed at 1 Fighter Wing, Marville, France, were required to relearn a role that the RCAF hadn't performed since the Second World War. Equipment such as the Vinten camera pod was developed and ex-CF-101 pilots and navigators were trained as "photo interpreters."

Low-level flying at such high speeds made the Starfighter an unforgiving plane to fly. Pilots had seconds to take corrective action or eject. In its 25 years of service, there were 110 accidents and 37 pilot fatalities, giving the plane the nickname, "The Widowmaker." Despite these statistics, Canada had one of the lowest accident rates among those who flew the CF-104 in Europe. RCAF Starfighter pilots were well-respected for their skills. In 1986, the CF-104 Starfighters were officially retired and replaced by the CF-18 Hornet. As the last of the Century Series of Fighters in Canada, the CF-104 leaves behind a legacy that continues today.

A World-Renown Flight Safety Program: Trusting a "Just Culture"

Between 1953 and 1957, the RCAF lost 476 aircraft and 405 personnel. Regardless of their circumstances, the Air Force had to do something about these grim numbers.

The first formal recognition of the need for a Flight Safety (FS) organization occurred in 1942 with the formation of the Aircraft Accident Investigation Board (AIB). Unfortunately, the Second World War ended with little progress made by a dwindling team of six members until the 1950s, when the Directorate of Flight Safety (DFS) was established. The DFS resurrected the AIB and based on the losses suffered after the Korean War, made the development of a FS Program its highest priority.

Change happened quickly. AIB investigations became more thorough. Pilots and engineers were trained to help uncover the cause of accidents so that preventative action could be taken in the future. The program was so successful that in 1958, only 42 aircraft were lost compared to 81 in 1957. The downward trend in losses continued over the next decade, and inquiries moved away from assigning blame and recommending punishment. This philosophical shift deepened during unification, when the program introduced a *Manual of Flight Safety for the Canadian Forces* and expanded the reporting system.

The cornerstone of the FS program today is based on a "Just Culture," which supports the open reporting of incidents without fear of recrimination and investigation that occurs independent of the chain of command. No other air force boasts an equivalent privilege of information or has created such a spirit of trust. The RCAF's FS program is well-respected and modelled around the world.

While FS has come a long way since the disasters of the mid-1950s, its mandate remains the same: to prevent accidental loss of aviation resources while accomplishing the mission at an acceptable level of risk. The FS program continues to reduce accident rates and inform aircraft operations and maintenance practices. Recently, it has taken on a broader focus that includes risk management to help the RCAF build stronger operational processes and improve its ability to prevent accidents.

Did You Know... the RCAF Kicked off the World's First Fitness Craze?

It was called the RCAF 5BX Plan.

In the late 1950s, Dr. Bill Orban was tasked with making fitness available to every member of the RCAF. It was widely believed that physical fitness would improve the mental alertness of aircrews and give them a reserve of energy to draw from in emergency situations. Since many RCAF members were stationed in remote parts of Canada with limited access to a gym, the program couldn't rely on facilities or equipment. And the regimen had to fit into busy schedules of training and operations.

Dr. Orban created the 5BX (five basic exercises) Plan for men and the XBX (ten basic exercises) Plan for women. The innovative programs were based on his observation that intensity of exercise had a greater effect on fitness than time spent exercising. Resembling today's hugely popular high-intensity interval training (HIIT) workouts, participants in 5BX complete reps of basic exercises like push-ups, sit-ups, and running on the spot. The entire workout can be completed in just 11 minutes (12 minutes for the woman's program). As participants progress, levels of difficulty are introduced by variations of each exercise.

Because the 5BX workout could be completed anywhere—from barracks to backyards—it became popular with civilians. The booklet (as seen above) was published in the United States, translated into 13 languages, and distributed around the world. Many adopted the workout and continue to incorporate its philosophy of leading a balanced and healthy lifestyle through fitness today—including celebrity Helen Mirren and British royals King Charles III, Prince William, and his wife Catherine, Princess of Wales.

NORAD: One of the Most Enduring Defence Partnerships in the World

Featured in movies like *War Games*, *Dr. Strangelove*, and *Interstellar*, NORAD's bunker is a fan favourite. And it's no wonder. Its original command centre, the Cheyenne Mountain Operations Centre, discretely carved out of a granite mountainside, captured the imaginations of many. The entrance to an underground operations room—row upon row of monitors, maps, and radar systems—is protected by actual blast doors. Romanticized on the silver screen, NORAD is, in fact, one of the oldest and most enduring defence partnerships in the world.

At the outset of the Cold War, Canada found itself on the frontlines between the Soviet Union and the United States. The new Soviet long-range bombers brought the nuclear threat home to North America. In 1958, both countries formalized the integration of an air-defence force under a joint command, NORAD. It was agreed that NORAD's Commander-in-Chief would always be an American four-star general and the deputy commander, a Canadian three-star general—the only non-American officer approved to release American nuclear weapons in an emergency.

To identify and warn of any attacks against North America from aircraft or coastal approaches, NORAD coordinated fighter interceptors, a system of radar lines called the Pinetree Line, Mid-Canada Line, and finally, the Distant Early Warning System, and maritime long-range patrols to counter Soviet nuclear submarines. Additional detection capabilities included the Ballistic Missile Early Warning System and the Missile Defence Alerting System, a U.S. satellite constellation able to detect missiles from space. In 1981, to represent its mission more accurately, NORAD incorporated the term "Aerospace" into its name. After the 9/11 terror attack, operations expanded to include internal threats and a maritime warning system. Today, NORAD provides security at major events including the Olympics, assists law enforcement with smugglers,

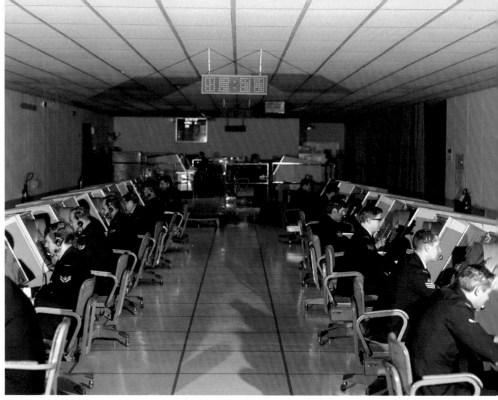

SAGE "Blue Room" in NORAD Underground Complex at CFB North Bay, Ontario.

and on the lighter side, tracks Santa on Christmas Eve to the delight of children around the world.

NORAD is coordinated in Canada through 1 Canadian Air Division at its headquarters in Winnipeg, Manitoba, with fighter squadrons stationed in Cold Lake, Alberta, and at Bagotville, Quebec, flying the CF-18 Hornet. In North Bay, Ontario, 22 Wing is home to the Canadian Air Defence Sector and is responsible for the North Warning System, a radar system that stretches from Alaska to southern Labrador.

After moving to Peterson Air Force Base in 2012, NORAD Headquarters was renamed the Eberhart-Findley Building, in part after RCAF Lieutenant-General Eric Findley for his stellar performance on 9/11. More than 50 years after its formation, NORAD continues to epitomize the trusted coordination of defence between Canada and the United States.

Pinetree Radar Station.

Close up of the radar antenna with the dome in the background. This DEW Line Site is located at Cambridge Bay in the Arctic.

Pinetree Line, DEW Line, and the North Warning System

Building an Integrated Air Defence System

When the Soviet Union tested its first atomic bomb in 1949, the need for an early warning system became a reality. Suddenly, many cities in North America fell within range of Soviet nuclear weapons. Under NORAD, the Canadian and U.S. governments agreed to build a Continental Radar Defence System called the Pinetree Line. In 1954, the RCAF and USAF worked together to implement a network of 33 radar stations that ran from Newfoundland to Vancouver Island, north of the Canada-U.S. border, close to the 50th parallel.

As the threat of attack grew, so did the requirement for an integrated defence system. The Canadian Mid-Line was built in 1957 along the 55th parallel to complement the Pinetree Line. That same year, construction began on the DEW Line to protect the Arctic North. Establishing 63 radar stations covering 8,000 km (3,000 miles) from the Canadian Arctic to Greenland was a massive job. Over 460,000 tonnes of equipment and supplies were hauled in, including enough gravel to build two Great Pyramids of Giza. Constructed amidst snowstorms in the dark, Arctic winters, the Dew Line became an important part of NORAD and the integration of the RCAF into a complex defence system.

With the Mid-Line closed down, low-flying cruise missiles rendered the remaining Pinetree and Dew Lines obsolete. In 1985, Canada and the United States agreed to a modern radar line, the North Warning System (NWS). Replacing the old radars, it ran along Canada's Arctic Coast at 70° N. Of its 52 stations, 47 would be in Canada and 11 would be staffed. Five northern airfields were established by the RCAF and outfitted with quick-reaction hangars to house CF-18s. For over 50 years, the NWS served as a deterrent in the North. In 2022, addressing a changing threat environment, which included cyberattack and sea-lane approaches, NORAD announced plans to overhaul its aging radar stations as part of a modernization of continental defence. The NWS will be replaced by two radar systems, one northern and one polar that can "see" over the horizon to track cruise and hypersonic missiles launched from outside of North American Airspace. The RCAF continues to support the Canadian government and NORAD in fulfilling its requirements for nationwide defence and sovereignty in the North.

The BOMARC Missile: Canada's SAM Squadrons

The Boeing CIM-10B BOMARC was a supersonic long-range surface-to-air missile (SAM) used during the Cold War for the air defence of North America. In 1958, the Canadian government cancelled the Avro Arrow and made the controversial announcement that the BOMARC nuclear missile would replace the jets. North Bay's Underground Complex was command-and-control centre for two CIM-10 BOMARC SAM missile squadrons: 446 SAM Squadron at RCAF Station North Bay and 447 SAM Squadron at La Macaza, Quebec. Each site was equipped with 29 BOMARC missiles: 28 for combat and a 29th for training purposes. Armed with a 10-kiloton W-40 nuclear warhead, in the event of an attack, the 56 missiles would be launched into the air and their warheads detonated to destroy as many bombers as possible. Although the BOMARCs were housed in Canada on 24-hour standby, their warheads were stored separately under the control of the USAF. No BOMARCs were ever launched in Canada.

The first site in the United States was operational in 1959, with the RCAF squadrons fully operational by 1963. By the time all missiles were introduced into service, however, the system was largely obsolete. The nuclear politics of the Diefenbaker era were officially over when Prime Minister Pierre Trudeau withdrew Canada from the nuclear role in 1969, with many Canadians unaware of the fact that the country was ever in the nuclear role. In 1971, all BOMARC sites were closed down, both RCAF squadrons were disbanded, and the warheads were removed from Canada.

Aerospace Control Operator

Aerospace Control Operators operate radar, computer, communications, and other sensor systems for the surveillance and control of airspace. They work in the control tower as data operators or ground controllers, recording flight plans, interpreting weather reports, maintaining records, and helping to keep vehicles and aircraft on the airfield moving smoothly and safely.

"I'm Corporal Ryan Braid from Ottawa. I'm an Aerospace Control Operator currently serving at 22 Wing, North Bay, Ontario. We are in charge of tracking all aircraft inbound into North America, whether it's a foreign aircraft entering airspace, a ship in distress in a search and rescue component, or if there's an airliner that's in trouble—we're ready to answer the bell. Dealing with aircraft on a daily basis has been a passion in which I've invested all my time and skillset. Every day is different. We could come in one day and it's just a normal few exercises or fighter missions; the next day we have a real, live emergency that we need to spring into action. That's when the weapons pit is activated and the order may come down to scramble our fighter jets to go check out what's going on."

Military Police at the blast door located in the entrance to the SAGE Military Complex.

A Canadian and an American work together on a Canada West Regional Operations Control Centre radar console, 1987.

CFB North Bay: Home of "The Hole"

Although "The Hole" at CFB North Bay sounds anything but covert, uncommon, or cutting edge, don't be fooled by its nickname. Officially NORAD's North Bay Underground Complex, The Hole is one of the most secure operations centres in Canada, built to withstand a 4-megaton nuclear blast. Incidentally, that's hundreds of times more powerful than the bomb dropped on Hiroshima.

After the NORAD agreement was signed, Canadian and U.S. forces needed a home for their system of supercomputers. Called SAGE, the system coordinated the two nation's military response to a nuclear attack. CFB North Bay was selected as the site for the underground complex and construction began in 1959. Located 60 storeys beneath some of the Canadian Shield's toughest granite, it took four years to build the sprawling facility, which is roughly the size of a shopping mall. It was comprised of two parts: the Main Installation with the control and communications equipment, and the Power Cavern which supplied the bunker with its very own energy grid.

In the event of a nuclear war, The Hole was designed to support 400 people living underground for a month. Facilities included a cafeteria, medical clinic, a gym, and a barber shop. By the early 2000s, the nuclear threat had lessened and the operations system was out of date. Expensive to run, The Hole was decommissioned. These days, while decommissioned it continues to find use and was featured in a 2012 sci-fi film, *The Colony*. At the time of writing, the National Trust for Canada had appealed to the government to save it. Even with The Hole out of commission, CFB North Bay remains one of the most important military bases in Canada with respect to our national air defence. Renamed to 22 Wing in 1993, the base is the centre for all NORAD operations in Canada, under the Canadian NORAD Region Headquarters. It is also home to Detachment 2 of the USAF's 1st Airforce.

The CF-105 Avro Arrow.

The Avro Arrow

A Marvel of Modern Engineering

Long and sleek with a massive, bladed tail, the Avro Arrow captured the imagination of Canadians. In March 1958, 13,000 people gathered outside the Avro Aircraft Plant in Malton, Ontario—the site of Pearson International Airport today—to witness the Arrow's first test flight. Pilot Janusz Zurakowski was at the controls, escorted by "Spud" Potocki and RCAF pilot Jack Woodman in a CF-100 Canuck and an F-86 Sabre. As it took to the skies, the futuristic Arrow promised to thrust Canadian innovation to the forefront of the aerospace industry.

The CF-105 Avro Arrow was a twin-engine, long-range, all-weather supersonic interceptor. Intended as a replacement for the RCAF's Avro CF-100, the Arrow's mission was to counter Soviet bomber threats in Canadian airspace during the Cold War. In 1953, the best and brightest Canadian minds came together to design this marvel of modern engineering. The Arrow boasted advances in aerodynamics, computer-assisted technology, flight control, engine design, and speed. It was built to fly at Mach 2 and reach altitudes of 18,000 m or 60,000 ft. The Arrow pioneered fly-by-wire technology, the first aircraft with an onboard computerized control system that enabled pilots to control the plane electronically. Five pre-production Arrows were outfitted with J-57 engines while the sixth was equipped with Orenda Iroquois engines—although it never flew.

On the same day as the Arrow's debut, the Soviet Union launched the world's first satellite, Sputnik 1, and overnight, ballistic missiles replaced bombers and interceptors as the primary threat to North America. The Canadian government of John Diefenbaker, struggling with the massive cost of the program, worried that the Arrow might become obsolete in the face of this new threat and in 1959, abruptly cancelled production of the Arrow. The talented engineers who worked on the Arrow headed south to work on NASA's Gemini and Apollo space programs. Production on 31 more aircraft was halted, as were Avro's top secret projects, some of them straight out of science fiction—including a lunar rover, a flying saucer called the "AvroCar," and a hovering truck.

The Avro Arrow was ahead of its time in stealth, weapon deployment, and fly-by-wire technology. Many of these innovations live on in aircraft design and development today—and, as we now know, the Canadian government was wrong about the pending obsolescence of air superiority fighters.

The NRC's National Aeronautical Establishment

Innovating for RCAF Airworthiness, Safety, and Readiness

The NRC's National Aeronautical Establishment in Ottawa, Ontario.

"The NRC's Aerospace Research Centre (ARC) is a vital source of R&D expertise for the Directorate of Technical Airworthiness and Engineering Support (DTAES) in areas such as Aerospace Structures and Materials Performance, Flight Research, Aerodynamics, and Gas Turbine Research. The strong relationship that has developed and continues today between the NRC's ARC and several organizations in the Canadian Defence team has contributed to improved sustainment of numerous RCAF fleets and enabled the introduction of new technologies and capabilities for military aviation in Canada." – Martin Breton, Director of DTAES, Department of National Defence, Government of Canada

Since its establishment in 1951, the NRC's National Aeronautical Establishment, which later became the NRC's Institute for Aerospace Research (IAR), has been instrumental in establishing research excellence in aerodynamics, structures, materials, aeropropulsion, and flight research.

When the Flight Research Laboratory (FRL) was established in 1946, the RCAF had been conducting experiments on its own and welcomed the NRC's scientific research expertise, creative engineers, and unique test facilities. The FRL was one of five labs in the IAR, with two of them, the Aerodynamics Laboratory and the Structures and Propulsion Laboratory, predating the FRL. The propulsion section has been around since the days of the Avro Arrow and was used to test the aircraft's Iroquois engine in the 1950s.

In the 1960s, the IAR experimented with helicopter-based simulation at the lab to explore the limits of Vertical and Short Take Off Landing Technology. In the 1980s, when the helicopter industry arrived in Canada, the IAR developed a revolutionary fly-by-wire system that replaced manual flight controls with electronics, and the Bell 205 Airborne Simulator provided critical data for the handling of modern military "rotorcraft." As the RCAF continued to invest in helicopters, the need for advanced research grew with the IAR ultimately creating an R&D Platform for testing advanced avionics in flight.

For more than 75 years, the FRL has helped advance the RCAF's defence capabilities and aviation in Canada. The lab shaped modern flight data recording systems with the invention, almost 65 years ago, of the precursor to the "black box" flight data recorder. Analyzing cockpit voice recorders, the technology is still used by the lab's Flight Recorder Playback Centre to investigate incidents for the Canadian military. Since the lab's inception, the NRC has been investing steadily in facilities such as wind tunnels, electrodynamic shakers, engine-icing test centres, and hyperspectral imaging systems. A typical day in the FRL might involve training astronauts in a microgravity airplane, otherwise known as a "vomit comet," or a T-33 "sniffer jet" flying behind commercial airliners to measure pollution and emissions with airborne sensors.

The NRC's research into flight mechanics and avionics has led to better and safer airplanes being built. From fatigue testing CF-18s to assessing RCAF helicopter noise and vibrations to developing alternative fuels to help the RCAF maintain interoperability with its NATO Allies, the NRC is a vital partner to Canada's Air Force. It continues to help the RCAF meet its goals for airworthiness, safety, and high readiness levels for all its fleets and aircrew. Today, the IAR is concentrating on future-forward technologies that the RCAF can leverage, such as virtual reality, digital twins, 3D printing, and drone detection to pioneer advances in Canada's defence.

Larry Ashley: Delivering Air Power to the Navy
Lieutenant-General Larry Ashley, CMM, CD

Larry Ashley's story starts, where many cadets' stories do, at the Royal Miliary College (RMC) of Canada. After graduating as an officer in the Royal Canadian Navy (RCN) in 1959, Ashley's career took a different trajectory—one identified by unique intersections of the RCN and the RCAF.

Initially, Ashley hadn't considered a flying career; he was fascinated by the RCN's plans to modernize with a new class of destroyer escorts (DDEs). Ashley caught the flying bug from RCAF colleagues at RMC who left each summer for aircrew training. Serendipity came into play in his third year when the RCN changed Ashley's curriculum to General Science and Naval Engineering and selected him for RCAF pilot training.

Ashley was awarded his wings in 1960. From that moment on, his connections to the RCAF would be "varied and quite extraordinary." At the time, the RCN began to make all of their ships air capable, converting DDEs to helicopter destroyer escorts (DDHs) to carry Sea Kings. After a flying tour on the aircraft carrier HMCS *Bonaventrue*, Ashley circled the globe in 1964 in the prototype DDH, HMCS *St. Laurent*, as Air Officer.

Ashley's next stint with the RCAF came in 1965 when he was selected for the Long Telecommunications Course at RCAF Centralia. "So, for a year, I was once again a dark-blue-suited guy in the Air Force community. That course propelled me into flight test and aerospace engineering." In 1967, Ashely became a test pilot for the Sea King helicopter at United Aircraft in Montreal.

As a naval officer in the newly unified Canadian Armed Forces (CAF), Ashley had several appointments on destroyers and commanded both 406 and 423 Maritime Helicopter Squadrons at CFB Shearwater. He was approached by RCAF Lieutenant-General Bill Carr to help incorporate Naval Air into the air arm of the unified CAF. In 1975, he joined Carr's staff in Winnipeg, Manitoba, as Senior Staff Officer Maritime Helicopters when Air Command was formed. A year later, he was appointed Commander of CFB Shearwater—taking operational command of an Air Command formation without ever having officially been in the RCAF. If Ashley had an *alma mater* it was Shearwater and he appreciates its 100-year history as the home of many innovations in maritime air warfare, including the development of the Beartrap helicopter hauldown system.

Ashley has flown 3,800 hours on various aircraft, with a good many spent in the Sea King, tracking Soviet submarines in the North Atlantic during the Cold War. The maritime helicopter holds a special place in Ashley's heart. "Everybody who flew the Sea King fell in love with it. It was very reliable—big, robust, and wonderful to fly—all very comforting at 40 ft on a dark, North Atlantic night."

After leaving Shearwater, Ashley was appointed Director of Air Force Requirements at National Defence Headquarters in Ottawa and Project Director of the CF-18 Program. In 1981, he was seconded to NATO to manage the complex Airborne Warning and Control System program. Two years later, he was appointed Chief Air Force Doctrine and Operations and in 1986, Commander of Air Command. In 1989, Lieutenant-General Ashley took early retirement from the CAF to form Lockheed Canada as Chief Executive.

Lieutenant-General Larry Ashley.

CFB Shearwater Base Commander Colonel Larry Ashley in front of a CH-124 Sea King.

The RCAF represents the zenith of Ashley's career. "Of course, I am proud of my naval roots and training, but I am humbly honoured to have served as Commander of Air Command. The RCAF is an enormously complex and competent organization made up of highly professional people who undertake a myriad of domestic and global missions in support of Canada's interests and commitments. For 100 years, air power has been essential to Canada's security, growth, and prosperity. Today and into the future, the RCAF will continue to meet that vital responsibility."

HMCS *Regina* "Beartrap" hauling in a Sea King.

The Beartrap: How to Snag a Sea King

What do a beartrap and a helicopter have in common? A lot when you're attempting to land a 10-tonne Sea King with a rotor span of 19 m (that's 62 ft) on the deck of a warship in high seas. The "Beartrap" is the world's first Helicopter Hauldown and Rapid Securing Device and one of Canada's greatest contributions to naval aviation.

Sea Kings were housed on aircraft carriers until a group of "Crazy Canucks" suggested they could land on the decks of destroyers. The Beartrap was developed in the early 1960s by members of the RCN's Experimental Squadron 10 at Shearwater and Dartmouth's Fairey Aviation. The system consists of a steel hauldown cable, an aircraft locking probe, a winch below deck, and a locking trap on deck. Once the helicopter is secured to the probe, it is winched from a high hover to a low hover, maintaining synchronicity with the ship's pitch and roll before the pilot is cleared to land. Upon landing, the trap closes on the probe, locking the helicopter firmly to the deck.

According to former RCAF Commander Lieutenant-General Larry Ashley, using the Beartrap could be, "very smooth, very fluid, even in severe weather. It was essential to know deck movement—the ship's pitch and roll—before landing. Every ship has a characteristic pitch and roll and some, like the Bonnie (HMCS *Bonaventure*) had a signature corkscrew motion. Experience taught all aircrew that knowing their ship's motion was essential to successful operations."

The Sea King was the first helicopter to use the Beartrap. It was later adopted by navies around the world, including the United States, Australia, and Japan, with many others developing similar hauldown systems.

RCAF CP-122 Neptune.

Long-Range Patrol and Anti-Submarine Warfare

The Neptune, Argus, and Aurora

What do gods and goddesses have to do with Anti-Submarine Warfare (ASW)? Plenty when it comes to hunting submarines and defending the world's longest coastline. During the Cold War, the RCAF used Neptune, Argus, and Aurora aircraft for long-rage patrol. Aptly named, they were the all-seeing, all-knowing eyes of ASW and deterrence.

The RCAF and the RCN consolidated ASW under Maritime Command. Responsible for its air arm, the RCAF initially converted Lancasters from the Second World War for ASW and maritime reconnaissance. In 1955, the RCAF replaced the aging Lancasters with 33 Lockheed P2V Neptune aircraft. Named after the Roman god of the sea, the Neptunes were armed with torpedoes, mines, depth charges, internal bombs, and rockets under their wings. Radar mounted on the aircraft's belly enabled it to detect submarines from considerable distances. A total of 25 Neptunes served with the RCAF on 404 "Buffalo," 405 "Eagle," and 407 "Demon" Long Range Patrol Squadrons.

In 1958, the RCAF developed its own maritime patrol aircraft, the Canadair CL-28 (later CP-107) Argus. The most advanced anti-submarine patrol bomber of its time, the Argus was fitted with an array of sensors for detecting submarines and consequently named after the

hundred-eyed giant of Greek mythology. The Argus was a redesign of the Bristol Britannia, modified to increase its low-altitude range and space for weapons and electronic equipment. It could carry up to 3,600 kg (8,000 lb) of weapons, including torpedoes and depth charges. Other ASW equipment included powerful radar, underwater listening devices, electronic countermeasures equipment, a magnetic anomaly detector, and a searchlight that could identify a periscope up to 2.8 km (1.7 miles) away. A mainstay of the RCAF during the Cold War, 33 Argus flew critical missions off of all three Canadian coasts.

As faster, nuclear-powered submarines replaced conventional ones, Maritime Patrol added short-range patrols that flew from HMCS ships. In 1962, the HMCS *Bonaventure* was outfitted with Grumman CP-121 Trackers and Sikorsky HO4S ASW helicopters, which were later replaced by Sea King helicopters. Between 1962 and 1966, all RCN *St. Laurent* class ships were converted to helicopter-carrying destroyers and fitted with a hangar and landing deck.

Although there were tense ASW moments during the Cold War, the most significant was the Cuban Missile Crisis, during which the RCAF raised its readiness alert level and ramped up surveillance patrols in the North Atlantic Ocean. Argus crews flew six hours to a mid-Atlantic Station, patrolled for eight hours, then returned home.

To counter the threat from ballistic missile-firing submarines, the RCAF replaced the Argus with the CP-140 Aurora in 1980 and the planes remain in operation today. Named after the Roman goddess of dawn, the Aurora is Canada's only strategic Intelligence Surveillance and Reconnaissance (ISR) aircraft and is operated by both 405 and 407 Maritime Patrol Squadrons. Able to cover great distances at high speeds, the RCAF's fleet of 14 Aurora aircraft conducts long-range missions over land, water, and coastal areas. It fills a wide variety of roles for the RCAF, including maritime and overland ISR, ASW, strike coordination, and SAR. The Aurora is also used to assist government agencies in combatting illegal fishing, pollution, drug trafficking, and more. Two Auroras were deployed to the Middle East as part of Operation IMPACT and flew over 800 sorties.

RCAF CP-107 Argus.

CP-140 Aurora.

The Sea King: 55 Years and 550,000 Hours of Dedicated Service

The CH-124 Sikorsky Sea King has a legacy unlike any other RCAF aircraft. Over the last five decades, the maritime helicopter has revolutionized the concept of air support for naval forces.

The first Sea King arrived in Shearwater, Nova Scotia, in 1963 when the RCN purchased a fleet of 41 Sea Kings during the Cold War. Introduced to counter the newer, faster Soviet nuclear-powered submarines, the Sea King proved itself to be more than capable in ASW. During its tenure, modifications and upgrades included radar, GPS, tactical navigation computers, acoustic detection equipment, Forward Looking Infrared (FLIR), homing torpedoes, and, most notably, it's innovative "Beartrap" system.

Following the Cold War, the Sea King became a multi-purpose maritime helicopter and earned its reputation as one of Canada's hardest-working aircraft. Its crews have flown an incredible 550,000 hours on operations around the world, including in Somalia, the Persian Gulf, Timor-Leste, the Adriatic, Haiti, and Libya. Domestically, Sea Kings have contributed to SAR, disaster relief, counter-narcotic operations, and fisheries and pollution patrols.

When the venerable chopper was retired in 2018, RCAF Lieutenant-General Al Meinzinger acknowledged a widespread appreciation for the aircraft and its crew: *"No other fleet has served as long as the Sea King, and its 55 years of service are a monument not only to its durability and capability, but to the men and women who operated, maintained, and supported this incredible helicopter."* Having operated from the aircraft carrier HMCS *Bonaventure*, St. Laurent-class destroyer escorts, Iroquois-class destroyers, and auxiliary oiler replenishmen supply ships, the Sea King was replaced by the CH-148 Cyclone as the RCAF's principle ship-borne helicopter.

Airborne Electronic Sensor Operator

Airborne Electronic Sensor Operators use advanced electronic sensor systems on board long-range patrol aircraft, maritime helicopters, SAR aircraft, and remotely piloted aircraft. Their missions include underwater warfare, above-water warfare, ISR, and SAR.

"I'm Master Corporal Johanna Flawn from Annapolis Valley, Nova Scotia. I'm an Airborne Electronic Sensor Operator at 406 Squadron in Shearwater, Nova Scotia. The biggest thing with the helicopter being on the ship is that it is an extension. We're there to find submarines, ships, do search and rescue if need be. And we also just get to do a lot of really cool stuff. When you're hunting a submarine and you've done countless exercises, simulations, and training to work towards that moment, it's just a giant game of hide-and-seek and when you find them, you win. Flying off the back of a ship is the most exhilarating portion of being a sensor operator, as well as being able to go out on missions that have specific things you have to accomplish and getting home as a crew after accomplishing that."

Opposite: 12 Wing Shearwater personnel, 423 Maritime Helicopter, and 12 Air Maintenance Squadron commemorate the Sea King's 50th anniversary.

4 Wing Baden–Soellingen

CF-18s above Hohenzollern Castle in Germany.

RCAF's Klein Kanada

The Rhine Valley in Germany is home to one of the RCAF's most scenic air bases in Europe, CFB Baden–Soellingen. Nestled between the picturesque Black Forest and the Rhine River, meandering through vineyards and castles, the base was built in 1953. Located just outside of the small farming community of Soellingen in the province of Baden, it was named Baden–Soellingen. The base became home to 4 Fighter Wing, one of the most outstanding units in 1 Canadian Air Division serving NATO during the Cold War.

Once the base was built, RCAF personnel and their dependants settled into 400 apartments that lined the airfield. As 4 Wing continued to grow, the settlement developed into its own independent community, complete with a mayor and town council. It featured a cinema, swimming pool, tennis courts, ball diamonds, library, post office, a bank, and (of course) a hockey arena. The first school opened in 1954 and was lauded as one

of the most modern in Baden. The RCAF village became known as "Klein Kanada" to neighbouring German towns, with RCAF members and their families participating actively in local civic, economic, and social life.

By 1962, 1 Canadian Air Division moved its headquarters to Lahr, Germany, and 2 Wing disbanded, its two squadrons joining the Wings at Zweibrücken and Baden–Soellingen. Five years later, 3 Wing was closed and its squadrons dispersed among the remaining Wings. In 1970, 1 Wing disbanded and the Canadian Air Division was reformed into 1 Canadian Air Group (1 CAG), consisting of 4 Wing squadrons, 421 "Red Indians," 409 "Nighthawks," and 439 "Sabre Toothed Tigers" Squadrons.

The 1980s saw a ramp-up in defence spending and CF-18 Hornets replaced the CF-104 Starfighters of 4 Wing, heralding in a new and exciting era in fighter plane aviation in Europe. The Nighthawks formed the first CF-18 squadron at Baden in June 1985. The

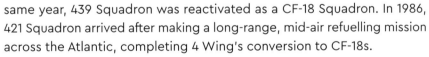
Master Corporals Reg Rivard (left) and Lon Elliott (right) discuss repairs to be made to a damaged F-404 engine from a CF-18 Fighter.

CF-18s fly by the tower at CFB Baden–Soellingen, Germany, for the last time, 1993.

same year, 439 Squadron was reactivated as a CF-18 Squadron. In 1986, 421 Squadron arrived after making a long-range, mid-air refuelling mission across the Atlantic, completing 4 Wing's conversion to CF-18s.

A potent fighter of its time, RCAF CF-18s in Europe were optimized for air defence missions and armed to counter any Soviet strike carried out by MiG and Sukhoi fighters. By practising air-to-air and air-to-ground strike operations, 4 Wing became extremely combat capable, receiving excellent Tactical Evaluation results in NATO and other evaluations. The three squadrons continued to operate into the early 1990s with at least two involved in deployments to the Middle East in support of Desert Storm in 1991.

After the Berlin wall came down, the Cold War thawed enough for Canada to cease flying NATO operations from Baden–Soellingen. European bases were shut down and RCAF fighter forces were consolidated in Canada. Following the closing of CFB Baden–Soellingen in 1993, CFB Cold Lake, Alberta, became the home of 4 Wing.

Remnants of CFB Baden–Soellingen remain in Germany in local displays, such as the CF-104 in the village of Soellingen, each one a tribute to the close relationship between Germans and Canadians with the RCAF.

CHAPTER 4
UNIFICATION
Maintaining Canadian Sovereignty

UNIFICATION
MAINTAINING CANADIAN SOVEREIGNTY

In the mid-1960s, Canada's Minister of National Defence, Paul Hellyer, tabled a white paper to parliament that recommended the unification of Canada's military to save money and improve efficiency. Unification was made official on February 1, 1968, when the *Canadian Forces Reorganization Act* came into effect. The Royal Canadian Navy (RCN), the Canadian Army, and the RCAF were consolidated into one service, the Canadian Armed Forces (CAF). The RCAF's five commands—Air Defence, Air Transport, Air Division, Air Training, Air Material, and the Office of the Chief of Air Staff—were abolished.

The RCAF, along with the flight organizations of the army and navy, became collectively known as the "Air Element." The remainder of the RCAF, the RCN's Air Arm, and the Army's helicopter and light fixed-wing air assets were distributed between the new Mobile Command and Maritime Command. Along with its name and uniform, much of the RCAF's rich heritage was lost under unification. Canada would not have a recognizable Air Force again until 1975, when, under the command of Lieutenant-General Bill Carr, Air Command was stood up.

Despite its fragmented identity, the RCAF continued to expand its capabilities in the areas of transport, medical evacuation, and Search and Rescue (SAR). The heavy duty transport aircraft, the CC-130 Hercules, joined the ranks of Canada's Air Force with the initial purchase of the "B" models in the late 1960s. Able to carry just about anything, the Hercules became the Air Force's lifeline, delivering much-needed aid and rescue during humanitarian crises and natural disasters. The aircraft helped to maintain Canada's sovereignty in the North through countless transport missions to the CAF's Station in Alert, Nunavut—missions that continue to this day. With the purchase of the "HT" model, the Hercules expanded its versatile role to include Air-to-Air Refuelling (AAR). This would become a key capability of the Air Force, enabling its fighter jets (and allied fighters) to complete longer missions farther north and across both oceans. Later, this AAR role would be shared with the CC-150 Polaris.

A milestone achievement of this era was the purchase of a fleet of new fighter jets, the CF-188 Hornet, also known as CF-18s. In 1977, the Canadian government called for the acquisition of a single

Photo of two female Pilots in front of the CF-18 aircraft.

multi-role fighter to replace three existing and largely outdated Air Force fleets: the Voodoo (employed in the North American Aerospace Defense Command, or NORAD, defence), the Starfighter (supporting the North Atlantic Treaty Organization, or NATO, in Europe), and the Freedom Fighter (which was providing tactical support for the army, NATO, and used in fighter pilot training). The hugely complex project was called the New Fighter Aircraft (NFA) program. Then Brigadier-General Paul Manson was appointed NFA Program Manager and given $2.34 billion and a dedicated team to find Canada the right fighter jet. In three short years, the major procurement was secured from McDonnell Douglas for its CF-188 Hornet, despite two federal elections held during that time. The acquisition would launch an unheard of five decades of combat effectiveness for Canada's Air Force.

The NFA program was one of the most expensive military procurements since the Korean War. Not without controversy, it procured a fleet of 138 CF-18s in Canada, complete with state-of-the-art software, increased weapons and reconnaissance capabilities, and airborne self-protection jamming. Training in the new fighters began and the CF-18s soon became integral to Canada's missions abroad and at home. The fighter jets participated in northern sovereignty exercises and provided a security element organized through NORAD to protect events like the Winter Olympic Games in Operation PODIUM.

During the 1970s, Canada's military was working towards becoming more gender inclusive. A Royal Commission on the Status of Women recommended that the CAF standardize its military enrolment criteria, allow women to attend Canadian military colleges, and make all military trades and officer classification available to women. In 1980, the CAF opened up the pilot classification to women. Three women became the first RCAF pilots: Captain Dee Brasseur, Captain Leah Mosher, and Captain Nora Bottomley. As CF-18 pilots, Captains Brasseur and Jane Foster became the first women in the world to fly fighter jets since the Second World War. Lieutenant-Colonel Karen McCrimmon was the first woman air navigator and the first woman to command an Air Force squadron as Commander of 429 Transport Squadron in Trenton, Ontario. Lieutenant-Colonel Maryse Carmichael became the first female Snowbird pilot and eventually Commanding Officer, and Major-General Nancy Tremblay was the first woman to reach the rank of Colonel within the aerospace engineering occupation. The list of women serving in the RCAF continues to grow today as they carry the torch of those who served before them, opening doors to a wide range of opportunities to serve.

In 1982, Canada adopted the *Canadian Charter of Rights and Freedoms*, which prohibits discrimination based on race, national or ethnic origin, colour, religion, sex, age, and mental or physical disability. This significantly widened the scope of inclusivity in the CAF. Previously, the Canadian military had a policy of releasing LGBTQ2+ members, which peaked during the Cold War, over concerns of susceptibility to blackmail. In 1990, after being discharged because she was a lesbian, Michelle Douglas launched a successful lawsuit against the Canadian military, which ended the discrimination against the military's LGBTQ2+ members. In October 2016, the House of Commons Defence Committee voted unanimously to amend the service records of LGBTQ2+ ex-military members who had been dishonourably discharged because of their sexual orientation. This led to the 2017 formal apology by Prime Minister Justin Trudeau and a $145 million settlement from the government.

In the early 1990s, Air Command witnessed military cuts that reduced its strength from 23,000 to 13,500 personnel. Fleets of aircraft were retired and numerous bases, including Lahr and Baden–Soellingen, Germany, were closed. Although the "Air Element" returned to wearing its blue uniform in 1985, shedding the army green of unification, it wouldn't be until 2011 that the Air Force would be restored to its much-loved and time-honoured roots as the Royal Canadian Air Force.

When the RCAF Disappeared

General Paul David Manson, OC, CMM, CD

General Paul Manson, Chief of the Defence Staff.

In celebration of the 100th anniversary of the Royal Canadian Air Force, I wonder how many Canadians realize that the RCAF didn't exist for 48 of those years.

In the mid-1960s, Canada's Minister of National Defence, Paul Hellyer, convinced the government of the day to unify Canada's armed forces and unification came into effect on February 1, 1968. One immediate result was the disappearance of the RCAF as a constituted organization. Whereas the Canadian Army and Royal Canadian Navy, while losing their historic names, retained their basic structures as Mobile Command and Maritime Command, respectively, Canada's major Air Force elements were either parcelled out to these new land and naval commands or were turned into stand-alone air organizations. Formally, therefore, the RCAF ceased to exist.

It wasn't all bad. Unification did succeed in one of its principal objectives, which was to diminish the unhealthy interservice rivalry that had existed. Another benefit was unifying essentially identical services that had existed separately in each of the army, navy, and air force, such as medical, dental, supply, financial, and chaplaincy. The traditional RCAF rank titles were also gone, but this change was largely welcomed. Squadron leaders no longer led squadrons, wing commanders didn't command wings, and the resort to American-style rank titles brought certain benefits in dealings with allies who already wore these ranks.

But the Air Force paid a heavy price in other ways beyond the loss of the RCAF name. The disappearance of the associated central organization was painful, and much of the pain was psychological. Staunch members sensed a heavy impact on their history, heritage, and custom, which from the beginning had been at the heart of their pride in the RCAF's outstanding operational performance in war and peace, and their devotion to duty. The absence of high-level command leadership was also disturbingly evident. Lost too was the distinctive light blue uniform, being replaced by a tri-service green version that was widely disparaged.

So the disappearance of the RCAF in 1968 was a great challenge during the ensuing years. Yet in 2024, as veterans, serving airmen and airwomen, and Canadians celebrate a very real RCAF on its centenary, it is apparent that the challenge was clearly met in a lengthy process, which restored the RCAF name in August 2011. How did it happen?

A huge first step occurred in 1975 when Lieutenant-General Bill Carr, one of the nation's greatest airmen, masterfully convinced the Chief of the Defence Staff to bring the military's air resources back together in a new organization called Air Command. It wasn't quite the old RCAF, but it restored the central Air Force structure that veterans and serving personnel needed and wanted. A few years later, a government edict brought back distinctive service uniforms; Air Force members past and present rejoiced at the return of the traditional light blue dress.

In 1995, the next logical move occurred: reversion to the familiar title Chief of the Air Staff, denoting the Air Force's senior commander. That was followed in 2011 by the ultimate step in the process, the Air Force's return to its historic name, the Royal Canadian Air Force, which remains its familiar and beloved identifier

Opposite: Paul Manson in his CF-104 Starfighter.

as the force's centenary is celebrated in 2024.

In many ways, Canada's Air Force today is very different from what it was in 1968, for perfectly understandable reasons. The force's top-ranking officer is now quite appropriately called Commander of the Royal Canadian Air Force. Most of the aircraft employed in those earlier days have been replaced by highly advanced modern craft. Women now serve in greater numbers and in much higher ranks. Operational roles have changed in a world that presents new and strategically challenging threats to Canada and our allies.

What hasn't changed is the simple fact that, in spite of the official absence of the RCAF name for almost half of its existence, the RCAF itself never did disappear in all that time. It was there all along, very much alive, deeply embedded in the minds and hearts of those who served, sustained in the traditional quality of that service, and remembered as a part of the history being celebrated on the 100th anniversary of the RCAF.

Bill Carr: The Father of the Modern Air Force
Lieutenant-General William Keir Carr, CMM, DFC, OStJ, CD

Lieutenant-General William Carr.

Although Lieutenant-General William "Bill" Keir Carr would say his career was no different to any other war heroes, it most definitely was. When he graduated, his wings were pinned on by none other than Billy Bishop himself. Carr flew Spitfires on 143 recon missions deep into Nazi territory in broad daylight, earning him the Distinguished Flying Cross in 1944. He returned home and flew Norsemans with 413 (Photographic) Squadron over Canada's North to survey remote, unmapped areas—the risky flights meriting a lake, "Carr Lake," being named after him in Nunavut. Flying Queen Elizabeth II, French President Charles de Gaulle, and Prime Minister John Diefenbaker around the world as Commander of 412 (VIP) Squadron didn't define Carr's historic contribution to the RCAF. Despite his distinguished RCAF career, Bill Carr is best known as the "Father of the Modern Air Force."

Being a great leader and change agent for the RCAF took part in the latter half of Carr's career, post-unification. Under a new command structure, a decentralized Air Force suffered from inefficiency, low morale, and the inability to establish a unified air authority. Carr noted that the division of assets according to function wasn't working. Doctrine was not taught, there was no oversight on flight safety, aircraft were being misused, and some units failed to maintain required levels of flying proficiency.

As a broken Air Force limped along, Bill Carr was appointed to Deputy Chief of the Defence Staff in 1973. Now in a position of power, he decided the time was right for an organizational change. Carr documented examples of inefficiency and abuse of fleets and recommended incorporating an air element into the CAF. Along with Major-General Dave Adamson, Chief of Air Operations at National Defence Headquarters, and Norm Magnusson, Commander of Air Defence Command, Carr was able to persuade his navy and army colleagues that it was time for a Unified Air Command. After overcoming the final hurdle—gaining the approval of the Cabinet, the Chief of the Defence Staff, and the Minister of National Defence—Lieutenant-General Carr was charged with implementing Canadian Forces Air Command and appointed its first Commander in 1975.

As Commander of Air Command, Carr was given authority on all Canadian Forces air activities, including the former Naval Fleet Air Arm and Army Flying Corps. Headquartered in Winnipeg, Manitoba, Carr united disparate units and assets under Air Command in a command-and-control structure of five groups: Fighter Group (FG), Maritime Air Group (MAG), Air Transport Group (ATG), 1 Canadian Air Group (1 CAG), and 10 Tactical Air Group (10 TAG). The Air Reserve Group was established the following year and Air Command's structure remained in place until 1997.

The second point of order was to restore the ailing morale for Canada's Air Force. RCAF heritage, symbols, and traditions were adopted by Air Command. In 1985, the RCAF's distinctive blue uniforms were restored. Lieutenant-General Bill Carr had left his indelible mark on the RCAF as the "Father of the Modern Air Force"— and indeed, the entire Canadian Armed Forces.

For a description of the organization of the RCAF, see Appendix 4: RCAF Organization and Ceremonies.

Al DeQuetteville: Launching the CF-18 Era—Five Decades of Fighter Combat Effectiveness

Lieutenant-General Al DeQuetteville, CMM, CD

Lieutenant-General Al DeQuetteville.

By the 1970s, the RCAF needed to replace its fleet of fighter jets—CF-104 Starfighters, CF-101 Voodoos, and CF-116 Freedom Fighters. Brought into service in the 1960s, all three were at the end of their service lifecycles. To maintain Canada's fighter capability, the Department of National Defence introduced a New Fighter Aircraft (NFA) competition. The McDonnell Douglas CF-18 Hornet won in what Lieutenant-General Al DeQuetteville describes as "a model procurement," launching five decades of fighter combat effectiveness in Canada.

DeQuetteville spent six years in the NFA acquisition process, first in the Directorate of Air Requirements and subsequently as Operational Requirements Manager in the NFA Program Office. From seven original candidates in 1977, the F-16 and the F-18 made the shortlist. Contracts were drafted for each by the team, something that "distinguished the procurement because the government could choose a fighter and sign a contract without lengthy negotiations." In April 1980, the contract was signed, two months after a new federal government took office. Thirty months later, the first two of 138 CF-18s were delivered, timing that Al considers "unprecedented, even with the election curveball thrown in." When the first CF-18 arrived in Ottawa in 1982, DeQuetteville was in it, along with Chief Test Pilot Jack Krings.

The CF-18 "ticked all the boxes" with the best fighter capability, contract, budget ($2.4 billion), risk mitigation, and industrial benefits for Canada. It also brought the RCAF into the digital age. Designed for the U.S. Navy to operate off of aircraft carriers, the CF-18's arrestor gear, landing gear, and wing-fold mechanism made it ideal for operating in Canada's cold climates. But the plane's *pièce de résistance* was its avionics. "Running fourteen different computers, it was state-of-the-art at the time."

The fighter helped restore Canada's prestige in 1988 when CF-18 squadrons received the first-ever A1 rating in both air-to-air and air-to-ground roles during NATO's yearly tactical evaluation assessment in Europe. This dual capability "took the RCAF back up to the pinnacle of success." Back home, CF-18 squadrons conducted NORAD's air sovereignty and defence missions with air-to-air refuelling support, something that was new to the RCAF and "a huge force multiplier." Canada's fighter jets could now fly non-stop from Canada to Europe or as far north as they needed to go.

In 1991, after deploying to the Gulf War, advances in technology rendered some of the CF-18's avionics and armaments incompatible with evolving threats. The Incremental Modernization Project was introduced to upgrade the fighter in two phases. Al expected this because "during the NFA competition, we measured the aircraft's growth potential. The CF-18 had excess capacity for computers and abundant power due to two modular engines—advantages that the RCAF has capitalized on over time."

In 1982, Al commanded 410 Squadron, the first CF-18 squadron, training subsequent CF-18 pilots at Cold Lake. He served as Base Commander/Wing

Commander 4 Fighter Wing at CFB Baden–Soellingen, and Commander 1 Canadian Air Division in Europe. In 1990, DeQuetteville was appointed Director General Force Development and in 1992, became Chief of Force Development. He was appointed Commander, Air Command in 1995, and Chief of the Air Staff in 1997 before he retired in 1998.

Ironically, Al never wanted to be a pilot. He was preparing to study engineering at Queen's University when his uncle suggested he pursue the CAF's Regular Officer Training Program. Al took the opportunity. After earning his wings, he was posted to Germany in 1967 flying CF-104s. For DeQuetteville, "life couldn't get much better. The RCAF hooked me and 37 years later, I was still there." He was 18 when he walked into the recruiting centre in Kingston, Ontario. After retiring from the Air Force, Al ended up "back in the heart of aerospace, working as Vice President of Boeing on programs that affected the RCAF. There isn't a day that goes by that doesn't connect me to the RCAF. It's everything."

Paul Manson, Bill Carr, and Al DeQuetteville are all mentioned in Appendix 1: List of RCAF Commanders and Command Chiefs.

CF-188: The Hornet with a Sting

The CF-188 Hornet, commonly called the CF-18, is a multi-role fighter that replaced the RCAF's three fleets of fighter jets in 1982. A variation of the American McDonnell Douglas F/A-18 Hornet, the CF-18 flies at speeds of 1,814 km/h or Mach 1.8, is highly manoeuvrable, and has target-tracking radar and modern communications. Well-suited to the modern battlefield, it's used by the RCAF for air defence, ground attack, tactical support, aerobatic demonstration, and aerospace testing and evaluation.

During the Cold War, CF-18s were optimized for defence missions to counter Warsaw Pact air forces. Since then, RCAF CF-18 Fighter Squadrons have participated in combat during the Gulf War in 1991, the Kosovo War in the late 1990s, and were part of the Libyan no-fly zone in 2011. They also flew bombing missions against ISIS in Iraq and Syria in Operation IMPACT. Back home, CF-18s were deployed on Operation NOBLE EAGLE, NORAD's mission to protect the skies over North America and saw action in Operation PODIUM, a security mission to protect the 2010 Winter Olympics in Vancouver.

At the time of writing, there were 88 CF-18 jets in use based out of 3 Wing Bagotville, Quebec, and 4 Wing Cold Lake, Alberta. Over the past few decades, the fleet has undergone a two-part modernization program which has made the CF-18 fully combat capable, employing the most sophisticated precision-guided weapons. Upgrades include structural improvements, an extensive overhaul and replacement of critical onboard systems, and cockpit improvements.

In January 2023, the Government of Canada announced that starting in 2026 the Lockheed Martin F-35 would replace the CF-18 Hornet. This procurement project for the RCAF—the largest in over three decades—will continue the 50-year-old legacy that the CF-18 maintained, defending our Canadian shores, enhancing our Arctic sovereignty, and meeting both NATO and NORAD obligations to protect against emerging threats.

RCAF CF-188 Hornet fighter.

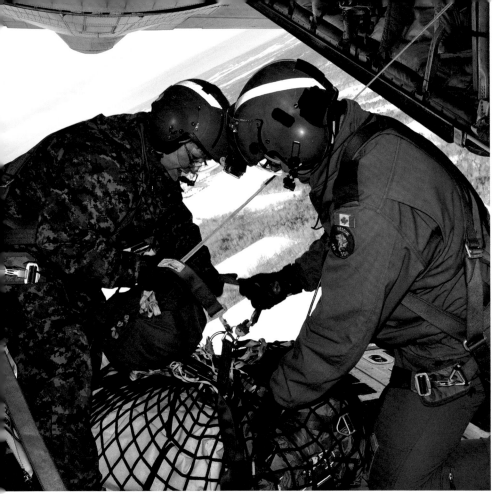

Loadmasters, Warrant Officer Nathalie Mallet (left) and Captain Bryan Aubin (right), prepare the parachute prior to dropping it over 14 Wing Greenwood, Nova Scotia, airfield during a training exercise on January 20, 2016.

Loadmaster/Traffic Technician

Traffic Technicians play a key support role in the Canadian Armed Forces, organizing the transport of materiel, equipment, and personnel around the world using every mode of transport. Traffic Techs are also employed as loadmasters on military transport aircraft. This specialty qualification enables Traffic Techs to fly as aircrew on aircraft like the CC-130 Hercules, CC-177 Globemaster, and the CH-147F Chinook helicopter. These technicians help to move everyone and everything—be it helicopters, vehicles, ammunition, humanitarian relief supplies, or people. Traffic Techs carefully plan and coordinate each mission to ensure the Canadian Armed Forces can operate anywhere in the world.

RCAF CC-150 Polaris fuelling CF-18 Hornets.

Polaris: The Airborne Gas Station

The CC-150 Polaris is the designation for the civilian Airbus A310−300s converted into multi-purpose, long-range aircraft for military passenger, freight, or medical transport for the RCAF. Two of the RCAF's CC-150s are equipped for AAR. Each Polaris can offload 80,000 lb of fuel to receiving aircraft over a 4,630 km (or 2,500 nautical miles) leg and is capable of ferrying four CF-18 fighter aircraft across the Atlantic Ocean. The tanker is a strategic AAR platform compared to the RCAF's CC-130HTs, which are used for both strategic and tactical AAR missions.

Polaris aircraft are also an essential strategic airlift asset supporting global operations. Five RCAF CC-150s are operated by 437 Transport Squadron at 8 Wing Trenton, Ontario. They have supported UN, Red Cross, and NATO initiatives, helped to enforce the no-fly zone over Libya in Operation MOBILE in 2011, and provided a key capability to the RCAF Air Task Force in operations over Iraq and Syria during Operation IMPACT.

One VIP-configured Polaris with the call sign "CAN Force One" is used to transport government officials and foreign dignitaries, including the Canadian Prime Minister, Governor General, and members of the Royal Family. While the Polaris has the flexible capacity for troop and VIP transport, it lacks the oversize cargo capacity required in more austere operations. For this, the RCAF relies on heavy lift aircraft such as the C-17 Globemaster.

A CF-188 Hornet from 425 Tactical Fighter Squadron refuels from a CC-150 Polaris from 437 Transport Squadron in the skies over Alberta during Exercise MAPLE FLAG 51 on June 15, 2018.

Air-to-Air Refuelling

Extending the Mission

Air-to-Air Refuelling (AAR) is a critical force multiplier for the RCAF. Its two AAR fleets, made up of the CC-150 Polaris and the CC-130HT Hercules aircraft, support combat operations on both NORAD domestic missions and NATO expeditionary missions abroad. The tankers act as airborne gas stations, refuelling both foreign and Canadian fighters during a mission, enabling them to carry heavier payloads and complete more and longer sorties. Domestically, AAR helps Canada assert its sovereignty over its three coasts and the far north. With a range of 3,300 km (2,000 miles), CF-18s have to refuel as soon as they reach the Arctic from bases in Bagotville, Quebec, and Cold Lake, Alberta. Tankers often fly with the fighters in a "ferry-escort" role.

AAR first became a reality in Canada when the Canadian Forces acquired five CC-137 aircraft (converted Boeing 707s) in the early 1970s and modified two for an aerial refuelling capability. As part of the Multi-Role Tanker Transport Program (MRTT), 437 Squadron acquired five Airbus 310 (CC-150 Polaris) to replace the CC-137s for transport in 1992. That same year, five new Hercules CC-130HTs were purchased in the tanker configuration. In 2008, two of the five CC-150s were converted to AAR tankers.

Here's how a typical AAR procedure works: Each Polaris has two refuelling pods, one on each wing, which contain 23 m (or 74 ft) of hose. At the end of the hose is a basket or "drogue." A retractable probe on the receiving aircraft plugs into the drogue to receive fuel at approximately 2,000 lb/min. The Flight Refuelling Specialist operates and monitors the procedure using the tanker's cameras and sensors. A good deal of planning goes into each AAR flight. The specialist has to be able to update calculations to ensure that the right amount of fuel is passed to the right planes at the right time. The loadmaster acts as the specialist's eyes, watching the procedure as the aircraft connects with the tanker's hose. After the required fuel is taken, the receiving aircraft disconnects from the hose and moves to a safe zone away from the tanker. AAR is a complex process that involves a lot of moving parts, often with multiple tankers in the air supporting hundreds of sorties a day. The exercise requires some delicate flying from both the receiving fighter jets and the tanker.

The MRTT Program has been a gamechanger for the RCAF, reinstating its AAR capability lost when the CC-137s were retired. Like the Polaris, the Hercules tankers provide the RCAF with a flexible AAR asset, also using drogue-style refuelling pods. Currently, 437 Transport Squadron is equipped with two CC-150 Polaris tankers and 435 Transport and Rescue Squadron has completed decades of tactical AAR with the five CC-130HT Hercules aircraft, including providing AAR support for the defence of North American airspace in Operation NOBLE EAGLE.

Ron Slaunwhite and the CF-18: The DND's Big Spender

Brigadier-General Ronald Slaunwhite, CD

Brigadier-General Ron Slaunwhite.

Brigadier-General Ron Slaunwhite's fascination with engines began early in life. As a teenager, he would help his father, Sherman, overhaul boat engines. Spending summers on McNabs Island, Nova Scotia, Ron remembers the military presence and the anti-aircraft guns in Halifax Harbour during the Second World War. He later combined these two interests—mechanics and the military—in an RCAF career that led him to successfully manage the hugely complex CF-18 Program in the 1980s.

While studying science and engineering at St. Mary's University, Halifax, Ron enrolled in the Regular Officer Training Plan. He completed Basic Officer Training at the Royal Military College in Kingston and took aeronautical engineering at RCAF Station Alymer, Ontario. In 1957, Slaunwhite was posted to No. 1 Air Division in Metz, France, as Aircraft Maintenance Staff Officer.

After graduating, Ron became Air Repair Officer at RCAF Station Penhold, Alberta, and he was "responsible for the maintenance, repair, and airworthiness of 92 aircraft." Slaunwhite then served as Programs and Management Officer at 6 Repair Depot, Trenton, Ontario, where he enjoyed the challenges of balancing projects, schedules, and budgets. In 1965, Slaunwhite was the RCAF's first-ever Exchange Officer posted to USAF Tactical Air Command Headquarters at Langley Air Force Base, Virginia. As Configuration Control Chief, he "managed the deployment and replacement of fighter and reconnaissance aircraft to Southeast Asia for two years during the Vietnam War."

Slaunwhite returned to Canada and held several senior roles. He was chosen to attend National Defence College (NDC) as a member of course No. 31, Canada's most senior government course with extensive travel. After completing NDC, Ron became Director of Aircraft Engineering and Maintenance at National Defence Headquarters, Ottawa. In 1980, he was promoted to Brigadier-General and appointed Project Manager of the CF-18 Program. The acquisition of 138 CF-18 Hornets from McDonnell Douglas was Canada's largest defence contract with a budget of $5.194 billion. For Ron, "Being selected to manage it was exhilarating." He created the project infrastructure, which had to "meet all contract objectives, along with the delivery of the aircraft and industrial benefits for Canada."

Slaunwhite commanded a project team in Ottawa and three detachments in the United States. "One of the largest challenges I faced was keeping control of the budget because other departments were constantly seeking funding. I said 'No' frequently." Slaunwhite and his team accomplished everything the original contract set out to—seven years ahead of time. The project was transformational for both the RCAF and the Canadian aerospace industry. "The new fighter jets cost $3 billion and, in turn, $5 billion was invested in employment, technology, and industry expansion in Canada."

As the RCAF turns 100, Ron is proud to have been there for nearly one-third of those years. "Its training made me a better, more qualified officer. I worked hard to ensure that the RCAF had the air capabilities it required to perform its many roles, and that included introducing the new CF-18 fighter jets to Canada and Europe."

Above: Colonel Slaunwhite with his family of Air Cadets.

Below: Flying Officer Slaunwhite inspecting an engine.

Aerospace Engineering Officer

Aerospace Engineering Officers are responsible for all aspects of the engineering, maintenance, and management of military aircraft, and all of their support equipment and facilities during military operations.

"I'm Lieutenant Keisha Chin-Yet from Halifax, Nova Scotia. I'm an Aerospace Engineering Officer, currently posted to 450 Tactical Helicopter Squadron in Petawawa, Ontario. Our main job here is to meet operational needs for aircraft. So, if pilots want to fly the aircraft, we need to make sure that those aircraft are ready for every single mission that's planned. We have to manage snags—if something breaks on the aircraft that is unforeseen—and then also complete planned maintenance. Every 200 hours we do an in depth inspection. And we schedule those so we don't have all of our aircraft down at the same time for maintenance."

A CF-18 Hornet fighter jet prepares to refuel in the air over Vancouver during Operation PODIUM.

Operation PODIUM

Protecting the Montreal 1976, Calgary 1988, Vancouver 2010 Winter Olympics

In the aftermath of the terrorist event at the 1972 Munich Olympics and later, the September 11 attack on the World Trade Center, three of the largest peacetime security operations in Canada—the Montreal 1976, Calgary 1988, and Vancouver 2010 Winter Olympics—were carried out, in part, by the army, navy, and air force arms of the Canadian Forces (CF). In all three events, security was integrated into a massive effort headed by the RCMP with operational support from the CF, Department of National Defence, Canadian Security Intelligence Service and the Canadian Border Services Agency, municipal police units, and the private sector. In a system that is typical in domestic security operations, the only difference between each event was its historical context.

During the 1976 Summer Olympics, Montreal was in the midst of the Front de libération du Québec Crisis and federal political figures were potential targets. In light of this, the CF were sent into Montreal to provide security for the games. Once again in Calgary in 1988, Olympic security was comprehensive and tight with the CF playing a more discreet role. For the 2010 Vancouver Olympic Games, the post-9/11

security framework was based on experience gained during the 1976 Montreal and 1988 Calgary Winter Olympics. The CF's contribution to overall security of the Vancouver 2010 Olympic and Paralympic Winter Games in support of the RCMP-led Integrated Security Unit was called Operation PODIUM.

The Air Component Command in Op PODIUM consisted of airlift, medical evacuation, and area surveillance for the RCMP while NORAD fighter jets ensured airspace security through joint U.S. and Canadian surveillance. Extensive airlift and air security was provided by CH146 Griffon, CH-124 Sea King, CP-140 Aurora, and CC-138 Twin Otter aircraft. Along with deployable radar units, CH-146 Griffons, CC-130 Hercules, and CC-150 Polaris tankers delivered aerospace warning, control, and Air-to-Air Refuelling support for CF-18s patrolling in defence of the localized event. As part of Op PODIUM's Air Component, the RCAF worked with security and public safety agencies to provide a safe environment while the world celebrated sporting excellence at the Olympics.

NRC's Trisonic Wind Tunnel
Extending the Life of the CF-18

NRC's Trisonic Wind Tunnel with a CF-18 test model.

The National Research Council of Canada's (NRC) Aerospace Research Centre (ARC) is a leader in the use of wind tunnel technology to study aerodynamics. Its 1.5 m Trisonic Wind Tunnel was built in 1962 to help in the development of supersonic fighter aircraft. It's a pressurized tunnel capable of running in subsonic, transonic, and supersonic flows from Mach 0.1 to 4.25. Today, the wind tunnel plays a fundamental role in the development of RCAF aircraft and defence systems and is part of the program that has extended the lifespan of the CF-18 Hornet fighter jet.

Virtually every aircraft built in Canada has been tested in NRC wind tunnels, which has made possible the prediction and optimization of aircraft performance and safety. After the RCAF acquired the CF-18 in the early 1980s, the fighter jet was used outside of its design specifications with unprecedented flight times and cycles. In 1989, the Department of National Defence (DND), concerned with overall fatigue of the jet,

commissioned the NRC's ARC to test its longevity by investigating events that impacted the aircraft's integrity and other phenomena, such as corrosion. The wing test was instrumental in certifying the CF-18 and providing the data required for preventive modifications which resulting in savings in the purchase of components and maintenance.

Called the International Follow-On Structural Testing Program, it has become one of the longest running programs in the world. As part of this program, the NRC's structural life extension program on CF-18 fighter jets has helped to ensure safety and gained years of usage for the current fleet. The partnership between the NRC and the RCAF has led to ongoing projects to validate, certify, and support the lifetime of the CF-18 fleet, along with other exciting initiatives, including testing the aerodynamics of a new sniper pod on the CF-18 Hornet.

Robert "Scratch" Mitchell: A Richly Storied Fighter Pilot Career

Lieutenant-Colonel Robert Mitchell, CD

Snowbird Lead Major Rob "Scratch" Mitchell.

As a boy, Robert "Scratch" Mitchell knew there was something special about flying military airplanes—from seeing the sparkle in his Grandpa's eyes when he talked about flying Spitfires in the Second World War to feeling the house shake as his dad flew in CF-101 Voodoos overhead. Being a fighter pilot was exciting and generationally ingrained. In his early 20s, Scratch continued the Mitchell family legacy and enlisted in the RCAF where he enjoyed a 20-year career, high-lighted by tours as a CF-18 air demonstration pilot and as lead of the legendary Snowbirds. After retiring from the Air Force, Scratch channelled his creativity into film and television, blending his roles as aviator, performer, and storyteller in productions like the Discovery Channel's *Airshow* and Roland Emmerich's film, *Midway*.

Mitchell is drawn to stories that explore the human condition. He uses universal themes like "Man Versus the Machine" to describe the challenges he faced as a pilot in training. Competition was stiff. Only one graduate in his class would become a fighter pilot. Scratch was lucky; flying came naturally to him. But it required more than technical ability "to figure out the jet's interface, blend with the machine, and develop a mastery of it early on. I was able to connect to the jet, find it limits, and know what those were." Scratch had to know his own limits, too. "A lot of people call me a daredevil when they see me flying in air shows. But in the course of being a military pilot, I've learned my limits. That's the wherewithal you get in that discovery of 'Man Versus Himself.' Not only do you find

the edges of the machine, but you also find the edges of yourself."

Landing the coveted fighter pilot spot as top of his class, Scratch completed three tours in CF-18 Hornets, with two as an instructor. In 1999, Scratch was asked to be the CF-18 demo pilot for the RCAF's 75th anniversary air show season, a role that sparked his passion for performance. "I found I could tell a story to hundreds of thousands of people." Engaging with the audience as the public face of the RCAF was deeply fulfilling for Scratch. Performing with the Canadian Forces Snowbirds aerobatic team was the next logical step in his career.

After flying one tour with the Snowbirds, Scratch returned as Commanding Officer/Team Lead in 2007, his most challenging role. Along with administrative duties, he had to "lead the formation and fly it flaw-lessly every time." The true test of his leadership came when the Snowbirds suffered a fatality during practice and lost Captain Sean McCaughey. Scratch instructed everyone to land and meet at the 5 Jet for an "over-wing" debrief. The last plane in, Scratch will never forget what followed: "I walked up and there were 22 pairs of eyes staring at me. They all said the same thing: 'What do we do now, boss?' And I realized that leadership wasn't just showing up to do your job, it was doing your job under horrible circumstances when everyone depended on you."

Scratch was prepared for that moment by the RCAF. "I was given so much exposure to leadership styles, positions, and challenges, I was ready to deal with something horrific. The military trains you to deal with adversity." The camaraderie of the squadron helped, a constant experience in the RCAF made up of "moments of extreme living, good and bad. In both cases, they bond you with your peers so tightly it changes your life."

After leading the Snowbirds, Scratch was promoted to Lieutenant-Colonel and selected as an Exchange Officer for postgraduate training in Australia. It was there that he decided to retire from the RCAF and pursue a career in film and television. Since then, Mitchell has transferred his RCAF skills and talents into acting, producing, and directing. He continues to tell the story of the RCAF. His latest project, the film *Valiant Skies*, celebrates the RCAF's 100th birthday by showcasing its many capabilities in a fictitious "day in the life" of the Air Force. For Scratch, the film is a labour of love. A way to give back to the RCAF for instilling in him qualities that he carries throughout his life—honour, integrity, authenticity, camaraderie, and leadership. Scratch closes the loop of gratitude when he considers the opportunities he was given: "I think in the RCAF, I was able to make a difference."

Lieutenant-Colonel Robert Mitchell (left) stands with his father, Bob, and grandfather, Fred.

Karen McCrimmon: The Example of Leadership is Service to Others

Lieutenant-Colonel Karen McCrimmon, OMM, CD

Lieutenant-Colonel Karen McCrimmon.

Karen McCrimmon joined the Royal Canadian Army Cadets on a dare. Just 17 years old, she told her brother, "I can do that," demonstrating a confidence that would shape her military career. But it was fellow soldier and friend, Suzanne, who made the start to that journey tolerable. Together they graduated from cadets and joined the Windsor Regiment as Reservists. McCrimmon credits their camaraderie—and other women she bonded with in a male-dominated military—as critical to her success in becoming the first female air navigator and, later, the first woman to command a squadron in the RCAF.

When the RCAF opened aviation training to women, McCrimmon was accepted as a Navigator and admits that it was tough at times. Some RCAF members were hard on women because they believed they didn't belong in the military. "We had to go the extra mile to prove ourselves." But McCrimmon is quick to credit the majority of her colleagues as welcoming the opportunity to depart from the accepted norms of the past.

As she climbed the ranks, trailblazing a path for other women to follow, McCrimmon was not satisfied with the status quo. A strong proponent of "service leadership," McCrimmon believed that leaders should serve their teams, not be served by them. In 1998, McCrimmon was promoted to Lieutenant-Colonel and given command of 429 Transport Squadron, flying CC-130s in Trenton, Ontario. She put service leadership into practice. "It was up to me to provide the kind of environment the team needed to excel."

As the first woman to command a Canadian Forces flying squadron, McCrimmon knew that she would have to build trust with her team. She likens the process to a trust bank account in which "you make deposits by being reliable, respectful, honest, helpful because one day, you're going to make a mistake. But if you've invested in your trust bank account, you'll have something to withdraw against."

This approach applied to McCrimmon's international posts as well. Serving overseas in Germany as a Senior Staff Officer at the NATO Air Headquarters, McCrimmon built trusted relationships with participating nations. She used her experience with strategic and tactical airlift at 429 Squadron to set up a deployed air mobility coordination cell for the International Security Assistance Force in Afghanistan.

In 1995, McCrimmon was made a Member of the Order of Military Merit, in part for her contributions to the incorporation of the Trenton Family Resource Centre. Another venture McCrimmon is proud of is the 429 Squadron reunion of veterans who served in Bomber Command during the Second World War. Her squadron, and particularly her secretary, Gloria Hewson, whom McCrimmon considers "a fine leader," tracked down 71 veterans and coordinated a weekend reunion. The experience exemplifies McCrimmon's respect for the RCAF. "All these veterans still felt connected to the Air Force. I share their sense of pride in the RCAF. My mother used to say, 'it's not happiness that makes you grateful, its gratefulness that makes you happy.' I'm grateful for the experience, the camaraderie, community, and all the opportunities I had to serve this country and other people. To learn and to be a better person. I wouldn't have any of that without the RCAF."

In 2006, after a 31-year military career, Karen McCrimmon retired as a Lieutenant-Colonel. She continued to serve Canada as a Member of Parliament from 2015 to 2021.

Lockheed CC-130 Hercules 130307 taxiing into the Canadian Air and Space Museum in Ottawa for retirement on April 5, 2016.

Lockheed CC-130 Hercules
One Aircraft, Many Capabilities

For those in need, the distinct roar of the four-engined turbo-prop military aircraft, the Hercules, is a welcome sound. It means that help has arrived in its required form, be it food, fuel, medicine, supplies, or firepower. Affectionately called the "Herky bird" or "Herk," the dependable CC-130 Hercules has an admirable history of saving lives all over the world, delivering supplies and infrastructure to remote areas in Northern Canada, airdropping troops and equipment into hostile territory, conducting search and rescue (SAR) operations, supporting flood and fire evacuations, and completing countless humanitarian missions.

Designed by Lockheed Martin in 1959 as a troop, medevac, and cargo transport, the CC-130 Hercules is a beast of a plane. It can airlift 92 ground troops, 64 paratroopers, 74 patients, or 45,000 lb of cargo in a hold that's 4,500 ft³—roughly the size of a boxcar. The rear ramp and door allow for easy loading and unloading and aerial delivery via parachute when landing isn't possible. If you can name it, chances are the Hercules has

moved it—soldiers, other planes, armoured vehicles, and trucks. It's even hauled a live whale. The CC-130 can fly in severe weather and operate from short, primitive airstrips of gravel, sand, or dirt. One of the most amazing feats this machine can accomplish is air-to-air refuelling (AAR), transferring hundreds of gallons per minute to two aircraft simultaneously in midair.

In 2020, the CC-130 Hercules celebrated 60 years of service in the RCAF. Back in 1960, 435 Transport Squadron welcomed the first "B" model Hercules into its family. Today, the RCAF uses the upgraded "H" model Hercules for SAR and AAR and the newest "J" model for tactical transport. While these new Herks might be able to fly faster, higher, and carry heavier loads than the older CC-130s, it's a comfort to know that the mighty Hercules will continue to fly in the skies over Canada, fulfilling the RCAF's mission as embodied in its original motto—*Per Ardua Ad Astra*—to rise "through adversity to the stars."

Nancy Tremblay: Forging New Roles for Women in STEM

Major-General Nancy Tremblay, CD

Major-General Nancy Tremblay.

Nancy Tremblay was 15 when she told her parents she wanted to go to military college. Having no military background, they were surprised. In 1987, looking for adventure and a guaranteed job on completion of her studies, Nancy enrolled in the Canadian Armed Forces (CAF), and she hasn't looked back since. Focusing on science and technology, Tremblay would graduate and blaze the trail for young women in the RCAF to follow.

Tremblay spent five years at the Collège militaire royal de Saint-Jean studying math and physics. She flourished under the leadership opportunities offered and was Cadet Wing Commander in her last year. After college, Nancy spent a year studying to become an aerospace engineer at Canadian Forces School of Aerospace Technology and Engineering (CFSATE). From the two streams available for CFSATE graduates—maintenance operations or engineering support—Nancy chose maintenance.

Her first posting was Aircraft Maintenance Engineering Officer of 438 Tac Hel Squadron at CFB St. Hubert. The first woman to serve in this role, Nancy managed a maintenance organization of 80 technicians. According to Tremblay, "one out of every two people in a blue uniform is a technician." Although they are not the public face of the RCAF, maintenance technicians are its unsung heroes. They work long hours and rarely falter in their exceptional attention to detail. Nancy sums up their critical importance: "An operational Air Force relies on a solid aircraft maintenance community. We practice preventative maintenance

programs, routine inspections, and corrective maintenance on everything from engines to mechanical systems to avionics and armament systems, ensuring that aircraft continue to be airworthy and available for operations. Everyone in the RCAF understands that it couldn't exist without its technicians."

A few years later, Nancy worked as the Aircraft Maintenance Standards Officer at 1 Canadian Air Division. "Responsible for keeping maintenance policies up to date as technology evolved, I also worked with the Chief Warrant Officers and RCAF Senior Occupational Advisors, on how to best train and employ technicians." In 2010, Tremblay had the greatest privilege that an Aerospace Engineer Officer can aspire to, becoming the first woman to command 3 Air Maintenance Squadron (3 AMS) in Bagotville. During that time, with less than 24 hours notice, 3 Wing deployed seven CF-18 Hornets and a strong maintenance team in support of Operation MOBILE.

In 2013, Tremblay was deployed to Jordan with the Canadian Special Operations Forces Command. During this mission, she provided military advice to the Ambassador of Canada and improved relations between the Jordanian Armed Forces and CAF on the ground. In 2015, Nancy became the first woman to reach the rank of Colonel within the Aerospace Engineer occupation.

Before being promoted to Major-General as the Chief Materiel Program in 2021, Nancy held numerous positions, including Integrated Logistics Support Officer, Aircraft Engineering Officer, Director of

Lieutenant-Colonel Tremblay as Commander of 3 AMS in 2012.

Aircraft Structures Technician

Aircraft Structures Technicians (ACS Techs) are members of the air maintenance team who handle, service, and maintain CAF aircraft and associated equipment. If it's part of an aircraft's wings, fuselage, nose, tail or frame, it's the job of ACS Techs to keep it in mission-ready condition. They also take care of the upholstery, seat belts, and safety equipment on board.

"I'm Corporal Melissa Vautour originally from Dalhousie, New Brunswick, an Aircraft Structures Technician currently posted to 8 Wing Trenton, Ontario. The frontline units, they have a bit of a different ACS feel to them, and they might be doing stuff hands-on the aircraft, such as servicing and inspections and changing configurations in the layouts of the plane, whereas you have other people within the trade that are shop-based, and they might be doing fabricating, they might be prototyping...So there's so much versatility within this trade that each day is completely different and you're not going to find yourself in a monotonous, cookie-cutter kind of a work environment."

Fighters and Trainers, and Chief of Staff. Tremblay was the first woman to be nominated Chief Engineer of the RCAF and Director General Aerospace Equipment Program Management, a division within the Materiel Group responsible for the modernization and sustainment of RCAF fleets.

Despite graduating from college in the minority (women made up ten per cent of her class) and working in a male-dominated field, Tremblay always felt like she was "part of the team." Slated to retire soon from the RCAF, for Nancy, the Air Force embodies "dedication to operations, 24 hours a day, seven days a week, 365 days a year. There is no downtime in the RCAF. The commitments are too crucial—from protecting the sovereignty of Canada, to peacekeeping abroad, and search and rescue here at home." Nancy considers herself privileged to have served for 35 years. "I owe a lot to the RCAF for giving me so many opportunities to lead and serve my country with pride."

Steven Deschamps: Serving his Country with Pride

Lieutenant-Colonel (Ret'd) Steven Deschamps, CD

Honorary Colonel Steven Deschamps.

As a young Air Cadet in 1969, Steven Deschamps fell in love with the RCAF. He spent his teenage summers teaching other Air Cadets at CFB Trenton and Cold Lake. His passion for flying earned him a scholarship and he became a glider pilot at the age of 16. He rose through the ranks to Warrant Officer First Class. Deschamps donned his first RCAF uniform in 1975 as Training Officer for 325 Air Cadet Squadron in Cornwall, Ontario.

In 1979, Steve joined the Regular Force as a pilot trainee. He attended Canadian Forces Officer Candidate School at CFB Chilliwack and was top of his class of 300. Deschamps spent three months at 10 Tactical Air Group in St. Hubert before attending 3 Canadian Forces Flying Training School at Portage la Prairie, Manitoba. Deschamps was 23 at the time.

Just as his RCAF career was taking off, the unthinkable happened: Steve became a victim of the "Gay Purge." During the Cold War, paranoia prompted the government to identify and remove suspected LGBTQ2+ military servicemen and women. It was believed that because they had a secret, they were targets for blackmail and breaches in national security—even though there wasn't any evidence to support this.

According to Steve, "being a visible gay person in the 1980s was a difficult proposition. Prejudice, bias, and physical danger followed gay and lesbian Canadians." As part of the purge, exposed servicemen and women were subjected to interrogations and pressured to reveal fellow LGTBQ2+ members in service. They were given a choice between immediate honourable discharge or risking a court-martial and a potential dishonourable discharge. When a letter surfaced in Ottawa about his sexual orientation, Steve became the subject of an investigation that involved interrogations, illegal surveillance, and polygraphs. In 1982, he was purged from the CAF. Deschamps describes the experience as "devastating. Without anyone to confide in, I was demoralized, despondent, and alone. The Armed Forces had ignominiously fired me without just cause."

The military continued to release LGBTQ2+ members until the early 1990s. Demonstrating a determination and resilience characteristic of RCAF personnel, Steve decided to challenge the law. He re-enrolled in the Cadet Instructor Cadre aiming to table a Human Rights Charter Case. The same week he expected to fight a refusal to re-enrol, the famous Michelle Douglas case was settled in the Federal Court of Canada, leading to the reversal of discriminatory practices in the military. Deschamps was re-admitted to the RCAF, the first known homosexual accepted after the Douglas settlement of 1992.

Back in uniform, Steve excelled. He was instrumental in pioneering technology systems for the Air Cadets, pioneering a flight simulation program that became the standard across Canada. Deschamps continued to serve at RCAF headquarters and was promoted to Lieutenant-Colonel. He retired in 2013.

In 2017, the Government of Canada formally apologized and agreed to compensate those affected by the purge. Over 9,000 people had their careers destroyed and they were denied benefits, severance, pensions,and promotions. Many would go on to suffer from PTSD, addiction, criminalization, and homelessness; and sadly, some committed suicide.

In 2020, the Government of Canada awarded Deschamps the Pride Citation to acknowledge the injustices that the LGBTQ2+ Canadians suffered as they proudly served their country. The CAF today recognizes diversity as an essential factor in mission success, its requirement to reflect the population it serves, and the importance of cultivating of an ethos of respect, trust, and cohesion. For Steve, "the citation and the Prime Minister's apology, along with a change in attitude in the RCAF, has been an extraordinary catharsis." In 2021, the Commander of the RCAF approached Steve to serve as Honorary Colonel for 443 Squadron in Victoria, British Columbia. Steve proudly wears the Pride Citation on his RCAF uniform today.

Right: Second Lieutenant Steven Deschamps receiving the top candidate award at officer candidate school in CFB Chilliwack in 1979.

Below: Acting Sergeant (RCAF Reserve) Steven Deschamps at CFB Trenton in 1973.

Then Brigadier-General Paul Manson and Colonel Bauer wearing the post-unification air force green uniforms while attending a Freedom of the City ceremony in Chatham, New Brunswick, on August 16, 1978.

The old RCAF Colours being retired at Nathan Phillips Square on September 1, 2017.

Back in Blue! The RCAF Returns to its "Blue" Uniform.

As part of the unification of the Armed Forces in 1968, the RCAF and RCN exchanged their uniforms for army green—a day lamented by many who cherished the traditions of the RCAF. This persisted until 1985, when, at the direction of the government, the Canadian Forces adopted the Distinctive Environmental Uniform as a dress and duty uniform. Since soldiers, sailors, and airmen and airwomen belonged to a distinct environment of either land, sea, or air, respectively, their uniform should reflect this. And so, the RCAF returned to a more familiar colour, a version of blue, similar but not exactly the same as the pre-unification version.

Back in blue, RCAF personnel were issued a blue version of the CF greens, with blue workpants, a light blue shirt, black necktie, blue wedge cap, and, in some cases, and optional V-neck sweater.

Over the years, the colours of the RCAF uniform have ranged from the blue-grey, to unification green, tan, and the distinctive environmental blue of today. Tac Hel and other aircrew in combat operations wear camouflage uniforms and Search and Rescue Technicians wear bright orange suits for increased visibility. In 2022, the Department of National Defence announced the introduction of genderless uniforms for Canadian Armed Forces troops in a briefing called "Diversity and Inclusion." New guidelines were written to eliminate gender-specific clothes to allow non-binary soldiers, sailors, and aviators to pick and choose their clothing.

An RCAF Pipe Major.

The RCAF Tartan.

Did You Know... the RCAF Tartan was the First of Its Kind in the World?

The RCAF was the first air force in the world to have its own distinctive tartan. It happened one Robbie Burns Night in 1942 at No. 9 Service Flying Training School in Summerside, Prince Edward Island, when Station Commander, Group Captain Elmer G. Fullerton organized a mess dinner to celebrate his Scottish heritage. Though he was able to secure bagpipes for his station band to play, he was unable to find a suitable tartan to outfit the band. Fullerton took matters into his own hands and sketched the prototype using light and dark blue- and maroon-coloured pencils. The original sample of the proposed RCAF tartan was created by Patricia Jenkins and loom crofters of Gagetown, New Brunswick, with the weavers adding a white line in the design. Fullerton liked the addition and sent a sample of the tartan to RCAF Headquarters in Ottawa for approval. After the design was endorsed by the Air Council, Air Vice-Marshal J.A. Sully sent it off to Scotland's Lord Lyon, King of Arms, for approval in July 1942. This was granted on August 15, 1942 and the design officially registered as the RCAF tartan. Since then, the distinctive tartan has been worn by members of RCAF pipe and drum bands during ceremonies. See Appendix 4 for a description of Annual RCAF Ceremonies and Celebrations.

The RCAF Roundel
1945–1946

The RCAF Roundel
1946–1965

The RCAF Roundel
1967 Centennial
Variant

The RCAF Roundel
1965 to Present

The RCAF Roundel: A Living Symbol of Canada's Air Force

The RCAF Roundel is steeped in tradition and has its roots in the First World War when they were used to distinguish enemy aircraft from our own. The Royal Flying Corps (RFC) first arrived in France in 1914 and during battle, they were shot at from both allies and enemies alike. Clearly, a mark of identification was needed. The RFC borrowed the concept from the French who were using a roundel of red, white, and blue concentric circles to represent the flag of France. The British simply reversed the order of colours for their own roundel. During the Second World War, the RCAF was authorized to replace the RAF's red circle with the maple leaf. Canadian military aircraft updated their roundels in 1946, and in 1965, the 11-point maple leaf of the Canadian flag took centre spot on the RCAF Roundel, replacing the old maple leaf.

The RCAF Ensign
Steeped in Tradition

An ensign is the flag that identifies an organization's history and heritage. In 1921, the Canadian Air Force (CAF) ensign, identical to that of the RAF, was unfurled for the first time at Camp Borden, Ontario. The concept of a unique flag for the CAF was raised as early as 1921, when the Air Officer Commanding of the CAF, Arthur Tylee Gwatkin, proposed that the RAF ensign could be adapted to display a maple leaf at the centre of the roundel. This was soundly rejected by the British Chief of the Air Staff. During the Second World War, the need to identify itself became critical for the RCAF. In 1941, King George VI approved an RCAF ensign based on a customized version of the RAF's, as Gwatkin had suggested. It featured a maple leaf roundel (in the "fly") set against a field of air force blue and retained the Union Jack in the upper left corner (the "hoist" or canton).

With the creation of Air Command in 1982, the Canadian flag replaced the Union Jack. The roundel was updated to feature a more stylized maple leaf than the one displayed on the original roundel.

RCAF Ensign 1982 to Present

Royal Air Force Ensign

RCAF Ensign 1941 to 1982

Master Warrant Officer Kimberly Jones carries the Eagle Staff, representing Indigenous members of the Canadian Armed Forces, past, present, and future, during the Royal Canadian Air Force Colours Parade held in Toronto, September 1, 2017.

CHAPTER 5
EXPEDITIONARY OPERATIONS

Opposite: A two-ship of CC-130J Hercules aircraft prepares to take off for a parachute drop at Tancos Airfield, Portugal, during JOINTEX 15 as part of NATO's Exercise Trident Juncture 15 on October 28, 2015.

EXPEDITIONARY OPERATIONS

In 1989, the Berlin Wall came down marking the end of the Cold War. The RCAF's active North Atlantic Treaty Organization (NATO) units in Western Europe were no longer needed. By 1992, the last fighter squadron left Germany and the airfield at CFB Baden–Soellingen closed in March 1993. As tensions from the Cold War thawed, new threats were flaring up around the world. Governments, terrorist groups, and radicalized individuals were using new combat tactics, ones that avoided direct confrontation with a superior opponent and posed what was called an "asymmetric threat."

The RCAF moved quickly to meet these emerging global challenges. CF-18 fighter jets were deployed in the First Gulf War in 1990 (Op FRICTION), tactical airlift was sent to assist the UN during the Rwandan genocide of 1994 (Op SCOTCH), and fighter squadrons flew bombing missions over the Balkans during the Kosovo Campaign in 1999 (Op ECHO). The state-of-the-art CF-18s made the Air Force combat ready and the acquisition of strategic airlift capability with the CC-177 Globemaster III extended the RCAF's abilities to transport resources to anywhere in the world. The

RCAF was on its way to fulfilling its goal of becoming an agile, multi-functional, well-equipped, combat-capable Air Force that could deliver integrated missions at home and abroad.

Part of the Air Force's transformation was organizational. Thirteen RCAF bases were designated Wings in 1993 and consolidated under a command-and-control structure called 1 Canadian Air Division. The Commander of Air Command moved to National Defence Headquarters in Ottawa and was given the title of Chief of the Air Staff, restoring a position that had not been used since 1968.

The terrorist attack on September 11, 2001, changed defence on a global scale. The North American Aerospace Defense Command (NORAD) responded by sending patrols of CF-18s into North American skies as Canada provided refuge for diverted domestic flights. Transport Canada estimates that over 33,000 passengers on 224 flights arrived in Canada on September 11. The CF-18 fighters were placed on high alert that day were part of a NORAD operation that came to be known as Operation NOBLE EAGLE.

By January 2002, the RCAF had returned to the

Persian Gulf to conduct counterterrorism operations. Canada sent troops to Afghanistan as a member of NATO's International Security Assistance Force while the RCAF transported troops and assets into Kabul and Kandahar. The RCAF also stood up a 450-person Joint Task Force Afghanistan Air Wing (JTF-Afg AW) operating out of Kandahar, supported by CH-146 Griffons, newly acquired CH-147 Chinook helicopters, CC-130 Hercules aircraft, and Unmanned Aerial Vehicles. Before it stood down in August 2011, the JTF-Afg AW ushered in a new era of air support for combat operations with helicopters playing a defining role in a fully integrated Canadian Armed Forces response.

Between March and November 2011, transport units flying the CC-177 Globemaster, CC-150 Polaris Airbus, and both H and J models of the Hercules aircraft supported missions in Afghanistan and Libya. The C-17 Globemaster played a major role in solidifying the RCAF's strategic airlift capability, flying supply missions in Afghanistan, Libya, Iraq, in humanitarian operations, as well as disaster response in the Philippines, in Operation BOXTOP, and more. At home, the Air Force maintained a variety of domestic operations that included surveillance and patrol of Canadian airspace, airlift of CF personnel and materials, support of the army and navy, search and rescue, and operations for government departments.

On August 16, 2011, the Canadian government reinstated "Royal" to Canada's Air Force, bringing the term "RCAF" back into use. In November 2014, for the fifth time since the end of the Cold War, the RCAF engaged in combat operations as part of the coalition fighting Islamic extremists in Iraq and Syria. With its domestic commitments and global reach, the RCAF continued to be a fundamental part of expeditionary operations while being the guarantor of Canadian sovereignty at home.

An aviation systems tech from HMCS *Calgary*'s embarked air detachment, prepares a CH-148 Cyclone helicopter for flight.

The First Gulf War
Operation (Op) FRICTION

In the summer of 1990, Iraq invaded Kuwait. The UN Security Council immediately demanded that Saddam Hussein withdraw his troops, and when he failed to comply, the UN mandated the use of force against Iraq. Keeping its commitment to restoring peace in the Middle East, Canada joined a coalition and sent 4,500 troops to the Gulf War in Operation FRICTION—the first time Canadian Armed Forces had gone to war in 40 years.

As part of Operation FRICTION, the Royal Canadian Navy (RCN) contributed warships and the RCAF deployed fighter jets. In September 1990, 409 Squadron flew from Baden–Soellingen, Germany, to a base in Qatar. Meanwhile, destroyers HMCS *Athabaskan* and HMCS *Terra Nova*, the supply ship HMCS *Protecteur*, and five Sea King helicopters, sailed from Halifax to the Persian Gulf. By mid-October, these warships were assisted by 24 CF-18 Hornets in "sweep and escort" patrols over the Gulf, the combined CF-18 force nicknamed the "Desert Cats."

Overall, the Desert Cats flew 6,000 sorties, 1,944 air-to-air combat missions, and 56 air-to-ground missions, dropping hundreds of tonnes of bombs. They averaged 70 hours of flight time per day with a 98.8 per cent serviceability rate. These missions were risky, with CF-18s often targeted by Iraqi surface-to-air missiles. The skilled Desert Cats were able to complete their missions and evade the intense anti-aircraft fire with no accidents or fatalities.

The RCAF also provided in-theatre transport and air-to-air refuelling. A CC-144 Challenger with 412 Squadron flew over 300 hours in transport missions to Canadian headquarters in Qatar, while 437 Squadron deployed its Boeing CC-137 air-to-air refuelling tanker, which delivered over 2,000 tonnes of fuel to coalition aircraft in 87 missions. All of this was supported by the RCAF's entire CC-130 fleet which built an airbridge from Trenton, Ontario to Lahr, Germany to Akrotiri, Cyprus, and finally, on to Qatar.

A CF-18 fighter taxis along a temporary trackway laid by the military in Doha, Qatar, 1990.

In 1991, just days after the U.S.-led Operation DESERT STORM's ground invasion began, President Bush declared the liberation of Kuwait. An armistice was negotiated in March, after which the Canadian military helped re-establish a diplomatic mission in Kuwait City.

"Events happened quickly and a non-stop airlift of 550 personnel and 3 million pounds of freight was flown into theatre in 79 Hercules and ten Boeing loads in October. The early arrival of personnel and freight allowed the coalition forces to reach combat ready status as soon as possible in a manner that established Canadian credibility.

For the first ten days of the Gulf War, the Desert Cats had aircraft on 15-minute and one hour alert and flew combat air patrol missions over the Persian Gulf, 12 to 24 hours a day, and when tasked, 24 hours a day, using our refuelling aircraft. On January 12, 1991, the Desert Cats armed their 26 CF-18 fighters in 12 hours and were congratulated by General Horner,

Commander, USAF, U.S. Central Command, for being the first Wing in the Middle East to achieve 100 per cent "ready to launch" readiness status. Truly a feather in the RCAF's cap, the manner and quickness that the Desert Cats flew combat missions speaks for itself.

The RCAF's performance in the Gulf War was highly professional and mission-focused at every turn. All ranks of the 713 men and women, as part of the Canadian Air Task Force Middle East in Qatar, worked all out, non-stop, to be the best. The RCAF is blessed with a broad spectrum of mission training and solid leadership aimed at mission success and returning home together." – Colonel Philip Engstad, MSM, CD, Commander, Canadian Air Task Force Middle East, Op FRICTION

A Canadian CC-130 Hercules was the only aircraft in the world flying into Kigali during the worst of the conflict in Rwanda.

The Airbridge to Rwanda
Operation (Op) SCOTCH

The horrific Rwandan genocide of 1994 killed an estimated 800,000 to 1 million people. A great number of people were displaced, including 3 million people internally and 2 million refugees, creating a devastating humanitarian crisis. The UN Assistance Mission in Rwanda (UNAMIR) remained onsite staffed by 460 personnel. In early April, aircraft from the UN arrived to evacuate their own civilian and military personnel. They departed two weeks later, leaving only a small RCAF Air Transport detachment remaining to support UNAMIR, operating out of Nairobi, Kenya, providing an airbridge to Rwanda.

The Canadian Air Lift Command Element (ALCE) detachment from 8 Wing Trenton, Ontario, supplied UNAMIR with tactical airlift in Op SCOTCH, helping them maintain a UN presence in Kigali, the capital city of Rwanda.

"As Commander of the ACLE to run Operation SCOTCH, our mission was to assist in the evacuation of Canadian nationals from Rwanda. I assembled my team of 23 personnel, a CC-150 Polaris from 437 Squadron and two additional countermeasures systems (CMS) equipped CC-130 Hercules aircraft—with armour plating, sensors, and warning systems—from Trenton. We arrived in Nairobi on April 12 and the two Hercules arrived the next day. Supported by a groundcrew of 71 personnel, we flew evacuation and medical resupply missions into Kigali, Rwanda, and Bujumbura, Burundi. On April 14, our CC-150 departed Nairobi with Canadian and American evacuees—mainly missionaries, aid workers, and Rwandan orphans, many of whom were babies.

By April 17, the initial role of evacuation of Canadian ex-patriates and missionaries and delivering humanitarian supplies was complete. Events led to a new mission, however, when Op SCOTCH was extended to assist with the drawdown of UNAMIR forces. During the next several days, we airlifted the Bangladeshi battalion from Kigali to Nairobi and began to resupply UNAMIR. Following the mortar attack on the Kigali airport on April 24, civilian aircraft suspended their UNAMIR support flights and the RCAF CC-130s became the UNAMIR lifeline for evacuation and resupply.

Our support flights into Kigali were becoming more perilous as the Rwandan Patriotic Front began its push to take Kigali. On April 25, several mortar rounds hit the airport shortly before and after our Hercules was on the ground. The windows on the terminal were blown out, but the ramp and runway were not damaged. The next day saw more attacks on the airfield as the Rwandan Government Forces used the airport as a strategic defensive position. For the next several weeks, our Hercules flew two chalks a day to Kigali, bringing much-needed humanitarian supplies, and food and water to the UNAMIR troops, with only one bullet hitting a Hercules during the airlift missions.

In one of the more satisfying air evacuations, with the support of a team from Médecins Sans Frontières, we airlifted 31 children (15 on stretchers) out of Kigali. While we evacuated various non-governmental organization civilian and military personnel, we were also bringing in VIPs to witness the situation in Rwanda, including Rwandan Patriotic Front representatives for peace talks later in July." – Colonel John Roeterin, OMM, CD, ALCE Commander, Op SCOTCH

In May, nearly four months after the crisis began, UNAMIR received approval to expand to 5,500 peacekeepers under the new name UNAMIR II. The ALCE continued its airlifts until the end of September, completing 312 flights, carrying 5,871,200 lb (2,663 kg) of freight and 6,340 passengers. Without the airlift—carried out by a single RCAF Hercules—UNAMIR would have been unable to remain in Kigali to assist with the humanitarian crisis.

Tactical Airlift in the RCAF: No Bridge Too Far

Airlift is the organized delivery of supplies or personnel using military transport aircraft. There are two types of airlift: strategic and tactical. Strategic airlift involves moving supplies long distances, whereas tactical deploys resources and supplies into very specific locations with precision. If movement by road, rail, or sea is unavailable, airlift is the only way to provide essential support, such as food, water, troops, and medical evacuation (medevac) to ongoing military operations.

Airlift as an RCAF capability has expanded since Rwanda. Within the transport community, the tactical-airlift component in 1994 was based on 30 CC-130 Hercules. While 13 aircraft were being used for domestic search and rescue, only 17 were available for tactical missions. Of those 17 aircraft, the Hercules outfitted with CMS equipment were 25 to 30 years old. Today, 17 upgraded CC-130 J Model Hercules are dedicated to tactical airlift with five CC-177 Globemaster III aircraft, capable of carrying much heavier payloads, expanding RCAF's transport capabilities. Tactical airlift in Canada has never been better equipped.

The Kosovo Campaign in 1999

Operation (Op) ALLIED FORCE/Task Force Echo

During the spring months of 1999, NATO conducted combat operations over the Former Republic of Yugoslavia to force an end to ongoing genocide of Kosovar Albanian people in the province of Kosovo. Operation ALLIED FORCE leveraged the combat capability of NATO air forces amassed in Italy, southern European air bases, and from the aircraft carrier USS *Theodore Roosevelt*. While the Canadian contribution was called Task Force Echo, the combat operation was universally known as Operation ALLIED FORCE.

"The Canadian fighter force contributed 18 CF-18 fighter jets and was manned as a composite unit of pilots and technicians, affectionately known as the Balkan Rats. During the period of combat operations, the force cycled almost every combat qualified CF-18 pilot into theatre to support operations. The CF-18 force flew 678 combat sorties, a disproportionate ten per cent of all attack missions, while making up just two per cent of the available fighter forces.

The Balkan Rats were thrust into combat operations with little preparation and training after many years of peacetime operations. CF-18 aircraft flew day and night, executing air-to-ground bombing missions as well as air-to-air combat air patrol sorties.

Above: The Balkan Rats around a CF-18 Hornet in Kosovo as part of Task Force Echo.

Below: CF-18 on the ramp at Aviano Air Base, Italy, 1999.

The long distances into enemy territory forced aerial refuelling on virtually every mission from NATO refuelling tanker aircraft, integral to the operation. Coalition attack packages comprised of fighters and support aircraft from many NATO nations made up the attack formations each time.

Canadian fighter pilot professionalism was recognized early in combat and led to RCAF flight leaders being tasked to serve as mission commanders for 50 per cent of the missions that Canadians flew. The Balkan Rats' groundcrew provided an astonishing 99.4 per cent sortie rate through the combat period, unheard of in peacetime or war—a testimony to the skill and dedication of RCAF maintenance crews. Not a single RCAF aircrew or aircraft was lost. The NATO bombing campaign brought the Serbian Army to its knees and showed that combat success could be achieved from air operations alone. For its professionalism under fire in combat, the contributing units of the RCAF were awarded battle honours by Queen Elizabeth II." – Lieutenant-Colonel Billie Flynn, CD, Commanding Officer, Balkan Rats

Above: Fully armed Hornet preparing to taxi out for combat operations over Kosovo.

Below: Major Steven Lawrence, Lieutenant-Colonel Sylvain Faucher, Captain John Hutt, and Major Paul Prevost pose for a group photo on November 10, 2000, before Lieutenant-Colonel Sylvain Faucher's last flight in Aviano, Italy.

Lieutenant-General Rick Findley.

Rick Findley: Outstanding Response on 9/11

Lieutenant-General Eric A. "Rick" Findley, CMM, MSC, CD

The early morning hours of Tuesday, September 11, 2001, were anything but typical for Rick Findley, Director of Combat Operations for NORAD. At midnight on September 10, NORAD was in the middle of conducting a global strategic exercise called Vigilant Guardian. At the same time, the command was monitoring Russian strategic bombers in a real-world counter-air operation. While it was highly unusual for Findley to be overseeing a simultaneous exercise and operation, what came next was even more unexpected.

It was during breakfast at NORAD in Colorado Springs when the first call came in from the Federal Aviation Administration (FAA) requesting assistance for a hijacking. The flight out of Boston, Massachusetts, was the first domestic hijacking in North America in years. Decades even. NORAD's typical tactical response was to shadow the hijacked aircraft with an unarmed fighter. Findley's team was asking the National Command Authority in Washington for permission to proceed with the intercept when the first plane hit the North Tower of the World Trade Center in New York.

The gaping hole in the North Tower perplexed Findley. On such a clear, sunny day, why didn't the pilot steer around the tower? When NORAD asked the FAA if this was the hijacked plane, their answer was inconclusive. When the South Tower of the World Trade Center was hit, the whereabouts of the original hijacked plane remained unconfirmed. It quickly became clear to Findley that critical national institutions had poor situational awareness of the attacks that were occurring. Based on this, he made the decision to take immediate action—ordering "battle stations" and launching the alert fighters.

As reports of a third hijacking came in, action was required on a massive scale. Findley improvised, adding more U.S. fighters under NORAD's command and implementing Emergency Security Control of Air Traffic. The RCAF also jumped into action, arming every serviceable fighter in Canada while preparing to launch. Under Major-General Findley's guidance, NORAD directed several hundred military aircraft (fighters, air control aircraft, and aerial tankers), along with warships that included four U.S. Navy aircraft carrier battle groups, into position to protect vital points in the United States and Canada. Findley achieved all of this in one hour and 50 minutes, calling it "the longest and shortest day of my life."

For outstanding leadership and performance on 9/11, Major-General Findley was awarded the Meritorious Service Cross in June 2002. Like many exceptional leaders, Findley credits the people he worked with for their dedicated service on 9/11. Entire units in the USAF and RCAF reported for duty, including those who were officially off-duty. Dedicated American and Canadian staff pulled together all of the resources that were made available to muster the largest peacetime air defence response in North American history.

Along with the Meritorious Service Cross, Rick Findley was also honoured with the Commander of the Order of Military Merit. Findley joined the Canadian Forces in 1968 and flew with 408 Tactical Helicopter Squadron (CFB Edmonton); 444 Squadron RCAF (CFB Lahr); 403 Squadron RCAF (CFB Gagetown) and commanded 427 Squadron RCAF (CFB Petawawa). Major-General Findley also commanded aviation units in the Sinai, Central America, and Haiti. Promoted

Findley flying with 408 Squadron.

to Lieutenant-General in 2003, his last appointment was as Deputy Commander of NORAD and Head of the Bi-national Planning Group. Findley is the first Canadian to have a U.S. Combatant Command building dedicated with his name, an honour he shares with USAF General Ralph E. Eberhart. HQ NORAD/USNORTHCOM has been named the Eberhart-Findley Building.

"When speaking at a Wings graduation, I encouraged graduates to be fiercely proud of all they had accomplished. Then I told them to acknowledge their families in the audience. I reminded them that they didn't get to where they were without their support. Along with all the other people who had contributed to their training—instructors, maintenance crews, etc. And this was just a sample of what the RCAF is about. They were becoming a part of this bigger team for life, one that could deploy anywhere in the world. Something that few nations have managed to achieve." – Lieutenant-General Rick Findley

Aerospace Telecommunication and Information Systems Technician

Aerospace Telecommunication and Information Systems Technicians (ATIS Techs) help create the backbone of communications in the RCAF. As a critical component of modern military operations, they keep networks and information systems running smoothly 24/7—from sending vital information or processing and compiling this information so that other RCAF personnel can make educated decisions.

"I'm Corporal Zachary Bernard-Demers from Montreal. I'm an ATIS Tech from 14 Wing Greenwood in Nova Scotia. We work with everything that has to do with technology, from desktop computers and monitors to the airfield side where we work with radar equipment. I was on Op Impact in Kuwait. There was a team of eight of us and we had to manage desktop support networks, classified materials, radios, as well as cell phones—everything that had to do with technology on a daily basis for every member that was deployed there. And it's a very rewarding feeling to know that you were a part of the team that went out there and basically helped the entire operation be successful."

General Raymond "Ray" Henault presides over his first NATO meeting as the newly appointed Chairman of the Military Committee.

General Raymond "Ray" Henault: Canada's Longest Serving Four-Star General

General Raymond "Ray" Henault, CMM, MSC, CD, is a 40-year veteran of the Canadian Armed Forces. Beginning his RCAF career in 1968, Ray served as a fighter pilot, and later completed multiple tours as an instructor and helicopter pilot. Within the Air Force, Henault climbed the ranks from Commander of 444 Tac Hel Squadron to Chief of Staff Operations at Air Command Headquarters before becoming Deputy Chief of the Air Staff and Deputy Chief of the Defence Staff (DCDS). As DCDS, Ray was the public face of the Canadian contribution to the Kosovo campaigns and other significant NATO missions, including the Stabilization Force in Bosnia-Herzegovina.

In June 2001, Ray was appointed Chief of the Defence Staff and commanded the Canadian Forces on 9/11. After heading the CF response to the terrorist attacks for four years, he was elected Chairman of the NATO Military Committee, representing NATO Chiefs of Defence at NATO headquarters in Brussels, Belgium. General Henault held this position until 2008, when he retired from the Canadian Forces as the longest-serving four-star General in Canadian history.

Aviation Systems Technician

Aviation Systems Technicians handle, service, and maintain CAF aircraft, ground equipment, and associated support facilities.

"I'm Corporal Tera Moussignac-Cimello from Dartmouth, Nova Scotia. I'm an Aviation Systems Technician at 12 Wing Shearwater. We work on all the mechanical components of an aircraft—wing and rotors, engines, transmissions, etc. You very much have to put your ego aside to be a good tech because whether you have mechanical background or not, you are accountable for people's lives. So you have to be willing to do everything by the book, and never be afraid to ask questions. We fly missions every day—jumping through all the hoops. Getting over all the obstacles to get an aircraft ready to go on the back of the boat for its six-month sail is probably the coolest thing we do."

CH-135 Twin Huey.

CH-135 Twin Huey: Simple but Rugged

Legendary for its role in the Vietnam War—and reputed to be able to fly with holes in its rotor—the Bell UH-1N Twin Huey first flew in 1969. Simple but rugged, it was the first military helicopter used in mid-intensity combat. In 1971, the Canadian Armed Forces (CAF) purchased 50 of the CUH-1N Twin Huey (later the CH-135 Twin Huey). The U.S. Army used the nomenclature "HU" for "Helicopter Utility" in the 1950s, hence the nickname "Huey" derived for the Bell UH-1 Iroquois as the Twin Huey. The CAF customized its U.S.-built specifications to incorporate Canadian-built turbine engines. Used for troop and cargo transport, reconnaissance, medical evacuation, and Search and Rescue (SAR) in Canada, the Twin Huey was replaced by the newer Bell CH-146 Griffon helicopter in 1996. One of the highlights of the Twin Huey's career in Canada was its SAR operations in Goose Bay, Newfoundland and Labrador, in the 1970s.

David Fraser: The Indispensable RCAF

Major-General David Fraser, CMM, MSC, MSM, CD

Major-General David Fraser.

When asked to describe the RCAF's contribution to Operation MEDUSA outside Kandahar, Afghanistan, retired Major-General David Fraser uses one word: "Indispensable." Specifically, he was referring to the CC-130 fleet that ferried soldiers and supplies to the southern province of Kandahar. "They gave new meaning to the phrase 'Crazy Canucks,'" Fraser adds with a grin. Also critical to the mission was "Dune" Howell, a CF-18 fighter pilot who was on Fraser's staff as the J3 Air 2. "I couldn't have done my job without him." As Brigadier-General, Fraser commanded over 2,000 coalition troops in Operation MEDUSA, the largest battle fought by Canadian forces since the Korean War. Fraser was Commander, Regional Command South comprising the six southern Afghan provinces and nine coalition partners totalling over 10,000 troops.

Operation MEDUSA's aviation task force fell under Fraser's command. This included over 40 helicopters—Apaches, Chinooks, and Black Hawks—flown by the Dutch, Australians, and the Americans. As part of the task force, three RCAF CC-130s Hercules operated out of Camp Mirage in the United Arab Emirates, providing intra-theatre airlift for personnel and equipment. Typically, American and Australian Chinooks were responsible for airdrop using the Container Delivery System, delivering palettes of supplies into drop zones using cargo parachutes. But Fraser had an idea. Instead of Chinooks accomplishing this role, why not use the RCAF's CC-130s? This would free up the Chinooks to complete other high priority jobs. Fraser pitched this to the CC-130 aircrews and they accepted.

This meant that in addition to daily flights into Kandahar, the CC-130s were now flying airdrop missions with a substantially increased level of risk. Aircrew from both 429 and 436 Squadrons boldly flew their CC-130s straight up the Afghan valleys, necessarily exposing themselves along the entire route. "They flew the Hercules like it was a Ferrari," Fraser says. "To see a big aircraft being flown like it's a small, nimble Formula 1 race car is absolutely spectacular—unless you're a passenger. It was very aggressive flying. And it was all Nap-of-the-earth, a type of low-level flight used to avoid enemy attack. Every other nation looked at the Canadian CC-130 aircrews and shook their heads in disbelief." They were up to the task due "to the high quality training and determination of great aircrew who not only made a tremendous tactical impact, but also gave me a strategic voice at a table where the Americans appreciated Canada's contribution. The CC-130 fleet garnered huge respect."

Although the RCAF didn't fly fighter jets in Operation MEDUSA, fighter pilot "Dune" Howell, served as Fraser's Air Liaison Officer. Dune didn't have an airplane, but he did have a radio. His job was to assist Fraser in asking for Air Force assets during ground operations. Describing a situation to a pilot who is flying at 10,000 ft is a complicated job, but Dune called in every fighter plane in the sky. Fraser recalls, "I told all the fighter pilots in Cold Lake, you weren't there physically but your spirit was there in Dune. And through his technical skills and abilities, he

Supplies are dropped from a Canadian Forces CC-130 Hercules aircraft over an undisclosed location in Afghanistan.

Air Weapons Systems Technician

Air Weapons Systems Technicians maintain aircraft air weapons systems. They also perform explosives storage and handling and provide Explosive Ordnance Disposal duties for the Air Force.

represented all of you. He was one of the only international officers that the Americans trusted. This was a commentary on the RCAF's outstanding capabilities."

Prior to Operation MEDUSA, Canada had a reputation as peacekeepers. But after the mission, this changed. According to Fraser, "Everyone, including the RCAF aircrew, demonstrated remarkable abilities in the combat arena. When I went down to Australia for a debrief after the mission, the Australian Vice-Chief of the Defence Staff said to me, 'Where the hell did you guys come from? You show up with this whole-of-government approach and lead the fight in Operation MEDUSA. You got all of our attention. We didn't follow you before but we do today.' Now that is respect. And the RCAF played a key role in earning that."

"I'm Corporal Palmer Clements from Belleville, Ontario. I'm an Air Weapons Systems Technician currently posted to 4 Wing Cold Lake, Alberta. As an Air Weapons Systems Technician, my job is maintaining all the onboard systems, the computers, and the functionals that have to do with armaments. On the flight line, we do most of the loading of bombs, missiles, and ammunition onto the aircraft. So, as a first-line Air Weapons Systems Technician, your day-to-day is going to be directly dictated by the flying schedule—whether they want two jets, four jets, 15 jets, chaff and flare in the jets, inert bombs, live bombs—whatever the pilots are calling for is your day-to-day objective."

Camp Mirage

United Arab Emirates, 2001–2010

With Canada's overseas commitment to the War on Terror, the RCAF supported Canadian Forces' operations in Afghanistan. Early in 2002, Canada established Camp Mirage at the Al Minhad Air Base in the United Arab Emirates (UAE), although the identity of the host nation has never been officially acknowledged. Designated "Theatre Support Element South West Asia," Camp Mirage served as the support base for operations in Afghanistan and the entire Gulf Region.

The base was originally used for surveillance by the Long-Range Patrol Detachment Southwest Asia with CP-140 Aurora maritime-patrol aircraft until the first CC-130 Hercules arrived. Home to approximately 250 CF members, the base was a busy stopover point for troops and supplies flown from Canada. CC-177 Globemaster III and CC-150 Polaris aircraft flew from 8 Wing Trenton and other air bases in Canada to Camp Mirage to drop off and pick up cargo. This was subsequently loaded onto a Hercules for final delivery to Kandahar Airfield in southern Afghanistan. The flight ran around 740 km (400 miles) southeast over the Gulf of Oman, past the Iran-Pakistan border, and north over Pakistan airspace for the remaining 930 km (500 miles) to Kandahar. Sorties for the CC-130s consisted of four or five round-trip flights weekly.

"During my tour as one of its first Commanders, Camp Mirage grew to accommodate approximately 300 personnel. Initially, the camp on the operations side relied on CAF generators with limited water supply and services, but by the end of my tour, it was modernized to include aircraft maintenance facilities, extra barracks, a dining hall, ball-hockey rink, and lighted basketball court. We facilitated the movement of over 30,000 personnel per year as they transited to and from theatre, along with thousands of tonnes of cargo. Camp Mirage also hosted numerous VIP visits and supported emergency relief missions into the Bam region of Iran following a disastrous earthquake in December 2003." – Lieutenant-General Andre Deschamps, CMM, CD, Commander, Camp Mirage, November 2003 to May 2004

On November 3, 2010, the UAE abruptly banished Canada from the base and barred Canada's Minister of National Defence from flying over the country. Camp Mirage closed after almost nine years of operations.

Tac Hel
Potent Tactical Aviation in Combat

The RCAF has always evolved to meet changing threats at home and abroad. Unification and the arrival of 10 Tactical Air Group (10 TAG) saw Canada's Air Force expand beyond a fixed-wing culture that dominated the Cold War.

Tac Hel's roots are solidly enmeshed in the history of army aviation in Canada. In 1944, the RCAF introduced 664, 665, and 666 Air Observation Post Squadrons, which flew Taylorcraft Auster light aircraft. Since then, there has been a long history of cooperation between the Canadian Army and the RCAF.

Postwar, a focus on joint operations led to the opening of the Joint Air School at RCAF Station Rivers in 1947, which later became the Canadian Joint Air Training Centre (CJATC). The CJATC taught close air support and trained helicopter pilots. In the 1950s, the Light Aircraft School taught army officers basic flying techniques, training later assumed by the RCAF's primary flying school at Centralia, Ontario. In 1961, after the army's purchase of 21 Hiller CH-112 helicopters, pilot training was given by the RCAF's Basic Helicopter Training Unit.

The unification of the Canadian Forces and the creation of Force Mobile Command saw Canada's helicopter forces rise in importance. A purchase of ten CH-118 utility helicopters was made in 1967 to transition aircrew to flying helicopters and develop operational procedures for proposed new Tactical Helicopter Squadrons. The first one was designated as 403 Helicopter Operational Training Squadron in Petawawa. Many pilots who started in Tac Hel squadrons were cross-trained navigators and radio officers (with backgrounds in the Flying Boxcar, Hercules, Argus, Neptune, and Canuck). Some had been flying instructors or flown Sabres or Starfighters, while others were RCN pilots or army fixed-wing or helicopter pilots.

Unification transformed the Canadian Army into a joint force with an air component of six helicopter squadrons and 113 helicopters, along with two fighter squadrons and one transport squadron. Although it was never designated an official branch of the RCAF, army aviation was a distinct

A CH-146 Griffon helicopter returns to Kandahar Airfield.

function for 25 years, with nine units consisting of 80 aircraft and 200 pilots, along with supporting technicians, flight engineers, loadmasters, and observers.

In 1975, Air Command organized its command-and-control structure into five groups. One of those groups was 10 TAG, headquartered in St. Hubert, Quebec, and responsible for the operation of Mobile Command's air assets. As part of 10 TAG, 1 Wing began flying the CH-135 Twin Huey and the CH-36 Kiowa helicopters for tactical aviation, which were replaced by the CH-146 Griffon in 1994. In 1997, 10 TAG disbanded and 1 Wing moved to its new home at CFB Kingston, Ontario. Today's self-contained and field-deployable Tac Hel Squadrons that make up 1 Wing train and integrate with army brigades. They are tasked with combat operations, peacekeeping missions, internal relief, and support for government departments and the Royal Canadian Mounted Police (RCMP). In 2017, a fleet of CH-147F Chinooks became fully operational at 1 Wing.

The advanced tactical aviation capabilities of the RCAF's Tac Hel squadrons have made invaluable contributions to Operation (Op) ATHENA in Afghanistan; Op HALO in Haiti; Op FORGE in Northwest Ontario; Op NANOOK in Canada's Arctic; and Op RENAISSANCE in the Philippines in the wake of Typhoon Haiyan, to name just a few.

Scott Clancy: There's No Hell Like Tac Hel
Major-General Scott Clancy, OMM, MSM, CD

Major-General Scott Clancy.

Major-General Scott Clancy served in the RCAF at a seminal point when military aviation was becoming a critical and ubiquitous part of a changing Air Force. As a young boy, Scott was inspired to join the Air Cadets by Pappy Boyington, a U.S. fighter ace who led the infamous "Black Sheep Squadron." Fulfilling his dream to serve his country, Clancy graduated from the Collège militaire royal de Saint-Jean in 1989. At primary flight school, instructor and mentor Herm Harrison convinced him to consider Tactical Helicopters (Tac Hel). "I got a ride in a helicopter and that was it. I was hooked." Scott received his wings in 1990 after completing the basic helicopter course.

Clancy served on 427, 430, and 403 Tactical Helicopter Squadrons. Between 1986 and 2001, deployments to Somalia, multiple deployments to Haiti, and sustained operations in Bosnia and Kosovo stretched the Tac Hel community to its limits. At 427 Squadron, Scott flew Twin Huey helicopters and when the unit deployed to Somalia, he was sent on the Advanced Aviation Course instead. At home, Clancy spent "months firefighting, evacuating floods, and doing surveillance for the RCMP or in the counter-drug mission." As part of 430 Squadron, the first operational unit to receive Griffon helicopters, Scott prepared forces for deployment to Haiti. Domestically, the squadron flew operations in Quebec, Ontario, as well as the Atlantic ice storms, Saguenay floods, and the Red River flood of 1997.

In 1997, 1 Canadian Air Division was stood up to provide operational command of all Canadian Forces (CF) air assets. Tac Hel and Land Aviation services transferred from 10 Tactical Air Group to 1 Wing. This centralization of air power changed everything "because there was one set of rules. Air power was harmonized at the operational level." Clancy served as Contingency Planner in Canadian Air Division/ Canadian NORAD Region, became Wing Operations Officer and then, Chief of Staff at 1 Wing Headquarters.

Scott took over as Commander of 1 Wing in 2014, overseeing 85 aircraft and hundreds of aircrew. "On any given day, 60 or 70 of those aircraft could take off and land a hundred times." The non-stop tempo of domestic operations set Tac Hel apart from other RCAF wings. Another difference was Tac Hel's army-infused culture. "We train, live, fight alongside the army. Tac Hel attends the army's professional development course to create that operational focus." Training that is critical because "when things go wrong, you're an infantryman in a heartbeat." While these elements made it challenging for the RCAF to incorporate military aviation into its Air Wing structure, they persevered to create an operational culture that persists in Tac Hel today.

In 2008, Canada decided to deploy helicopters to Afghanistan to support ground troops in Operation ATHENA. As Chief of Curriculum Development at the Canadian Army Command and Staff College, Clancy was selected by mentor, Lieutenant-General Alain Parent to plan the deployment of Chinooks

Fighting ISIS in Iraq and Syria
Operation (Op) IMPACT

When the Islamic State of Iraq and Syria (ISIS), also known as the Islamic State of Iraq and the Levant or its Arabic acronym Da'esh, defeated the U.S.-trained Iraqi army to control parts of Iraq and Syria, there was more at stake than the survival of the Iraqi government. The world watched in 2014 as the radicalized terrorist organization threatened international security, committing human rights violations with a looming humanitarian crisis in its rise to power. NATO and the UN had to act. And they did so with an indispensable tool: air power.

"Imagine my surprise and honour when I was offered command of Air Task Force-Iraq (ATF-I) in 2015. In October, I joined a very professional team already well-established in the operational theatre and based in four different locations in the Middle East. The threat in Iraq was clear, ISIS was a violent extremist group that had dangerously and quickly spread and taken control of key areas across Iraq and Syria. While ISIS had taken hold, the coalition could not stand by and watch as innocent Iraqis and Syrians suffered under this tyrannical and cruel regime.

In October 2014, the Government of Canada approved CAF military operations in support of the coalition mission to counter ISIS and the RCAF established ATF-I with a mix of key air power capabilities joining the coalition team, including the CF-18 Hornet to conduct kinetic airstrikes, the CP-140 Aurora providing surveillance and reconnaissance support, and the CC-150 Polaris providing air-to-air refuel support. By the time I joined the Rotation 2 team, ATF-I was a well-oiled machine

and every member of the team stepped up to ensure the delivery of high-quality air power to ensure the coalition defeat of the ISIS threat. I was proud to be a member of this battle-proven team and was in awe of the commitment and performance of each of the air warriors deployed on this important operation. I will never forget their operational focus and camaraderie." – Colonel Shayne Elder, MSC, AM.

Under Operation (Op) IMPACT, the RCAF carried out airstrikes on ISIS targets in Iraq and Syria from October 30, 2014 to February 15, 2016. CF-18 fighter pilots flew a total of 1,378 sorties and made 251 airstrikes, 246 in Iraq and five in Syria, dropping 606 munitions to impact 267 ISIS fighting positions—destroying equipment, vehicles, and Improvised Explosive Device factories and storage facilities. CP-140 Auroras flew 881 sorties between 2014 and 2017, and the CC-150T Polaris aerial refueller flew 1,166 sorties between 2014 and 2019, flying over 7,050 hours and delivering 29,914,508 kg (65,950,200 lb) of fuel to coalition aircraft.

In 2022, the Canadian government extended Op IMPACT to March 2023, committing millions to stabilization programs in Iraq, Syria, and Lebanon. While CF-18s no longer fly under Op IMPACT, as of 2019, the RCAF had six aircraft in the Middle East, including two CC-130J Hercules transport aircraft and four CH-146 Griffon helicopters to move personnel and cargo through the region. At the time of writing, these aircraft were no longer there.

CF-18s and a CC-150 Polaris fly over Ottawa after returning from Operation MOBILE in Libya, 2011.

RCAF Operations in Libya, 2011

Operation (Op) MOBILE

When Colonel Muammar Gaddafi's government attempted to crush local "Arab Spring" protests by attacking protestors and civilians with air and ground attacks, the UN Security Council called for an arms embargo on Libya and imposed a no-fly zone to ensure the safety of its civilians.

Operation (Op) MOBILE was the designation given to the Canadian Forces' participation in the international response to the Libyan crisis. Though the RCAF began to evacuate Canadians and other foreign nationals from Libya in February 2011, it shifted to a combat role in March. The RCAF air detachment was called Task Force Libeccio, named after the strong southwesterly Mediterranean wind. Staffed by 200 CF personnel that included aircrews and ground technicians from 425 and 409 Tactical Fighter Squadrons, the task force became operational on March 21 when four CF-18s conducted escort and air interdiction patrols off of Libya's coastline.

Op MOBILE was one of the RCAF's most successful deployments. Armed with new weapons and upgraded avionics, CF-18 pilots were able to conduct their missions successfully and strike with precision. Besides giving fighter pilots the chance to refine their combat capability, Op MOBILE required the RCAF to tightly coordinate with other allied nations. CF-18 Hornets conducted ten per cent of all bombing missions, organizing strike packages with other NATO alliance fighter jets. RCAF CC-150 Polaris Tankers from 437 Transport Squadron were instrumental in filling a critical NATO alliance shortage, picking up the slack in air-to-air refuelling and distributing over 5,896,700 kg or 13 million lb of fuel to fighters from other nations. CP-140 Auroras excelled in their surveillance and reconnaissance role, helping to direct naval gun fire from NATO ships and monitor fighter jets during bombing missions, while CH-124 Sea King helicopters did critical work flying off the sterns of Royal Canadian Navy frigates. By October, the RCAF had flown

1,539 sorties, including over 946 CF-18 sorties, 389 refuelling sorties, and 181 surveillance sorties.

The Libyan government's response was ineffectual. Gaddafi's forces failed to shoot down a single NATO plane. Military intervention ended in October when Muammar Gaddafi was captured and killed in Sirte and Op MOBILE ceased operations in November 2011.

"When I received the call asking if I was available to deploy to Italy to participate in Operation (Op) MOBILE, I was serving as Commanding Officer of the Aerospace Engineering Test Establishment in Cold Lake, Alberta. I was given the job to go to Naples and from there, coordinate all of the administrative support for the three task forces that were in theatre: Task Force (TF) Libeccio, TF HMCS Charlottetown, and TF Naples. I arrived in Naples on April 12, 2011 and began meeting key members of the staff. The majority of personnel already on the ground were from 1st Canadian Division Headquarters in Kingston. Although some had limited understanding of command and control from an air power perspective, they had been instrumental in establishing the initial liaison with NATO HQ and its components. In the weeks that followed, I worked hard to build their knowledge and understanding of RCAF and air operations in general as well as how our Air Force fit into the overall campaign plan.

We operated out of the old Canadian Military Family Resource Centre, next to the Officers' Mess where Lieutenant-General Bouchard had established his HQ. In late April, Canadian Expeditionary Force Command announced that our detachment would be called the National Coordination Centre and Support Component (NCCSC). Our mission statement was to enable mission continuity and success by providing administrative, logistics, and CIS (communication and information systems) support and sustainment functions to the task forces assigned to this Operation. I salute the members of our Air Force who took part in Op MOBILE and those from our sister environments who went to Naples to support them. We learned much from this experience, and it is gratifying to see how these lessons learned have influenced our development since. The formation of 2 Expeditionary Wing was a great leap forward in shaping the RCAF as prepared as it can be for its expeditionary operations." – Major-General Paul Ormsby, OMM, CD, Commander NCCSC, Op MOBILE

An RCAF CC-177 Globemaster III from 429 Bison Squadron.

Boeing CC-177 Globemaster: 429 Bison Squadron

The Boeing CC-177 Globemaster III is a strategic airlifter that transports troops, cargo, and oversized combat equipment from CH-146 Griffon helicopters to three combat-ready infantry-fighting vehicles to the Leopard 2 main battle tank. The CC-177 aircraft was procured by the RCAF in response to increasing global transport needs and saw early action in Haiti, delivering the Disaster Assistance Response Team to the Philippines, and supporting combat operations in Afghanistan and elsewhere. The high-wing, four-engine aircraft with a T-tail and a rear-loading ramp has a payload of 74,797 kg (164,900 lbs). At 53 m (174 ft), the CC-177 is approximately 23 m (76 ft) longer than the CC-130J Hercules. Designed to fly long distances and land or take off from short runways in remote airfields, the CC-177 is an ideal transporter for military and humanitarian missions. Advanced digital avionics and cargo systems enable the aircraft to be flown by a cockpit crew of a pilot, a co-pilot, and a loadmaster.

The RCAF's fleet of five CC-177s have accumulated almost 50,000 flight hours since the first four were acquired in 2007. Beyond the strategic airlift role, allied air forces that fly the C-17 have begun to explore how it might increase its contribution to combat operations, with possibilities including the deployment of Joint-Air-to-Surface Standoff Missiles using a roll-on pallet or to launch small, unmanned aircraft from the cargo hold.

CH-146 Griffon: Dependable and Multi-Purpose

The CH-146 Griffon is a utility tactical transport helicopter that has been in service with Tac Hel since 1995. Though its primary role is the tactical transport of troops and materials, it can also be used for aerial firepower, SAR, surveillance and reconnaissance, counter-drug operations, medevac, and armed escort for other helicopters. Flown by a crew of three, the Griffon can carry up to ten troops and has a cruising speed of 220–260 km/h (140–160 mph). Griffons have been deployed in various operations in Canada since their introduction, including Operation SAGUENAY in 1996 and Operation ASSISTANCE in 1997. The helicopters played a key role in evacuations during the 1998 ice storms in Ontario, Quebec, and Atlantic Canada, and provided emergency services for victims of the 2016 Fort McMurray wildfire in Operation LENTUS. Griffons were also deployed to secure the 2010 Winter Olympics during Operation PODIUM.

A CH-146 Griffon helicopter takes off at Camp Castor in Gao, Mali, during Operation PRESENCE–Mali on August 13, 2018.

Aerospace Control Officer

Aerospace Control Officers contribute to air operations by providing air traffic control services and air weapons control. They're responsible for the conduct of aerospace surveillance, warning, and control of airborne objects throughout Canadian airspace. Army Enlistment Centre Officers also serve as Air Battle Managers in air defence and air operations command centres all over the world—both on the ground, and in the air on board command and control aircraft called Airborne Warning and Control System.

"I'm Captain Shannon Archer from Moose Jaw, Saskatchewan. I'm an Aerospace Control Officer currently posted at 14 Wing Greenwood, Nova Scotia. Some of the great things about becoming an Aerospace Controller are that we get to work domestically and help Canada with our mission, but we also have the opportunity to deploy. To support the Disaster Assistance Response Team, we were in Haiti where we set up an airfield and brought in aid. Each day when I come to work, I look forward to interacting with not only the people, but the different challenges and opportunities, the different environments that I get to work in. It's an exciting new challenge every day."

CH-136 Kiowa.

CH-136 Kiowa: Small but Mighty

Small in stature but mighty in capability, the Bell OH-58 Kiowa was the workhorse of 1 Wing's Tactical Helicopter squadrons as a single-engine, single-rotor military helicopter. A total of 74 were acquired by the Canadian Armed Forces between 1971 and 1972 to be used for reconnaissance, command and liaison, and artillery fire direction. Redesignated as the CH-136 Kiowa by the Canadian Forces, they were flown by 400, 408, 422, 427, 430, 438, and 444 Squadrons. The Kiowa, Chinook, Twin Huey, and the Griffon are included in Appendix 3: List of Aircraft (Current and Historical).

CF-188 Hornet aircraft and Romanian F-16s fly in formation.

Protecting NATO's Eastern Flank

Operation REASSURANCE (Air Task Force Romania)

Following the Russian invasion of Ukraine in 2014, Canada immediately transferred ships into NATO's standing fleet, deployed army personnel into Europe, and deployed a six-pack of CF-18s into Romania, all in support of the Alliance's assurance measures. This initial deployment evolved into Operation REASSURANCE, the Canadian response to Russian aggression. In 2017, the RCAF sent Hornets once again to Romania as Air Task Force Romania (ATF-R). The ATF-R assumed NATO enhanced Air Policing duties at Mihail Kogălniceanu Air Base, alongside the Romanian Air Force.

Since 2017, the RCAF has deployed seven rotations of CF-18s and personnel from squadrons across Canada from within the fighter force. A typical rotation of the ATF-R was comprised of approximately 150 to 200 personnel, including aircrews and groundcrews, as well as operations and logistical support personnel for the CF-18 fighters deployed.

Under NATO command and control, the ATF conducted surveillance of Romanian and allied airspace, trained with their NATO counterparts, and if required, intercepted, identified, and escorted aircraft that entered the Romanian Air Defence Identification Zone. In 2022, the ATF also consisted of a CP-140 Aurora long range patrol aircraft for missions over the Black Sea. The first ATF in Romania in 2017 was commanded by Lieutenant-Colonel Mark Hickey, who was also the Commander of 409 Tactical Fighter Squadron, 4 Wing, based in Cold Lake, Alberta.

Corporal Sean Adel, Corporal Matt Seguin, and Master Corporal Chad Peacey transport an aircraft engine to a CF-188 Hornet aircraft for installation at Mihail Kogălniceanu Air Base, Constanta, Romania during Operation REASSURANCE.

Lieutenant-Colonel Mark Hickey, Air Task Force (ATF) Romania Commander, gives the NATO Force Integration Unit a tour of the flight line at Mihail Kogălniceanu Air Base, Constanta, Romania.

Sergeant Trevor Williamson and Chief Warrant Officer Troy Zuorro collect ball hockey equipment destined for Romania.

The Canadian Spirit: Bringing Hockey to Romania

When the RCAF goes on deployment internationally, it always does its best to take a little bit of Canada with it. On the allied base in Kandahar, Afghanistan, one of the most popular locations was the Tim Hortons, a mobile coffee shop transported from Canada and staffed by civilians.

In Romania, at the RCAF's NATO Air Policing detachment, the deploying CF-18 Squadron arrived in theatre with some of their equipment containers sent by mistake to the Canadian Army detachment in Lithuania. In one of these containers was the Squadron's hockey equipment they used to play ball hockey tournaments while on deployment, a loss that the more than 200 members in the detachment would feel. However, back home, 8 Wing Trenton sprang into action. Within a few days, thanks to the help of some local sponsors (Honorary Colonels and local businesses), the Wing Commander and Wing Chief Warrant Officer visited the local Canadian Tire in Trenton and purchased the entire aisle of hockey equipment. When the Canadian Tire Manager learned why the purchase was being made, he provided a generous discount to the purchasers and wished the troops well on their deployment.

What happened? That equipment made it over safely and was put to good use by successive deployments hosting tournaments, including some against fellow allies in the U.S. Army and U.K. Royal Air Force squadrons—which the Canadians (of course) won. It was, after all, hockey. So Canadian.

CHAPTER 6
SEARCH AND RESCUE
AND HUMANITARIAN OPERATIONS

Opposite: An RCAF SAR Tech being hoisted by a Griffon helicopter.

SEARCH AND RESCUE AND HUMANITARIAN OPERATIONS

Canada is the second-largest country in the world with some of the most rugged and unforgiving terrain and extreme weather conditions found anywhere. Despite this, or maybe because of it, Canadians love to get outside. At work or at play, they fly into its northern wilderness, hike through its majestic mountain ranges, and sail on its countless waterways that include three oceans. Keeping Canadians safe is a daunting task. Coast-to-coast Search and Rescue (SAR) is a capability that the RCAF shoulders with dedication and pride.

It was during the Second World War that the RCAF's SAR capability began to take shape, partly in response to accidents experienced by aircrew enrolled in the British Commonwealth Air Training Program. Former bush pilot Wilfrid Reid "Wop" May was General Manager of the BCATP's No. 2 Air Observer School when the U.S. Army supplied bombers to the Soviet Union for the war. These planes were flown along the Northwest Staging Route from Edmonton, Alberta, to Snag, Alaska. Many of the pilots who flew these dangerous flights crashed their planes. If they survived, they risked dying of exposure. Wop May, as the "father of pararescue," organized an air rescue team of survivalists and trained them to parachute into a crash site. After seeing a demonstration of their work, the RCAF was so impressed that it took over May's rescue squad as the RCAF's first SAR unit.

After the war, the Canadian government decided to build upon this capability and create a national SAR service. With its postwar resources and experience gained through forestry patrols, surveillance and aerial photography of remote terrain, and transport operations to hard-to-reach areas, the RCAF was the obvious choice for managing Canada's SAR mission. The first three official RCAF pararescue jumpers were enrolled in 1944 and in 1945, the first pararescue courses were stationed in Dartmouth, Nova Scotia; Sea Island, British Columbia; and Edmonton, Alberta. Pararescue teams opened up to medical personnel, and this included five trailblazing nurses affectionately known as "the Parabelles." Around this time, the Fleet Air Arm of the Royal Canadian Navy (RCN) began to task its aircraft for SAR operations and perform joint operations with the RCAF.

In June 1947, the government officially made the RCAF responsible for the planning and coordination of SAR in Canada. The Air Force reorganized itself to take on the new SAR role, creating Rescue Coordination Centres in Halifax, Rockcliffe, Winnipeg, Edmonton, and Vancouver. The formation of the Canadian Coast Guard in 1962, along with civilian volunteer organizations, repositioned the SAR role into a shared responsibility. RCAF planes were outfitted with beacons, relying on early equipment such as Harry Stevinson's Crash Position Indicator and, later, the COSPAS-SARSAT satellite system to detect distress alerts, determine the location, and communicate this back to SAR authorities for rescue.

Today, Pacific and Atlantic maritime SAR is managed at Joint Rescue Coordination Centres (JRCC) at headquarters in Esquimalt, British Columbia and in Halifax, Nova Scotia. The centres are jointly staffed by RCAF and Canadian Coast Guard personnel. The Pacific JRCC covers 1,427,000 km² of mountainous terrain and 687,000 km² of the Pacific Ocean, while the Atlantic JRCC is responsible for 29,000 km of coastline—an area of 4.7 million km² that is 80 per cent water. A third JRCC is located at Trenton, Ontario, and is responsible for the Great Lakes and the North, some 10 million km² that forms the bulk of Canada's land mass.

Five dedicated RCAF SAR Squadrons are stationed strategically where they can respond most quickly to those in need: 103 in 9 Wing Gander, 413 in 14 Wing Greenwood, 424 at 8 Wing Trenton, 435 at 17 Wing Winnipeg, and 442 at 19 Wing Comox. Most squadrons are equipped with helicopters and fixed-wing aircraft, including the CH-149 Cormorant, CH-146 Griffon, and CC-130 Hercules, both the HT and J models. The squadrons and SAR aircraft are supported by 750 personnel, including groundcrew, aircrew, and approximately 140 Search and Rescue Technicians (SAR Techs).

SAR Techs are Canada's orange angels in the sky. Advanced pararescue specialists, they train in diving, mountaineering, rappelling, wilderness survival, hoist rescue, and various other rescue-related operations. SAR Techs undergo 11 months of gruelling training at the Canadian Forces School of Search and Rescue at 19 Wing Comox, British Columbia. In 1998, Tammy Negraeff graduated from the rigorous course as the RCAF's first woman Search and Rescue Technician (SAR Tech). Present on every primary SAR aircraft on a mission, SAR Techs have saved thousands of lives.

When required, SAR Techs work with local agencies and volunteers as part of a multi-layered rescue operation. They often participate in humanitarian SAR, an incident that is neither aeronautical nor maritime that is requested by another agency; for example, a ground search for a missing person led by the local police force. Natural disasters can occur without warning. Hurricanes, floods, snowstorms, and forest fires are common to certain regions and seasons in Canada. Depending on the severity, provincial and territorial authorities may require immediate support from the RCAF to help with domestic evacuation, recovery, and humanitarian aid. Across Canada, the RCAF and Canadian Armed Forces (CAF) have been on hand to help Canadians during the 1997 Red River flood in Manitoba, the 1998 ice storms in southern Quebec and eastern Ontario, Saskatchewan wildfires in 2015, Fort McMurray wildfires in 2016, the 2019 Hurricane Dorian in Nova Scotia, and the 2020 blizzard in St. John's, Newfoundland and Labrador.

In responding to a domestic crisis, the RCAF follows an established plan of action to support communities in need called Operation LENTUS. In the 2021 mudslides in the interior of British Columbia, as part of Operation LENTUS, 442 Transport and Rescue Squadron broke all previous records for the number of people rescued in one mission in the CH-149 Cormorant helicopter—airlifting 311 people, 26 dogs, and one cat to safety in one day.

Every day, the RCAF manages thousand of distress calls through their respective JRCCs, coordinating complex and effective SAR operations across the country to keep Canadians safe.

Master Corporal Jason Murray (left) answers a question posed by a Jamaican youth during the Jamaica Defence Force Air Wing Open Day.

"Wop" May: The Father of Canadian Pararescue

Captain Wilfrid Reid "Wop" May, OBE, DFC

Wilfrid Reid "Wop" May, Edmonton, Alberta, 1931.

Wilfrid Reid "Wop" May was a fighter pilot in the First World War. With 13 victories under his belt, "Wop" (nicknamed by a relative who couldn't pronounce "Wilfrid"), returned home a flying ace and one of the pilots involved in the dogfight that brought down the infamous Red Baron. Back in Canada, Wop quickly became a legend as a stunt pilot. He also worked as a bush pilot, delivering mail and other goods to remote parts of Northern Canada. He even conducted the first ever hunt for a fugitive from the skies and helped the RCMP track down the "Mad Trapper of Rat River." While May accomplished all of the above and served as an instructor with the British Commonwealth Air Training Plan in the Second World War, his quintessential contribution to the RCAF was his role in the creation of military search and rescue from the skies. Or what is now known as pararescue.

Long before he became the father of pararescue, Wop May demonstrated the courage, resourcefulness, and self sacrifice of modern-day Search and Rescue Technicians (SAR Techs). In the "Mercy Flight" of 1929, Wop May and co-pilot, Vic Horner, flew medicine to Fort Vermillion to prevent an outbreak of diphtheria. Their plane was open cockpit, and after the five-day flight in subarctic conditions, both men suffered from frostbite. In what has been called a "Race Against Death," May delivered the much needed medicine, but only after sacrificing his own health and welfare to save the lives of others.

During the Second World War, Wop was supervisor of all of the Observer Schools in Western Canada. The United States supplied fighters and bombers to Russia along the Northwest Staging Route, from Edmonton, Alberta, to Snag, Alaska. Many of the planes, flown north by American, Russian, and some Canadian pilots, crashed en route. Downed pilots stranded in the bush often died of exposure. For Wop May, this was unacceptable. In 1942, he established an air rescue team to parachute into the bush, provide medical aid, and extract the pilots.

Organizing and training a parachute squad was no simple task. Parachutes were relatively new at the time and planes weren't outfitted to carry jumpers. Windspeed was determined by tossing an old Eaton's catalogue out of a plane. The technology was primitive. But Wop ignored the inherent danger and called for volunteers. He formed his first rescue crew in 1943, made up of civilians from Canadian Airways Training Limited.

Despite rudimentary equipment and poor facilities, training continued, and in 1944 the Canadian government integrated Wop May's rescue team into the RCAF. In 1945, the first formal SAR course received 20,000 applicants, with only 12 selected to participate in the 15-week course. Candidates had to be between the ages of 22 to 30, in good physical condition, and have previous bush experience. These were the RCAF's first SAR Techs.

Along with the Distinguished Flying Cross, Wop May was awarded the Trans-Canada (McKee) Trophy in 1929 and appointed Officer of the Order of the British Empire in 1935. For his assistance to the United States, May was given the American Medal of Freedom, with Bronze Palm in 1947. He was inducted into Canada's Aviation Hall of Fame in 1974 and has been immortalized in a Stompin' Tom Connors song, "Wop May."

Mercy flight from Edmonton to Fort Vermilion, Alberta, January 2, 1929.

Men involved in the manhunt for Albert Johnson, the "Mad Trapper," 1932.

RCAF firefighters from Air Task Force–Iceland (in front) and Keflavik International Airport firefighters conduct an airfield crash exercise.

Firefighter

Firefighters prevent the loss of life or property due to fire. They perform a variety of tasks including aircraft rescue, structural and wild land fire-fighting, automobile extrication, hazardous material, and confined space rescue.

"I'm Corporal Lawrence Martin from Niagara Falls, Ontario, and I'm a Firefighter at 8 Wing Trenton. We do a lot more than fight fires in buildings. We drive and operate firefighting apparatus and respond to aircraft and vehicle incidents. We keep fire-detection and suppression systems in working order, respond to hazardous material spills, and maintain self-contained breathing apparatus. We're also trained for confined space and technical rescue as well as Emergency Medical Response. Every time the bells sound, your adrenaline rushes and you prepare to respond. It could be an aircraft in distress, a fire in a hangar, a medical emergency in the building next door. You don't know what you are walking into until you arrive at the scene."

The Parabelles in 1951, left to right: Marian Neilly, Isabelle Thomson, Marion MacDonald, and Anne Peeden.

Flying Officer Marian Neilly at RCAF Station Trenton in 1955.

The Parabelles

Getting the Jump on Gender Roles

Unlike the gentility implied by their name, the "Parabelles" were a group of intrepid women who volunteered as Canada's first pararescue nurses. At the end of the Second World War, the RCAF used pararescue teams for Search and Rescue (SAR). In 1951, the RCAF opened these units up to medical personnel and five qualified Nursing Sisters answered the call: Muriel Beaton, Marion MacDonald, Isabelle Thomson, Marian Neilly, and Anne Peeden.

The Parabelles underwent rigorous training in RCAF Pararescue Course No. 5, a precursor to today's challenging SAR Technician course. Training for survival in some of Canada's most difficult terrain, Muriel Beaton broke her leg in the 11-week "bush lore" portion of the program and had to quit. The four remaining Parabelles went on to train in parachute jumping, first from a tower in Edmonton and then from a bush plane, the Noorduyn Norseman.

The Parabelles jumped into dense bush wearing canvas suits made for men and padded caged helmets that resembled hockey masks. As the first Canadian woman to complete an operational jump, Parabelle Gracie MacEachern could attest to the ill-fitting equipment. During the rescue of a geologist on Mount Coquitlam, British Columbia, Gracie landed in a tree and slipped out of her harness. Dangling by a foot, it took her two hours to right herself and climb down. MacEachern spent the night in the wild, joining her colleagues to complete the mission the next day.

The Parabelles earned the right to wear the badge of qualified RCAF pararescue personnel. They were the first women officers in Canada to wear an emblem of aerial operations. As pioneers in pararescue, the Parabelles were part of an elite unit of survivalists who redefined gender roles in the RCAF.

NRC Engineer Henry Stevinson and his Crash Position Indicator.

Crash Position Indicators and Radar
Revolutionizing Search and Rescue

Onboard beacons revolutionized Search and Rescue (SAR), enabling downed pilots and aircrew to send a distress signal. At the close of the Second World War, RCAF aircraft carried primitive beacons until the 1950s. The British designed a system called SARAH (Search And Rescue And Homing), consisting of an onboard transmitter and a receiver installed in a SAR aircraft.

While the RCAF was implementing the SARAH system, engineer Harry Stevinson of the National Research Council of Canada's Flight Research Lab was busy developing a different kind of emergency beacon. His brainchild? The Crash Position Indicator (CPI)—essentially a rescue beacon that could be manually or automatically deployed from the outside of an aircraft.

Harry Stevinson was tired of stories about rescue missions gone wrong. Prior to the 1960s, when airplanes crashed in the remote wilderness of Canada, survivors faced a long wait, often injured in extreme elements, before they were rescued. Rescue teams had trouble locating crash survivors. Enter his rescue beacon.

Other rescue beacon systems had already been developed and deployed, but Stevinson felt these were ineffective. If a plane crashed into water, the beacon would sink with the aircraft, even if there were survivors on the surface. And on land, the beacon could be blocked depending on where it ended up (buried under parts of the plane or burned in a fire, for example). What was needed was an aerodynamic system that could be quickly detached from the plane after impact.

Available in 1959, Stevinson's first CPI was designed to detach from the aircraft when it sensed a crash, remain intact post-crash, and transmit a beacon to allow a SAR aircraft to locate it. The system included a flight recorder to capture details that might reveal what caused the accident. Stevinson's CPI was the forerunner to today's flight recorders inside an airplane's black box.

A CH-149 Cormorant helicopter.

SAR Techs That Others May Live

"Without regard for my personal comfort or self advancement, to the best of my ability and to the limitation of my physical and psychological endurance, I solemnly pledge to make every effort to return to safety, those victims of disaster entrusted to my care by the assignment of the mission to which I have consented. These things I shall do: 'That others may live.'" – RCAF SAR Pararescue

Search and Rescue Technicians (SAR Techs), the RCAF pararescue specialists, who wear the distinctive orange flight suits, are responsible for saving the lives of Canadians. Becoming a SAR Tech is not easy. In fact, the chances of making it through both the selection process and the training course are so slim, it is one of the CAF's most difficult units to join. And for good reason—it is also one of the Canadian military's most dangerous jobs.

Each year, after reviewing applications from Regular Forces or the Reserve Force for transfer into SAR, 24 to 30 people are chosen to attend a two-week pre-selection course in Jarvis Lake, Alberta. From there, only 12 to 16 SAR candidates are accepted into the 11-month training course at the Canadian Forces School of Search and Rescue (CFSSAR) at 19 Wing Comox. Candidates are trained to survive in the most remote areas of Canada and provide immediate medical care and pararescue to those in need. SAR Techs learn a myriad of skills. Depending on the emergency, they are diving, mountain rescue, or parachute rescue specialists and all round survivalist of artic, ocean, or bush conditions—all of which test their medical skills. There is never certainty in any SAR mission; SAR Techs must carefully balance risk with their chances of success in unforgiving and often deadly environments. Lucky for Canadians, they are highly skilled and selflessly dedicated to their missions.

When they graduate, SAR Techs receive their wings and orange berets. As well as training the new candidates, CFSSAR also trains current SAR Techs in courses for Team Leader, Dive Supervisor, and Parachute and Medical recertification.

Tammy Negraeff: Breaking Gender Barriers in SAR

SAR Tech Master Corporal Tammy Negraeff.

Search and Rescue Technicians (SAR Techs) are known as "angels in orange jumpsuits." The highly skilled survival experts drop out of the sky, specializing in extreme rescue on land and at sea. When conditions are at their worst, SAR Techs are at their best so "that others may live."

Tammy Negraeff never wanted to be a trailblazer, she just wanted to be a SAR Tech. When she was 17, Negraeff saw a picture of a technician repelling out of a Labrador helicopter on a SAR pamphlet, and thought, "that's what I want to do." She went down to the recruitment office to sign up, but the recruiter had other ideas. It's a tough field to get into, Negraeff was told. She needed to be a corporal and it was, at that time, an all male trade. After 45 minutes of convincing the recruiter, he finally took down Tammy's name.

Negraeff enrolled in the CAF and gained experience in three trades: Communications and Research, Infanteer, and Medic. After spending seven years training hard to improve her strength and fitness and completing an airborne jumping course, Tammy's diligence paid off. She was accepted into the gruelling 11-month SAR Tech training course at CFB Comox. Tammy graduated in 1998 as a Master Corporal and the first Canadian woman to become a SAR Tech.

SAR Techs learn all facets of rescue: parachuting, mountaineering, diving, and medical training. According to Negraeff, proficiency in training gave her the confidence to perform under pressure in situations that were beyond her control and changing, moment by moment. A calm disposition helped. "I always knew who I was before I put a uniform on," says Negraeff.

Posted as a SAR Tech to Cold Lake, Alberta, a day at the office for Tammy might consist of repelling into a ravine, parachuting from a helicopter, or snowshoeing across a snow-covered mountainside—or a combination of all three. In one particularly harrowing rescue, Tammy and her Team Leader, Lance Teichrib, were called out to rescue two occupants of a Cessna that crashed in the remote mountains near Lillooet, British Columbia.

In the three hours it took them to reach the wreck, Negraeff and Teichrib prepared their toboggans, medical equipment, and parachutes. They identified the downed plane and determined where to jump, only realizing the next day how dangerous the situation was. They landed just shy of a cliff with a sheer drop of 400 ft. Parachuting in that altitude was also risky because the thin air speeds up the jump. After landing safely, Negraeff and Teichrib spotted the survivors, a pilot and co-pilot, hiking down the mountain. One of them said, "you guys looked like angels flying out of the sky." Words Tammy Negraeff will never forget. For her, saving lives and closing the loop for the families involved were the rewards of a job well done.

In her 25-year military career, Negraeff was promoted to Sergeant, returned to CFB Comox to serve as an instructor, and later became a Warrant Officer at the Regional Cadet Support Unit. Perhaps Tammy Negraeff is best remembered for her sheer grit and determination. She overcome many obstacles to enter a traditionally male-dominated arena, serving as a role model for others to break the gender barrier.

The RCAF's Buffalo 461 and the Buffalo Nine

A Tribute to United Nations Peacekeepers

Canada has a long history of contribution to United Nations (UN) peacekeeping missions around the world. Each August 9th, we celebrate the contributions and sacrifices our peacekeepers have made on National Peacekeepers' Day. This particular date was chosen in honour of nine Canadians, known as the "Buffalo Nine," who lost their lives on August 9, 1974, when their plane—a Canadian Forces CC-115 Buffalo 115461 (known as Buffalo 461)—was shot down over Syria.

The Buffalo Nine served on the second UN Emergency Force with 116 Air Transport Unit. Supporting this important peacekeeping mission in the Middle East, Canadian Forces provided air, logistics, signals, and service support units. Three Canadian Buffalo aircraft were used to fly regularly scheduled flights from Ismailia, Egypt to Damascus, Syria, via Beirut, Lebanon.

In the early afternoon of August 9, 1974, UN Flight 51 was Buffalo 461's last call sign for the routine supply trip. Five aircrew and four military passengers were on board: Captain George Garry Foster (Pilot) and Captain Keith Mirau (First Officer) were joined by Captain Robert Wicks (Navigator), Master Corporal Ron Spencer (Flight Engineer), and Corporal Bruce Stringer (Loadmaster). The remaining four passengers, Master Warrant Officer Gaston Landry, Master Warrant Officer Cyril Korejwo, Corporal Michael Simpson, and Corporal Morris Kennington, served on active duty with the Canadian Contingent, UN Emergency Force at Camp Shams.

Shortly after Captain Mirau received clearance to enter Syrian airspace, the plane crossed from Lebanon into Syria and was immediately hit by a surface-to-air missile. Moments later two more missiles struck the plane, scattering wreckage across a large field in Al Dimass, Syria. All nine Canadians on board were killed. Though the missiles were launched from a Syrian airfield, a subsequent Canadian Board of Inquiry was unable to determine if they were fired in error or deliberately.

The missile attack is the greatest loss of life of Canadian peacekeepers in a single incident. The Buffalo Nine are intrinsically linked to Buffalo 461, or the "Buff" with CF registration number C-115461 on its tail. It has come to symbolize the sacrifice of those who have given their lives in service as Canadian peacekeepers. Only two pieces of the plane returned to Canada. A section of the Buffalo's tail fin is on display in the Violent Peace Gallery of Canada's War Museum in Ottawa and one of 461's propeller blades, inscribed with the names of the Buffalo Nine, is located at the National Air Force Museum of Canada at 8 Wing Trenton, Ontario.

Canadian Warplane Heritage Museum Recreation of Buffalo 461.

COSPAS-SARSAT

Using Satellites to Save Lives

Getting to an emergency incident quickly can mean the difference between life and death. The international satellite-aided search and rescue (SAR) system, COSPAS-SARSAT, helps minimize search times by trying to take some of the search out of SAR. Formed by Canada, France, the United States, and the former Soviet Union in 1979, the COSPAS-SARSAT Program relies on orbiting satellites to receive distress signals which are then relayed to ground stations, where coordinates are calculated and shared with SAR agencies. Previously, distress signals were limited to reception by passing aircraft. Relying on satellites has expanded the RCAF's SAR capability into a global capability.

After forming the program, each original participating nation was responsible for different aspects of the project. The United States built the ground stations, France and Canada managed data generation and coding, and the former Soviet Union produced the first satellite, COSPAS-1, which was launched on June 29, 1982. In September of the same year, COSPAS-SARSAT began tracking distress signals from Emergency Position-Indicating Radio Beacons and 121.5 MHz ELTs. On September 9, just nine days after testing began, the first distress signal was detected from an airplane that had crashed in northern British Columbia. The COSPAS-SARSAT satellite system provided coordinates and one day later, SAR Techs located the airplane and rescued three survivors.

With Canada's role in the COSPAS-SARSAT Program, the Canadian Mission Control Centre (CMCC) processes distress signals to alert SAR agencies over a dedicated network. At the CMCC, RCAF regular force, reserve, and civilian Department of National Defence members ensure year-round support, 24 hours a day, seven days a week, to rescue centres and international SAR partners.

Over the years, the program—a model of joint cooperation—has grown to include 45 countries and territories. Beacon technology has evolved to leverage Global Navigation Satellite System receivers such as GPS. COSPAS is an acronym for the Russian words "*Cosmicheskaya Sistema Poiska Avariynyh Sudov*," which translates to, "Space System for the Search of Vessels in Distress." SARSAT is an acronym for Search and Rescue Satellite-Aided Tracking.

The CC-115 Buffalo.

CC-115 Buffalo: 55 Years of Service

The de Havilland Canada DHC-5 Buffalo was a twin-engine, Short Takeoff and Landing (STOL) utility transport turboprop aircraft used by the RCAF. The RCAF's first 15 "Buffs," designated CC-115, were flown by 429 Squadron out of CFB St. Hubert as part of Mobile Command in a transport role. Based on its incredible STOL capability, by 1970, the aircraft took on an additional SAR role with 442 Squadron, 413 Squadron, and 424 Squadron. A stable platform for parachute jumps and equipment drops, the Buffalo was used in hundreds of SAR operations—dropping smoke markers, emergency communication gear, rescue kits and other SAR equipment, and conducting "valley shoots," flying low in tight areas to make visual contact during a rescue mission. Three Buffalos were dispatched on UN missions to the Middle East until 1979, bearing the distinct UN colours of blue and white. The CC-115 Buffalo flew its final operational flight on January 15, 2022 with 442 Transport and Rescue Squadron, 19 Wing Comox, British Columbia.

Sergeant Kevin O'Donnell, a SAR Tech from 103 Search and Rescue Squadron, based in Gander, Newfoundland and Labrador, is hoisted down from a CH-149 Cormorant helicopter during a search and rescue exercise in Iceland in February 2016.

SAR Aircraft: The Right Capabilities at the Right Time

Successful SAR missions depend on the RCAF having the right capabilities in place at the right time—and this includes aircraft. Along with the recently retired CC-115 Buffalo, the RCAF has access to its entire arsenal of aircraft to support SAR, including both the CC-130 Hercules H and J models, CH-146 Griffon and CH-149 Cormorant helicopters, the CC-138 Twin Otter, and the CP-140 Aurora.

While the CC-130H Hercules is used for transport missions, it also carries out search and rescue operations, offering specialized equipment such as air-droppable survival kits with life rafts and shelters. Able to fly in severe weather for more than 7,200 km (4,474 miles) and land on short runways, it's no wonder the CC-130H Hercules has been the mainstay of RCAF SAR. The CH-146 Griffon

and CH-149 Cormorant helicopters are the primary rotary-wing aircraft used for SAR with swift response times, hover and hoist capabilities, and dedicated SAR aircrew and Techs. The Griffon can be fitted to carry a powerful searchlight and a hoist to extract people and cargo. The Cormorant has capacity for up to 12 stretchers or a load of 5,000 kg (11,023 lb) and also has capability for hoisting operations. Both helicopters have rescued lost hikers, injured mountain climbers, and crews from shipwrecks. Other RCAF aircraft used for SAR include the CC-138 Twin Otter, which is based in Yellowknife and ideal for Arctic SAR missions, and the CP-140 Aurora, sometimes used in marine SAR operations. See Appendix 3 for a complete listing of RCAF aircraft.

RCAF personnel board a CC-177 Globemaster in Thule, Greenland, for a flight to CFS Alert during Operation BOXTOP on April 13, 2016.

Operation BOXTOP

A Lifeline to Canada's North

Imagine living in a climate so extreme that it's not suitable for human habitation. Welcome to Alert, a CAF Station on Ellesmere Island, Nunavut, named after the British ship HMS *Alert*, which anchored close by in 1875 on its quest for a route to the Pacific. Located 817 km (508 miles) from the North Pole, snow falls year round and winter months are spent in complete darkness. Those who live here are called the "Frozen Chosen," and many are Environment and Climate Change Canada researchers.

Along with the researchers, Alert is home to Canada's remotest military outpost, Canadian Forces Station (CFS) Alert. In April 2009, the RCAF took command of CFS Alert as a unit of 8 Wing, Trenton, Ontario. There are 55 full-time military and civilian personnel working at the station, with that number doubling during Operation BOXTOP. Operation BOXTOP is an RCAF mission to ferry supplies to CFS Alert. Every year since 1956, Operation BOXTOP has delivered fuel and dry goods to the remote

military station. A bi-annual operation, BOXTOP takes place in April and September. Nearby Thule Air Base (AB) in Greenland is used as a staging stop because its large runway and hangars can accommodate the supply planes.

RCAF CC-130 Hercules and CC-177 Globemasters are used on BOXTOP missions, working around the clock for two weeks to deliver hundreds of thousands of pounds of dry goods and close to one million litres of fuel to both CFS Alert and the Eureka Research Station. Each aircraft is limited to how much they can carry so many trips are made from Thule AB to CFS Alert. While air traffic controllers play a critical role in managing the airways in a place that is bombarded by high winds and constant snow, RCAF Meteorological Technicians help to ensure that the conditions are reported accurately in support of flying operations.

CFS Alert, the most northern permanently inhabited place in the world.

CFS Alert: The Base at the Top of the World

Alert was established as a weather station for the Joint Arctic Weather Station system in the 1950s. In 1958, Alert became a signals intelligence unit under the command of the Canadian Army, first as the Alert Wireless Station and then as Canadian Forces Station (CFS) Alert. During the Cold War, the base extended Canada's sovereignty over a largely uninhabited area. Since Alert is closer to Moscow than it is to Ottawa, its ability to pick up Russian communications made the base a key asset in the global ECHELON network, a Canada-U.S.-U.K.-Australia-New Zealand intelligence sharing alliance. Today, CFS Alert continues to play an important role in Canada's surveillance and control of its northern territories and approaches. The base maintains signals intelligence and geolocation facilities and can detect the location of objects of interest through High Frequency and Direction Finding, used for search and rescue and other military operations.

Meteorological Technician

Meteorological Technicians observe, brief on, and forecast weather conditions in support of operations at RCAF Wings and Squadrons, on Royal Canadian Navy Ships at sea, and in army facilities. Weather forecasts are a vital part of every mission where forces are deployed. Commanders rely on accurate and timely weather reports to make important decisions in real time.

"I'm Master Corporal Holly Wortman from Fredericton, New Brunswick. I'm a Meteorological Technician currently posted at the Joint Meteorological Centre in Gagetown, New Brunswick. Whether it's artillery, giving them information about the upper atmosphere so that their rounds land in the right spot, or if it's a helicopter deciding whether they're going to fly that day—or where they're going to fly or what adjustments they have to make for fuel or what they're packing—weather impacts every aspect of the military. Being right or wrong can make the difference between life or death or a successful operation or exercise."

BOXTOP 22
Daring Rescue in the High Arctic

On October 30, 1991, what should have been a routine 22nd BOXTOP flight turned into one of the longest and most daring disaster rescues ever undertaken in Canada's high arctic.

Around 4 p.m., in the black of winter with overcast skies, a CC-130 Hercules making its final approach into Alert from Thule AB crashed into unseen terrain. The plane broke into three pieces on impact. The internal bulk fuel tank it was carrying as part of a "wet lift" burst, dumping 3,400 litres on passengers, the plane, and surroundings. All 13 passengers were thrown from the plane and the cockpit caught fire.

For the next 30 harrowing hours, the survivors of the crash would huddle in sleeping bags in the mostly intact tail section of the plane. The arctic windchill was extreme with temperatures as low as −30°. In the post-crash confusion, the pilot, Captain John Couch, organized his crew for survival while Captain Wilma DeGroot, a doctor, did her best to tend to survivors despite her broken ankle. Two passengers were too severely injured to be moved, so the others built a shelter around them. Miraculously, they survived. Five other passengers would not be so lucky. Four people died within the first hour due to injuries sustained in the crash: Captain Judy Trépanier, Master Warrant Officer Tom Jardine, Warrant Officer Robert Grimsley, and Master Corporal Roland "Roly" Pitre, the crew's Loadmaster. Pitre was fatally injured because he was too busy with his crew duties to buckle himself in as the plane went down.

No distress call was heard by CFS Alert radio operators, but another BOXTOP aircraft reported a fire on the ground east of Alert. Within minutes, a massive rescue operation was underway with participants from across Canada, Alaska, and Greenland. Just as they were mobilizing, a brutal Arctic blizzard blew in.

Back at the crash site, Captain de Groot completed a roll call every hour to ensure that everyone was still alive. Captain John Couch, the Hercules' pilot, answered for several hours before finally succumbing to hypothermia—dressed only in the summer flying jacket he wore, having given his parka to an injured passenger. He died doing everything he could to ensure the survival of his crew.

Marking the 25th anniversary of BOXTOP 22 at the crash site near Alert in 2016.

Seven hours after the call went out, a Hercules carrying 12 SAR Techs from both 435 Transport and Rescue and 440 Search and Rescue Squadrons in Edmonton, Alberta reached the site. High winds and white-outs prevented them from parachuting in. Another Hercules from 413 Search and Rescue Squadron in Greenwood, Nova Scotia, joined the rescue. A ground rescue team was formed at Alert and set out over land for the crash site, guided by a Hercules.

The first overland rescue efforts were recalled due to extreme weather conditions. Eight hours after the crash, the Hercules from 413 Squadron arrived. Its six-person medical team parachuted in from low altitude. Any air-dropped supplies were blown away in fierce winds except for one toboggan. Despite suffering from minor injuries due to the difficult jump, the SAR Techs gave shelter and first aid to survivors. Shortly after, a second group of SAR Techs arrived. When the ground rescue team finally arrived, 21 hours after setting out and nearly driving into a ravine, there were 26 rescuers onsite. The injured were warmed, treated, and prepared for medical evacuation. The final survivor was airlifted from the site on November 1 in a rescue mission that lasted 51 hours and 45 minutes.

The wreckage of the downed Hercules remains on the crash site to this day. In 2016, on the accident's 25th anniversary, a cairn was unveiled by the Commander RCAF, Lieutenant-General Hood, at the crash site near Alert to honour the five souls lost on BOXTOP Flight 22, the 13 survivors, and the CAF members that bravely brought them home.

442 Transport and Rescue Squadron
311 People, 26 Dogs, and 1 Cat Rescued in a Day

It all came down to an atmospheric river known as the "Pineapple Express." Funnelling warm water vapour from Hawaii to North America's West Coast, the Pineapple Express is essentially a giant water pipe in the sky. In November 2021, it poured an entire month's worth of rain onto southern British Columbia in just one day. The record rainfall flooded entire communities, triggered mudslides, and stranded hundreds of people. Over 300 motorists were trapped between two mudslides on Highway 7, outside of Agassiz, British Columbia. RCAF Search and Rescue (SAR) crews from 442 Transport and Rescue Squadron were on hand almost immediately, braving unstable terrain, driving rain, and leftover debris to airlift hundreds of motorists to safety—311 people to be exact—along with 26 dogs and a cat.

According to Lieutenant-Colonel Jean Leroux, Commanding Officer of 442 Transport and Rescue Squadron, within 30 minutes of the emergency call, three Cormorant helicopters were airborne from 19 Wing in Comox, British Columbia. The mission was an unusual one based on the enormity of the damage and the amount of people needing rescue. And, of course, there was the weather. Aircrews expected a difficult landing with low visibility. Sergeant Nigel Donley, a Search and Rescue Technician (SAR Tech) onboard one of the Cormorants, described the highway as being very long and narrow, flanked by a rocky cliff face on one side and power lines on the other. The aircrew had to find an area wide enough to land. Once the landing was made, there was an overwhelming number of people waiting to be rescued. While they're used to extracting one or two people at a time, crews from 442 Transport and Rescue Squadron found themselves assisting hundreds. For most, including Major John McSheffrey, Aircraft Commander and pilot with the Vancouver Island-based squadron, the sheer numbers would top any other rescue in their career.

Captain Jeffrey Barth and his Cormorant helicopter, flown with a co-pilot and three other crew members, made eight trips, carrying an average of 15 evacuees on each trip to a spot where a bus waited to take them to an emergency shelter. Elsa Gilroy, an Air Operations Support Technician, and Cormorant helicopter 906 Pilot Amanda Harris were also part of the effort. Harris likened the rescue to an assembly line, with helicopters using the same area to land and pick up as many people as they could. By the end of the day, aircrews from 19 Wing Comox had flown for nine hours to get everyone out.

In this example of Canada's robust SAR system, 442 Transport and Rescue Squadron worked with the Joint Rescue Coordination Centre in Victoria as part of Operation LENTUS, the Canadian Armed Forces (CAF) multi-layered response to natural disasters in Canada. On the same day as the Highway 7 evacuation, 442 Transport and Rescue Squadron was managing simultaneous emergencies, with a boat in distress near Port Hardy and a plane in crisis in the interior of British Columbia—proving that they are on call for all Canadians, 24 hours a day, seven days a week.

Home to the 442 Transport and Rescue Squadron, 19 Wing Comox was formed in 1942 to defend Canada's West Coast after the attack on Pearl Harbor. With CC-130 Hercules and CH-149 Cormorant Helicopters, the squadron conducts SAR operations in the busiest region in Canada, from the British Columbia-Washington border to the Arctic, and from the Rocky Mountains to 1,200 km out into the Pacific Ocean.

A CH-149 Cormorant helicopter and its crew from 442 Search and Rescue Squadron provide support for Operation LENTUS, evacuating people out of Merritt, British Columbia, after heavy rain triggered mudslides along a highway within the province on November 15, 2021.

Air Operations Support Technician

Air Operations Support Technicians (AOS Tech) provide support in the areas of aircraft servicing and handling, assistance to Search and Rescue (SAR), airfield and base security, and transport and general duties. AOS Techs perform quality assurance checks along with aircraft handling tasks such as parking, towing, marshalling, starting, refuelling, and cleaning of aircraft.

"Hi, my name is Corporal Ashley Cameron. I am an Air Operations Support Technician at 424 Transport and Rescue Squadron in Trenton, Ontario. I come from a village in Perth-Andover, New Brunswick. Some of the work that I do at 9 Hangar would be parking an aircraft, which is marshalling an aircraft into its parking spot, starting an aircraft, standing in front of the plane, talking to the pilot, making sure their engines are running properly. AOS Techs have a variety of different roles within the trade. Along with supporting maintenance crews, AOS Techs can become a qualified spotter to search while on training or real Search and Rescue missions."

CHAPTER 7
THE RCAF TODAY AND TOMORROW

THE RCAF TODAY AND TOMORROW

At the dawn of the 21st century, the RCAF was stretched thin, serving in simultaneous North Atlantic Treaty Organization (NATO) operations in Afghanistan and Libya, along with humanitarian, North American Aerospace Defense Command (NORAD), and Search and Rescue (SAR) missions back home. A competing array of responsibilities demanded a balance between deployed and domestic operations. Relief came in the form of a new defence policy with a long-term commitment to creating an agile, combat-ready Air Force.

While the 2011 return to its designation "Royal" reconnected the RCAF to its distinguished past, it was time to look to the future and prepare for the challenges ahead. This became a period of transition for the RCAF as it made key acquisitions and modernized its fleet with next-generation technologies and autonomous systems. Amid a global pandemic and Russia's renewed aggression in eastern Europe, virtually every RCAF capability was in use in operations, both at home and abroad.

A measure of any air force is its aircraft. Across the RCAF fleets, capabilities in strategic airlift,

air-to-air refuelling (AAR), SAR, tactical aviation, and Intelligence Surveillance Reconnaissance (ISR) were strengthened. In 2016, the RCAF completed a major upgrade of all 17 of its CC-130J Hercules aircraft. As the mainstay of the RCAF's transport fleet, modifications were made to its navigation, mission-critical communications, and maintenance systems. Likewise, the CC-177 Globemaster III heavy logistic transport fleet received an upgrade to its navigation system. The Canadian-built CP-140 Aurora was modernized to fit an ISR role and outfitted with beyond line-of-sight satellite communications and tactical data exchange as part of the Aurora Incremental Modernization Project. Upgraded mission systems and sensors were combined with a structural life extension to 2030, ensuring the Aurora was well prepared for both its ISR and Anti-Submarine Warfare (ASW) roles.

Similar to what was happening in the private sector, digital technologies would introduce a deluge of data across the RCAF's combat, training, and operations networks. Along with new aircrew training systems, the RCAF would have to rethink traditional roles and open up occupations in specialized areas such as data

Corporal Errol Morgan, a Canadian Avionics Technician, provides a CF-18 briefing to an American military firefighting team in case an emergency situation arises.

management and analytics, signals, communications, cyber security, and electronic air warfare to capitalize on the potential of information to improve decision making, efficiency, and response times.

Most importantly, the Future Fighter Capability Project (FFCP) was stood up and tasked with procuring a fifth-generation fighter to replace the RCAF's fleet of CF-18 Hornets. The FFCP reached the final phase of the procurement in 2023, securing 88 Lockheed Martin F-35s in a contract with the first aircraft planned to arrive in 2026.

The outbreak of the COVID-19 pandemic in 2020 forced the RCAF to adjust to a new normal. Stringent health and safety measures were introduced and flying limitations were imposed. Functioning close to capacity, the RCAF continued to deal with a flood of COVID-19 responses and Operation LENTUS tasks. During the mudslides in British Columbia, for example, transport units rerouted the delivery of COVID-19 vaccines safely to Alberta. When India was devastated by the coronavirus, two RCAF CC-150 Polaris flights transported much-needed medical supplies to its overwhelmed health care system. Five CC-177s operated by 429 Transport Squadron worked non-stop—moving Griffons to and from British Columbia, distributing more than 82,000 kg (180,779 lb) of COVID-19 supplies across Central America.

Throughout the pandemic, the RCAF's operational tempo dipped but it never stopped. Overseas, RCAF Griffons and Chinooks returned to Canada after participating in a United Nations (UN) mission in Gao, Mali. In August of 2021, the RCAF helped to evacuate the remaining Canadian and Afghan nationals from Kabul under Operation AEGIS. In chaotic conditions, 429 Transport Squadron Globemasters, along with a 436 Squadron Hercules and a 437 Squadron Polaris, flew multiple sorties to bring 3,700 people safely out of Afghanistan. In Operation REASSURANCE, an Air Task Force of approximately 170 personnel and six CF-18s deployed to Constanta, Romania, participating in NATO's enhanced Air Policing mission.

At the peak of the pandemic, the RCAF's aerobatics flight demonstration team, the Snowbirds, celebrated their golden anniversary. Since William Barker led his first aerobatics performance over Toronto's waterfront more than 100 years ago, air show teams have graced Canadian skies—from the Siskins to the Blue Devils, the Golden Hawks, and the Golden Centennaires. For the last 50-plus years, this honour has belonged to Canada's beloved Snowbirds. Postponing their anniversary during the pandemic, the Snowbirds reconfigured their season into the Operation INSPIRATION tour of flypasts across the country to boost morale.

On February 24, 2022, Russia invaded Ukraine for a second time in a major escalation of the Russian-Ukrainian War that began in 2014. Not since the Cold War had Russia postured itself as such an imminent threat. In July 2022, the Canadian government renewed its commitment to NORAD with a modernization plan to spend $38.6 billion over the next 20 years upgrading Canada's continental defences. The overhaul would replace the North Warning System, a chain of radar stations in the far north, in the most significant upgrade to Canadian NORAD capabilities in almost four decades.

The Canadian military's response to Russia's invasion of Ukraine was called Operation UNIFIER. As part of the Canadian Armed Forces Joint Task Force–Ukraine, 30 members of 436 Transport Squadron set up a temporary base at the Glasgow Prestwick Airport in Scotland. Receiving both lethal and non-lethal aid transported from Canada on a CC-177 Globemaster, two J-model Hercules would complete the airlift to Poland, for onward ground transportation into Ukraine. At the time of writing, the two designated aircrews have moved over 900,000 kg, or just over 2 million lb of goods.

The war in Ukraine deepened the understanding that the war-fighting domain had grown much broader. Nations and public corporations slowly began to compete for their stake in space. The RCAF was officially made Canada's functional authority in this domain in 2017 and established 3 Canadian Space Division in July 2022. The new RCAF division was tasked with exploring how space-based capabilities can better support CAF requirements in communications, command and control, navigation, weather, and situational awareness. Through this initiative and partnerships with organizations and agencies to advance projects in both air and space defence, the RCAF continues to blaze a pathway to the stars. This is exemplified by its long-term collaborations with CAE and the National Research Council of Canada in such exciting areas as simulation, autonomous flight, digital twins, 3D printing, and drone detection.

The legacy of the RCAF is defined by its operations, aircraft, and innovations in aviation. But mostly, it is defined by its extraordinary people, of which this book illustrates the contributions of only some of these people. On any given day, whether it's June 24, 1944, when Flight-Lieutenant David Hornell spotted a German submarine, and despite being hit by anti-aircraft fire, sank the U-boat; or June 19, 1976, when Major Rudy Willhauk of 414 Squadron in North Bay, Ontario, reached 3,000 hours flying a CF-100 Canuck; or September 20, 2020, when Sergeant Brigitte O'Driscoll became the first woman to be certified as a Master Door Gunner on a Tac Hel Squadron, RCAF personnel are constantly making history. Many of their stories span generations, like Brigadier-General William "Fat Daddy" Radiff, who grew up on the base at Baden–Soellingen during the Cold War and went on to become a fighter pilot, coming full circle before serving as Brigadier-General in NORAD.

It's the people who make the RCAF what it is, with pilots like TOPGUN graduate Chris Swartz and test pilot Billie Flynn reaching the pinnacle of fighter aviation. Others, such as Chris Hadfield and Colonel Jeremy Hansen, test their limits in the frontiers of space. Despite its various roles—and today, there are 100 different occupations in the RCAF, from Mechanical Engineering Officer to Air Combat Systems Officer to Radiologist to a Musician in the RCAF band—its personnel remain committed to a common goal: to defend and protect the skies above Canada and provide peacekeeping and humanitarian assistance around the world. For the past 100 years, aviators and Canadians alike have been inspired by the achievements of those who have served and continue to serve in the Royal Canadian Air Force.

Governor General and Commander-in-Chief of Canada, David Johnston, accompanied by Lieutenant-General Mike Hood, Commander RCAF, stops to chat with an airman during his inspection at the RCAF Colours Presentation at Nathan Phillips Square in Toronto on September 1, 2017.

The RCAF Is Back!

Reconnecting to Its Rich History and Heritage.

On August 16, 2011, the Government of Canada announced that the RCAF would revert from "Air Command" to its original historic name, the Royal Canadian Air Force. The RCAF was back! Along with this change, "Maritime Command" became, once again, the Royal Canadian Navy and Land Force Command was renamed the Canadian Army. These changes were made to honour Canada's distinguished military history and reaffirm the importance of the individual services in the Canadian Armed Forces.

In 2013, the RCAF adopted a new badge, which was similar to the pre-unification badge showing an eagle with outstretched wings, but retained elements of Air Command, including the modern frame and the Latin motto *Sic Itur Ad Astra*, "such is the pathway to the stars." To reconnect current RCAF members with their celebrated predecessors, the RCAF unveiled new changes to the uniform in 2014. Launched for the 75th anniversary of the Battle of Britain, the uniform was a throwback to those worn when the RCAF was first created with the addition of small changes, such as the introduction of pearl-grey wings and ranks, and silver buttons. All designations remained the same, except for "Privates" who were to be now known as the gender-neutral "Aviator," designated by a single-stitch propeller. While main aspects of the uniform were drawn from pre-unification rank insignia, maintaining some modern elements and terminology served to strengthen the RCAF's heritage while honouring those who continue to serve.

In 2017, the RCAF received new Colours. Colours are consecrated ceremonial flags carried by designated CAF formations and units. In the military, colours matter. In early days, armies were led into battle by their colours and standard, which served as rallying points in time of danger. The RCAF carries two Colours: the Queen's Colour, a maple leaf flag with the Sovereign's cypher in the centre, which symbolizes loyalty to the Crown, and the Command Colour, a blue flag with the RCAF's badge at the centre, symbolizing the RCAF's pride, cohesion, and valour. The RCAF Colours replaced the Air Command Colours presented in 1982.

At the 2017 ceremony, Governor General and Commander-in-Chief of Canada David Johnston (as seen on the left) presented the RCAF with new Colours during a military parade at Nathan Phillips Square in Toronto. A flyover of every aircraft-type in the RCAF also figured prominently over the skies of downtown Toronto. The Mayor of Toronto declared September 1 to be Royal Canadian Air Force Day. City Hall lights, the Toronto sign in Nathan Phillips Square, and the CN Tower were illuminated in RCAF blue to mark the occasion.

Historically, the RCAF was the first of the Commonwealth air forces to be granted the privilege of carrying the King's Colour, which it received in 1950 together with the RCAF Colour. Both were presented in the name of King George VI on Parliament Hill, Ottawa, on the King's birthday, June 5, 1950, by the Governor General, Viscount Alexander of Tunis. These were replaced by the Air Command Colours in 1982.

Above: The current version of the RCAF badge with the Latin motto *Sic Itur Ad Astra*, which means "Such is the pathway to the stars."

Captain Chris "Lime" Schwartz flying an F/A-18E Super Hornet above the aircraft carrier USS *Abraham Lincoln*.

Captain Chris "Lime" Swartz

A Celebrated TOPGUN Graduate

RCAF fighter pilots are world class and some have the TOPGUN patch to prove it. On November 24, 2020, an RCAF aviator, Captain Chris "LIME" Swartz, made history by graduating from the gruelling U.S. Navy Strike Fighter Tactics Instructor program, otherwise known as TOPGUN, considered to be the pinnacle of fighter aviation in the U.S. Navy.

With the release of *Maverick* more than 35 years after the original movie was released, TOPGUN has experienced a resurgence in popularity. The real TOPGUN, the Strike Fighter Tactics Instructor program that origi-nated as the U.S. Navy Fighter Weapons School in 1969, teaches fighter tactics and techniques to select naval aviators and flight officers who then return to their fleet or to TOPGUN as instructors. The course is made up of hours of ground school and some of the most challenging live flying in the world.

Before graduating from TOPGUN, Captain Swartz joined the RCAF in

2006, earned his wings in 2012, completed fighter training in 2014, and was posted to 425 Tactical Fighter Squadron in Bagotville, Quebec. Flying CF-18s, Chris was deployed on Operation REASSURANCE in Germany and Operation IMPACT in Kuwait. In 2017, Swartz began an exchange tour with the U.S. Navy. After finishing F/A-18E Super Hornet training, Chris was posted to U.S. Navy Strike Fighter Squadron 143 (VFA-143) "Pukin' Dogs" at Oceana. He completed a ten-month mission aboard the USS *Abraham Lincoln* with Carrier Air Wing 7 from April 2019 until January 2020, the longest aircraft carrier deployment since the Vietnam War. Swartz excelled with VFA-143 and was nominated to participate in the distinguished TOPGUN course. Here, he would learn basic fighter manoeuvres, before moving on to air-to-air missions, with a final focus on air-to-ground tactics.

Captain Swartz wears his coveted TOPGUN patch with pride. Deeply honoured to have graduated from the course, Swartz credits

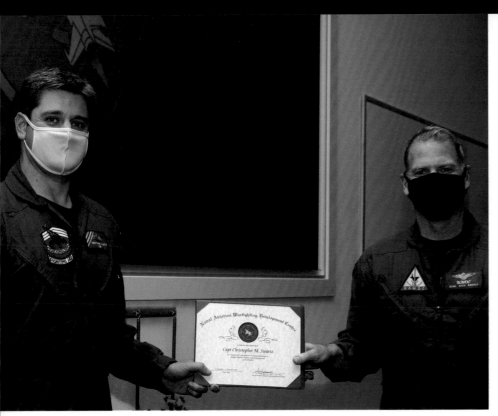

Captain Chris "LIME" Swartz receives his TOPGUN graduation certificate from Rear Admiral Richard Brophy, Commander, Naval Aviation Warfighting Development Center.

a professionalism and dedication to aviator training in the TOPGUN program that is "second to none." He compares taking off from an aircraft carrier to drag racing, calling it a "crazy ride" and crediting the Landing Signal Officers for being instrumental in getting him "up to speed on carrier operations, and in recovering the aircraft back aboard the boat safely."

The RCAF is incredibly proud of Swartz's dedication and drive to strive for excellence in his work. Chris is on exchange with the U.S. Navy with an RCAF Air Combat Systems Officer (ACSO). Two additional RCAF aircrew, also a pilot and an ACSO, are on exchange with the Royal Australian Air Force. These exchanges will help the RCAF gain advanced experience and help facilitate the introduction of a new fleet of F-35A fighter jets in Canada under the Future Fighter Capability Project.

Air Combat Systems Officer

Air Combat Systems Officers plan, coordinate, and direct the missions of aircraft and crew. They manage the operation of precision tactical navigation systems, sophisticated sensors, communication systems, electronic warfare equipment, and weapon delivery systems.

"I'm Captain Simon Wilson from Calgary, Alberta. I'm an Air Combat Systems Officer at 423 Maritime Helicopter Squadron in Shearwater, Nova Scotia. Air Combat Systems Officers, or ACSOs, are responsible for tactical decisions onboard aircraft and directing pilots where to fly. They operate on world-class, state-of-the-art tactical platforms like the Cyclone maritime helicopter and the CP-140 Aurora long-range patrol aircraft, as well as fixed-wing search and rescue aircraft. On a maritime helicopter, we fly with two pilots, an Air Combat Systems Operator, and an Airborne Electronic Sensor Operator. I'll direct the tactical mission and the sensor operator will devise and correlate tracks and be able to stitch together the maritime picture."

Billie Flynn: Canada's Very Own Top Gun

Lieutenant-Colonel Billie Flynn, CD

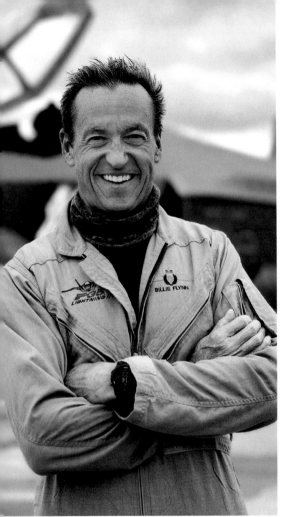

Lieutenant-Colonel (Retired) Billie Flynn as Chief Test Pilot of the F-35 Joint Strike Fighter.

If you've watched the movie *Top Gun* or its sequel, *Top Gun: Maverick*, you may be interested to know that Canada has its very own, real-life Top Gun. That pilot is Billie Flynn. In fact, the movie's script could have been based on his life.

Flynn was born in Germany. His parents, both RCAF veterans, were married in the church on the base at CFB Baden–Soellingen (where, incidentally, Billie would fly 25 years later). Billie's father was a fighter pilot. He flew F-86s, CF-100 Clunks, and CF-101 Voodoos, so Billie grew up around fighter jets and air bases. In fact, when asked where his hometown is, he often hesitates because it is somewhere between Cold Lake and Bagotville! As a young boy, Flynn would sit in fighter cockpits in the hangars on Sunday after church. He wanted to "live in that world," inspired to do so by his father's fellow RCAF pilots.

Billie took his love of flying jets to the RCAF. He graduated from Royal Military College in Kingston, Ontario, in 1981 with a Bachelor of Mechanical Engineering degree and became one of Canada's first pilots to fly the CF-18. He would go on to command a CF-18 Fighter Squadron in combat missions over Kosovo and the former Republic of Yugoslavia and then serve as a test pilot of future fighters, such as the Eurofighter Typhoon and the F-35 Lightning II. In fact, Billie was the test pilot and lead spokesperson for the F-35 for more than 15 years and travelled all over the world demonstrating what a fifth-generation fighter can do.

Flynn attributes his success in the RCAF to being "offered incredible opportunities as well as extraordinary timing." He was Commanding Officer of the Balkan Rats in Operation ALLIED FORCE, commanding men and women in combat. Getting into his plane every day knowing he might be shot at was lifechanging for Billie. It defined who he was for the rest of his life. The performance of the Balkan Rats was an exemplary display of the professionalism of the RCAF under the stresses of combat operations. What Flynn is most proud of was the honour and privilege of commanding in combat and "bringing them all home." As a test pilot, it is his contribution to the Automatic Ground Collision Avoidance System that he relishes most. As the lead test pilot for the Lockheed Martin famed Skunk Works project team, Flynn helped develop and test the innovative and lifesaving technology that found its way into the F-16, F-22, F-35, and later, the F/A-18 Super Hornet and CF-18 Hornet.

It's only fitting that, upon his retirement, Canada chose the F-35 as its next generation fighter. He played a major role in Lockheed Martin's F-35 Joint Strike Fighter Program, a complex defence program that demanded expansive testing by Flynn. Billie has flown over 80 aircraft for the RCAF, USAF, USN, Marine Corps, NASA, Eurofighter, and Lockheed Martin. His favourite fighter is the F-16 Viper but if he was going into combat, his choice would be the CF-18 Hornet.

Opposite: Billie Flynn salutes from the cockpit of his CF-18 Hornet fighter before taking off on a combat mission over the former Republic of Yugoslavia on April 28, 1999.

Siskin Aerobatic Team, left to right: Pilot Officer E.A. McGowan, Flight Lieutenant D.A. Harding, and Pilot Officer E.A. McNab.

A F-86 Sabre aircraft flies over the Strait of Georgia near Comox, British Columbia, April 23, 2009. The Sabre or "Hawk One" is refurbished and repainted in the golden colours of the legendary RCAF Golden Hawks, Canada's first jet aerobatic demonstration team.

RCAF Aerobatic Teams
A Tradition of Excellence from the Siskins to the Snowbirds

It's been over a century since Canada's most decorated flying ace, William Barker, dazzled viewers at the Canadian National Exhibition (CNE) with his daredevil solo aerobatics over the Toronto waterfront. In the same show, Barker led a formation of fellow First World War pilots. And just like that, the air show industry was born in Canada.

Barker belonged to the glut of experienced pilots who returned home after the First World War in search of an occupation. Many wanted to continue flying. So they partnered with other pilots, bought a couple of "Jennys" and became "barnstormers"—daredevils flying across North America selling airplane rides and performing hair-raising stunts, such as flying loops, walking out on their wings mid-flight, and transferring from one plane to another in the air.

Ten years after Barker's CNE performance, the RCAF formed its first official aerobatic team, the Siskins. Since then, air show teams like the Blue Devils, the Golden Hawks, and the Golden Centennaires have entertained millions of Canadians. Over the last 50 years, Canada's beloved Snowbirds have kept up this tradition of excellence in jet formation aerobatics.

Back in 1919, British aviators John Alcock and Arthur Brown flew a Vickers Vimy biplane from Newfoundland to England. To celebrate the tenth anniversary of this first non-stop flight across the Atlantic, the RCAF formed the Siskins in 1929 at Camp Borden, Ontario. The aerobatics team flew three Armstrong Whitworth Siskin biplanes, performing daring manoeuvres at over 100 air shows before being disbanded in 1932. Notably, the Siskins' Squadron Leader, E.A. McNab, was the first RCAF pilot to win the Distinguished Flying Cross during the Second World War.

In the 1950s, a number of RCAF squadrons contributed to Canada's rich heritage in aerobatic performance, including the Blue Devils, founded in 1949 at St. Hubert with 410 Squadron. The Blue Devils were the first RCAF team to use fighter jets, first the de Havilland Vampire and then F-86 Sabres in 1951—the same year the team was disbanded. The Fireballs were a European-based RCAF aerobatic team that flew red painted Sabres in shows out of Germany in 1954.

The Sky Lancers were another European-based aerobatic team, based out of RCAF Station Grostenquin in France. Formed in 1955 by pilots from

2 Wing, the team flew Sabres in 20 shows. In 1956, 4 Wing flew a team out of Baden–Soellingen, Germany, with the same name but new pilots and a different colour scheme for their Sabres. The team consisted of Flying Officers J.D. "Dale" McLarty (lead), J.H. "Jake" Adams, F.K. "Fred" Axtell, L.C. "Stretch" Price, and E.H. "Ed" Welters. Unfortunately, while practising a routine over the Rhine valley, a fatal accident resulted in the death of all team members except Flying Officer Price. The tragedy halted RCAF aerobatic teams for several years.

In 1959, aerobatics returned with the Golden Hawks. The RCAF celebrated its 35th anniversary, along with 50 years of powered flight in Canada, by creating the country's first national aerobatic team based out of RCAF Station Chatham, New Brunswick. The Golden Hawks symbolized the Golden Era of the RCAF, flying six gilded Sabre Mk. 5 aircraft (and later the Mk. 6) bearing a red-and-white hawk emblem on each fuselage. Squadron Leader Fernand "Fern" Villeneuve led the team as they revolutionized air show performances, perfecting manoeuvres like the head-on cross and pushing the limits of formation complexity and risk. Wherever they performed, the Golden Hawks stole the show. Supposed to only be around for one year, the team captivated audiences in 317 air shows until 1963. In 2006, the Golden Hawks received the Belt of Orion Award for excellence from Canada's Aviation Hall of Fame.

The legacy continued with the Golden Centennaires. The team was created by the RCAF in 1967 to mark the 100th anniversary of Canada's federation by performing at 100 air shows across the country. The Centennaires were led by Wing Commander O. B. Philp and flew a formation of six gold and blue CT-114 Tutor jets with two solo aircraft—a CF-101 Voodoo and a CF-104 Starfighter. The team performed at 103 shows across Canada, opening and closing Expo 67 celebrations in Montreal, and participating in air shows in the United States and the Bahamas before disbanding.

After the Centennaires split in 1967, Commanding Officer O.B. Philp established a seven-plane formation team using the same white CT-114 Tutor jets that the Snowbirds fly today. Philp selected veteran fighter pilot Major Glen Younghusband to lead the team. In 1971, after a naming contest at a local elementary school, the team became known as the "Snowbirds." The squadron expanded to nine aircraft and in 1975, the

The Golden Centennaires: Rear (left to right): Flight Officer Jim McKay, Flight Lieutenant Russ Bennett, and Flight Lieutenant B.K. Doyle. Front (left to right): Squadron Leader Clarence Lang, Flight Lieutenant Tom Hinton, Flight Lieutenant Red Dagenais, Flight Lieutenant John Swallow, and Flight Lieutenant Bill Slaughter.

RCAF Sky Lancers Aerobatics Team.

Snowbird pilot Captain Maryse Carmichael.

Women in the Snowbirds: A Team of Many Firsts

The Snowbirds are a team of firsts: The first aerobatic team to be designated a squadron; the first to perform to music; and the first to have a woman break the sky-high glass ceiling when in November of 2000, Captain Maryse Carmichael was selected as a demonstration pilot with the Snowbirds. In 2010, Lieutenant-Colonel Carmichael returned to 15 Wing Moose Jaw as Commanding Officer of 431 Air Demonstration Squadron. To this day, women have proudly filled every role on the Snowbirds' Squadron.

Snowbirds were officially designated 431 Demonstration Squadron based at 15 Wing Moose Jaw in Saskatchewan.

Few exemplify the thrill of formation flying better than Canada's iconic Snowbirds. The level of concentration required to complete each manoeuvre is extraordinary, considering the high speeds (up to 600 km/h or 370 mph) and close proximity of each plane. In their tightest formation, the Double Diamond Roll, their wing tips are a mere 1.2 m (almost 4 ft) apart. It's no wonder the Snowbirds are admired as the best in the world at flying precision aerial acrobatics.

Over 80 personnel support the 24-person Snowbird show team. The squadron's pilots, technicians, and support staff are hand-picked volunteers. As Canada's aerial ambassadors, the Snowbirds have flown across North America performing in shows to more than 153 million spectators. Carrying on the proud tradition of their predecessors, the Snowbirds have become a symbol of national pride for Canadians. In October 1999, the Snowbirds received their "Queen's Colours" for 25 years of service, and in 1994, Canada's Aviation Hall of Fame honoured the Snowbirds with the Belt of Orion Award for Excellence.

Canadian Forces Snowbirds.

Opposite: The Canadian Forces Snowbirds (431 Air Demonstration Squadron) performing over 19 Wing Comox.

"Fat Daddy": Full Circle—From the Cold War to NORAD

Brigadier-General William Radiff, MSM, CD

Brigadier-General William Radiff.

Brigadier-General Will Radiff's military career spans more than 32 years, stretching from the Cold War to today. He was first introduced to the RCAF as a seven-year-old boy living on the Base at CFB Baden–Soellingen, Germany, where his father taught. At the time, the threat of nuclear war was a stark reality. Radiff remembers "participating in nuclear attack drills at my on-base school where the teachers' voices were often drowned out by the sound of the fighter aircraft taking off or landing." All his friends were the children of at least one military parent and even though they were very young, they collectively understood why the RCAF was there: "to defend against Soviet attack."

Radiff knew he wanted to be a fighter pilot at nine years old, when he saw his first CF-104 Starfighter. During a field trip to the flightline, "the entire school was there and we were in awe when the action started. There were tactical helicopters flying low and fast, firing their door guns, and inserting troops. There were armoured personnel carriers transporting soldiers who jumped out and began firing their weapons and deploying smoke grenades. But most impressively to me, there were the CF-104 Starfighters flying overhead, conducting bombing runs with simulated bomb explosions." Will's classmates wanted to become soldiers or fly helicopters, but he "could only remember the fighter aircraft." Flying one became his life's mission.

That demonstration put Radiff on the path to becoming a pilot in the RCAF. "I never wavered from my goal and spent the next years doing all of the things necessary to become an RCAF pilot; I worked hard in school, played sports, did community service work, and had a part-time job." Radiff joined the Canadian Armed Forces in 1988. "At 18, I enrolled as a pilot trainee in the Canadian Forces to attend Royal Roads Military College. Completing my university education and pilot training some six years later, I was disappointed when my pilot course offered only helicopter and multi-engine slots. I chose helicopters and spent the next three years flying the very rewarding mission of search and rescue." However, Radiff hadn't given up his fighter pilot dream.

He spent the next three years as a pilot instructor on the CT-114 Tutor, at the end of which, Will was selected for fighter pilot training. In 2000, Radiff completed the fighter training course on a CF-18. Having finally "made it," he was posted to the CF-18 Operational Training Unit at 410 Squadron in 4 Wing, Cold Lake, Alberta, and later 433 Escadron d'appui Tactique at 3 Wing, Bagotville, Quebec. Will was part of the Government of Canada's Next Generation Fighter Capability Project, held positions at NORAD Headquarters in Colorado Springs, was Target Engagement Authority for Canadian flying operations during Operation IMPACT in Qatar—where he earned the Meritorious Service Medal—and commanded 409 Nighthawk Squadron in Cold Lake. In these role, he deployed many times in support of both NATO expeditionary operations and NORAD Northern Sovereignty Operations. In 2017, Will rose to the rank of Colonel and became Commander of 3 Wing, returning to Bagotville.

After finishing the National Security Programme at

Colonel William Radiff (second left), Air Task Force Commander and Captain Sylvain Rousseau (second right), ATF Public Affairs Officer, talk to Major Michael Wawrzyniak (right), Allied Air Command Chief Public Affairs Officer at the media gathering in Bodo, Norway on November 2, 2018 during Exercise TRIDENT JUNCTURE 2018.

the Canadian Forces College, Radiff was promoted to his current rank as Brigadier-General and Deputy Commander of NORAD Alaska Region—a posting that brings him back to where it all began. Throughout his career, Radiff often assumed the NORAD alert duty, reminding him of the fighters on alert at CFB Baden–Soellingen all those years ago. "Today, I sit in the role of the Deputy Commander of the Alaska NORAD Region. I have truly come full circle from that day beside the runway in 1977. It has meant a lot of hard work, some sacrifice, and many, many moves, but I would not trade it for anything. The RCAF inspired me as a young boy, and it still inspires me today."

Air Operations Officer

Air Operations Officers command, control, and coordinate air and space forces in tactical, operational, and strategic environments. They are experts in planning, directing, and leading air and space operations, leveraging experience developed at tactical units and formations to integrate those effects in higher-level joint, combined, and pan-domain operations and campaigns.

"I'm Major Kendra Bencun from Calgary, Alberta, an Air Operations Officer currently posted to 450 Tactical Helicopter Squadron in Garrison Petawawa, Ontario. The Air Operations Officer is essentially the orchestrator of everything that happens on an airfield or on an operation, and that means coordinating all elements that make everything flying work—from the meteorologists that will provide the baseline for decisions to launch aircraft to cleaning snow off the airfields to being able to launch the aircraft and then recover them at the end of the day."

Did you know... That NORAD Tracks Santa?

The North American Aerospace Defense Command (NORAD) tracks everything that flies into North American airspace—and that includes Santa Claus. Every Christmas Eve, eager children watch NORAD track Santa as he drops off gifts around the world. "NORAD Tracks Santa" is one of the oldest and most popular Santa tracking services. And it all started because of a typo.

On December 24, 1955, a little girl in Colorado set out to call Santa using a telephone number posted in a local Sears advertisement. Because of a misprint, she dialled the Continental Air Defense Command Operations Center instead. Many other calls came in, and rather than disappoint the Santa-seeking children, Harry Shoup (the "Santa Colonel") reported Santa's location back to them. And so began a tradition that was continued by NORAD when it was formed in 1958.

Today, NORAD uses high-powered radar, "Santa Cams," and sophisticated satellite systems with infrared sensors that follow Rudolph's nose to track Santa. When he reaches Newfoundland, Santa is received by Canadian NORAD fighter pilots in CF-18s and escorted on his rounds across Canada.

RCAF pilots report that on these very important missions, Santa does indeed slow down with a wave at initial interception. After being identified as "undoubtedly friendly," CF-18s return the greeting with a respectful tilt of their wings. For the duration of Santa's journey, RCAF pilots are on hand to assist in any kind of situation, as they did on one occasion in the 1960s when Santa made an emergency landing on frozen ice in Hudson Bay.

Leading up to Santa's arrival on Christmas Eve, volunteers at NORAD track Santa and staff phones and computers to answer calls from children. The official website, https://www.noradsanta.org, receives close to 15 million unique visitors from over 200 locations across the globe in NORAD's hi-tech spin on the Santa Claus legend.

Avionics Systems Technician

Avionics Systems Technicians are responsible for maintaining all onboard electronic systems—the nerve centres of all CAF aircraft. This includes aircraft communication, intercom, acoustic sensing, infra-red radar, electronic warfare, navigation, compass, flight control systems, and more.

"I'm Samantha Schaus from Trenton, Ontario, an Avionics Systems Technician here at 424 Search and Rescue Squadron at Canadian Forces Base Trenton, Ontario. Avionics Systems Technicians are the electricians of the aircraft. Essentially anything electronic, we are in charge of. Not only do I do the electrical maintenance on the aircraft, but I also do servicing, which would include liquid oxygen on the aircraft, fuelling the aircraft, etc. As an Avionics Systems Technician, I'm not assigned to just one aircraft, so in my career, I could end up working on the CF-18 or the Snowbirds' Tutor or the Chinook. The possibilities are endless."

NORAD Modernization
A Multi-Layer System of Defence

In 2022, Canada's Minister of National Defence announced that the government would invest $38.6 billion over 20 years to modernize NORAD in partnership with the United States, a seminal moment in the continent's defence since the formation of NORAD in the 1950s and the creation of the Dew Line almost 70 years ago.

NORAD is responsible for the defence of North American airspace, along with NATO's northern and western flanks. And defence, particularly of our homeland, has to keep pace with threats as they evolve. Hypersonic missiles, for example, fly faster than the speed of sound, are very long range, and can evade interception to reach the target. The war in Ukraine in 2022 has demonstrated how this threat environment is evolving, with Russian hypersonic missiles being launched from aircraft to cause massive casualties and destruction, giving an urgency to the need to upgrade NORAD's defence system.

NORAD was originally formed to protect North America from the threat of Soviet bombers during the Cold War. Its current surveillance system, the North Warning System, a chain of radar systems built in the 1980s, is unable to track the more modern threat presented by recent hypersonic missile technology.

In a joint declaration, Canada and the United States announced that NORAD's aging radar stations will be replaced with a new radar system that will feature two types of modern radars, both a northern and polar, that will have the ability to "see" over the horizon and detect new threats. The new multi-layer network will monitor Pacific and Atlantic approaches to North America as well as the Arctic. Along with these "Arctic Over-the-Horizon" and "Polar Over-the-Horizon" systems, a new system called "Cross-bow" will feature a network of sensors with classified capabilities, distributed across Northern Canada, as an additional layer of detection. NORAD's three systems will significantly improve Canada's situational knowledge of what enters North American air space and will also be complemented by space-based surveillance from satellites.

Dew Line Site.

Other upgrades will be made to meet NORAD's evolving requirements as the command takes on additional responsibilities, such as protecting against cyberattacks. Proposed changes include a sizable research and development component that will cover modernizing command-and-control systems, constructing new systems to help with air navigation in remote regions, enhancing satellite communications in the Arctic, and acquiring new digital radios and network equipment. Infrastructure will also be upgraded to support these proposed changes.

NORAD is also committed to working with Indigenous and northern communities. Because these communities play a key role in the defence of Northern Canada, NORAD's modification is set to include benefits for local Indigenous communities, while addressing their environmental concerns. Over the course of 20 years, the government's investment in NORAD's continental and northern defence will total $40 billion, with the RCAF front and centre as the guarantor of Canadian sovereignty.

Members of the Helicopter Air Detachment onboard HMCS *Montréal* conduct a foc'sle transfer with a CH-148 Cyclone helicopter during Operation REASSURANCE in the Mediterranean Sea on April 9, 2022.

CH-148 Cyclone
Canada's Maritime Helicopter

The CH-148 Cyclone replaced the Sea King as Canada's main ship-borne maritime helicopter, providing air support for the RCN. Its principal roles are to conduct Anti-Submarine Warfare, surveillance, and search and rescue missions from RCN warships. The helicopter also provides tactical transport for national and international security efforts. The Cyclone can be used for surface and sub-surface surveillance, search and rescue missions, tactical transport and more. Able to operate during the day or night and in any weather conditions, the Cyclone supports missions in Canada and around the world.

HMCS *Halifax's* aircrew unfold the CH-148 Cyclone Maritime helicopter on the flight deck during Exercise DOGU AKDENIZ 19 in the Eastern Mediterranean as part of Operation REASSURANCE on November 14, 2019.

Opposite: HMCS *Montréal's* CH-148 Cyclone helicopter, where aircrew conduct flight operations in the Mediterranean Sea during Operation REASSURANCE on April 4, 2022.

Chris Hadfield: The Sky Is Not the Limit

Colonel Chris Hadfield, OC, OOnt, MSC, CD

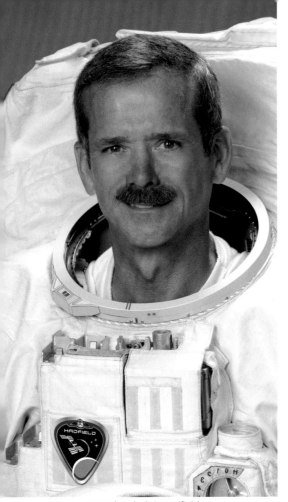

RCAF Colonel Chris Hadfield.

Imagine floating in space, over a million feet above the Earth and being afraid of heights. Unthinkable for many of us, though not Colonel Chris Hadfield, world famous astronaut and first Canadian ever to walk in space—who also happens to be afraid of heights.

According to Hadfield, the way to overcome your fears is to face them head on with a plan. For Chris, this meant understanding the difference between "perceived danger" and "actual danger." Concluding that a fear of heights is essentially a fear of falling, the remedy was straightforward. In Hadfield's own words, "all I need to do is clip myself on [to a safety line] and I can manage that fear."

Undeterred by a primal fear, Hadfield spent his life in pursuit of one goal: to fly to space.

Like so many kids, a young Chris Hadfield was inspired by the Apollo 11 lunar landing on July 20, 1969: "The burning fire that made me want to pursue this for my whole life was absolutely turned on by watching the race to the Moon, eventually seeing Neil Armstrong and Buzz Aldrin walk on its surface."

Hadfield's first step towards realizing his dream was to become a pilot. At 15, he was awarded a Royal Canadian Air Cadet glider pilot scholarship, and at 16, a powered pilot scholarship. Hadfield graduated from the Royal Military College in Kingston, Ontario, with an engineering degree, proudly wearing his great grandfather's sword in his graduation parade.

A strong sense of duty contributed to Hadfield's drive to serve as a fighter pilot with the RCAF. He took Basic Pilot Training at CFB Portage la Prairie, subsequently earning his wings and graduating with honours from 2 Canadian Forces Flying Training School at CFB Moose Jaw. Hadfield then trained with both 419 and 410 Tactical Fighter Operational Training Squadrons at CFB Cold Lake, flying the Canadair CF-5 Freedom Fighter and the CF-18 Hornet.

Hadfield was a combat fighter pilot in the Cold War, holding 24/7 alert, and did Canada's first intercept of a Soviet Bear bomber with a CF-18. In total, he flew fully armed CF-18s on eight different scramble missions versus Soviet Bears. Hadfield then attended the U.S. Air Force Test Pilot School at Edwards Air Force Base, receiving the 1988 Liethen-Tittle Award as top graduate, and served as an exchange officer with the U.S. Navy in the Strike Test Directorate at the Patuxent River Naval Air Station where he was Test Pilot of the Year (1991).

In 1992, Hadfield proved he was made of the right stuff. From a pool of over 5,300 candidates, he was accepted into the Canadian Space Agency alongside Michael McKay, Dave Williams, and Julie Payette. From thereon in, Hadfield would undergo the rigorous training required to spend time in space. "I was an astronaut for 21 years," he once stated, "I was only in space for six months."

Hadfield's lifelong ambition was realized when he flew into orbit twice aboard the space shuttle. On his first mission in 1995, Hadfield operated the robotic Canadarm and was the only Canadian ever to board the Russian Space Station Mir. In 2001, Hadfield flew on the *Endeavour* to deliver the Canadarm2 to the International Space Station (ISS) and completed the first-ever Canadian spacewalk. Floating in space,

Canadian Astronauts: Rear (left to right): Marc Garneau, Chris Hadfield, Bjarni Tryggvason, Steve MacLean. Front (left to right): Mike McKay, Dave Williams, Julie Payette, Robert Thirsk.

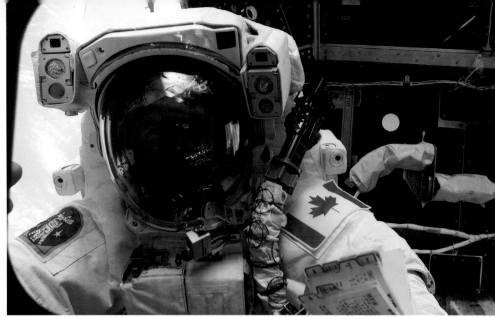

Chris Hadfield was the first Canadian to walk in space.

Chris made the first music video in space covering David Bowie's "Space Oddity." Released in 2013, the video has collected over 50 million views.

tethered by his feet to the ISS, Hadfield was installing the Canadarm2 when he suffered a bout of "space blindness." Instructed by mission control to open the purge valve on his helmet, Hadfield did so and the liquid in his eyes evaporated. The dauntless astronaut got right back to work.

For the last two months of his third spaceflight, Hadfield served as the first Canadian Commander of the ISS. Despite his long list of firsts, it was Hadfield's five-month stint aboard the ISS that made him a global celebrity. Recording a day in the life aboard a space station, Hadfield played his guitar, sang, conducted scientific experiments, and took breathtaking pictures of the Earth (45,000 of them). Perhaps what Hadfield is best known for is his evocative cover of David Bowie's "Space Oddity." Released in 2013, the video went viral, and at the time of writing has collected over 50 million views. As if being the first Canadian to walk in space wasn't enough, the charismatic Hadfield became the first person to record a music video in space.

After showing the world that the sky is not the limit, Hadfield retired. Today, he is a four-time bestselling author and an inspirational public speaker. He also is on the board of several space and technology companies, and helps run the global tech incubator The Creative Destruction Lab.

Lieutenant-General Al Meinzinger, Commander of the Royal Canadian Air Force, and Brigadier-General Mike Adamson, Commander of 3 Canadian Space Division, participate in a ceremony that marks the establishment of the RCAF's newest Division, 3 Canadian Space Division, at National Defence Headquarters Carling in Ottawa, Ontario.

Canada's Space Force: 3 Canadian Space Division

"The space domain is of critical importance, now more than ever, when considering its role in guiding military operations and enabling a vast range of day-to-day activities for Canadians. The establishment of 3 Canadian Space Division enables the Royal Canadian Air Force to ensure we have the right organizational structure to continually deliver spaced-based effects across the CAF, while also ensuring we are aligned with our allies who have established similar Space Commands." – Lieutenant-General Al Meinzinger, Commander, RCAF

Defending Canada includes defending space. Paving a true pathway to the stars, the RCAF established 3 Canadian Space Division (3 CSD) in 2022, marking an important date in the evolution of Canada's organization and defence of space. 3 CSD will build on space initiatives outlined in Canada's defence policy, improving its capability to deliver space effects and recognizing the importance of space in all Canadian Armed Forces operations.

3 CSD is a reorganization of the existing space-focused team within the RCAF's Director General Space. Supporting Canada's defence policy, 3 CSD will move the RCAF forward in ensuring that Canadian interests are protected in space, giving the country strategic advantage for both domestic and international operations. As new space technologies emerge from both private and public sector organizations, space is becoming a competitive, crowded, and potentially difficult domain to manage.

The new formation under the Commander of 3 CSD includes the stand up of 7 Wing, comprised of 7 Wing Headquarters, 7 Space Operations Squadron, and 7 Operations Support Squadron which includes the Canadian Space Operations Centre. The approximately 175 military and civilian personnel of 3 CSD will explore how capabilities in space support vital Canadian Armed Forces initiatives, including communications, command and control, navigation, weather, surveillance, and situational awareness. Operations will span search and rescue, monitoring coastal approaches to strengthen Canada's Arctic sovereignty, support for NORAD operations, and support in overseas operations. The RCAF division deepens Canada's commitment to the Combined Space Operations Initiative, cooperation on defence space operations between Australia, France, Germany, New Zealand, the United Kingdom, the United States, and Canada.

Colonel Jeremy Hansen
From RCAF Fighter Pilot to NASA Astronaut

From RCAF fighter pilot and now a senior RCAF astronaut, Colonel Jeremy Hansen is one of 14 graduates of the 20th NASA class and a proud representative of the Canadian Space Agency (CSA). While waiting for a flight assignment, Colonel Hansen represents CSA at NASA, and works at the Mission Control Center as Capcom—the voice between the ground and the ISS. In 2017, he became the first Canadian to be entrusted with leading a NASA astronaut class, which puts him in charge of the training astronaut candidates from both the United States and Canada.

As a young boy, Jeremy knew he wanted to fly. At age 12, he joined the Air Cadet Program. After obtaining his glider and private pilot licences at age 17, he was accepted by the Collège militaire royal de Saint-Jean, Quebec. Hansen graduated with a Bachelor of Science in Space Science (1999) and a Master of Science in Physics (2000) from Royal Military College in Kingston, Ontario.

Prior to joining the Canadian Space Program, Jeremy served as a CF-18 fighter pilot with both 409 Tactical Fighter Squadron and 441 Tactical Fighter Squadron, participating in NORAD Operations, Deployed Exercises, and Arctic Flying Operations.

In May 2009, Colonel Hansen was one of two recruits selected by the CSA through a Canadian Astronaut Recruitment Campaign. He graduated from Astronaut Candidate Training in 2011, an intensive program that includes instruction in ISS systems, spacewalks, robotics, physiological training, T-38 flight training, Russian language courses, and survival training.

To prepare for future space missions, Jeremy practices his spacewalks, continues to learn Russian, participates in expeditions in the High Arctic, and has even lived underground for six days as part of the European Space Agency's CAVES program. He also lived on the ocean floor in the Aquarius habitat off Key Largo, Florida, simulating deep space exploration for seven days as a crew member for NEEMO 19. Colonel Hansen maintains his pilot currency on the NASA T-38 jet aircraft as part of his astronaut training.

CSA astronaut Jeremy Hansen will fly aboard Artemis II with NASA astronauts Christina Hammock Koch, Victor Glover, and Reid Wiseman (sitting in front), April 18, 2023.

RCAF Band in the United Kingdom during the Second World War.

The RCAF Band

Entertaining the Troops—Overseas and at Home

Entertaining the troops is nothing new for the RCAF. It began during the Second World War, when the Canadian Army Show, with writers and performers Sergeant Johnny Wayne and Staff-Sergeant Frank Shuster (of the Wayne and Shuster comedic duo), completed a cross-Canada tour in 1943. While the Navy produced one show, *Meet the Navy*, few rivalled the RCAF in terms of forming spirited entertainment units. Personnel in all roles of the RCAF auditioned, from fitters and chefs to parachute riggers, airframe technicians, and trainee pilots. The troupes were managed out of RCAF Station Rockcliffe and given Entertainment Group numbers.

The *Blackouts of 1943* were the first RCAF musical revue to travel extensively. Seen by 70,000 service personnel as No. 1 Entertainment Group, this cast of singers, musicians, dancers, and comedians travelled to England for their premiere at the London Comedy Theatre. The RCAF Concert Trio put on 24 shows in Eastern Canada and the W-Debs of the RCAF performed for No. 6 Bomber Group shortly after they arrived in England. Another RCAF band called Swing Time played music in the style of Glenn Miller for troops stationed in Europe.

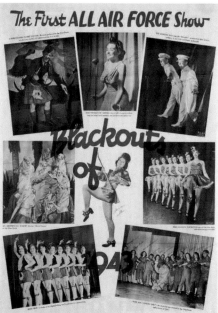

The *Blackouts of 1943* were the first RCAF musical revue and were based in RCAF Station Rockcliffe.

The Central Band of the Canadian Armed Forces and La Musique du Royal 22ᵉ Régiment perform during the opening ceremony of the Invictus Games at the Air Canada Centre in Toronto, Ontario, on September 23, 2017.

In 1946, Carl Friberg, a wartime bandmaster, was invited to form a professional band for the RCAF. He established the North West Air Command Band, a 30-piece band operating out of Edmonton. Their first gig was to accompany His Excellency, Viscount Alexander, the Governor General of Canada, on his 1948 tour of Western Canada. In 1955, the North West Air Command Band became the Tactical Air Command Band and increased to 55 members. They performed in an overseas tour in England, France, Belgium, and Germany. In 1975, the band was renamed The Air Command Band. In 2011, when the "Royal" designation returned to the Air Force, the band became the Royal Canadian Air Force Band.

For over 60 years, the RCAF Band has instilled national pride in Canadians and *esprit de corps* in its military. Based out of 17 Wing in Winnipeg, the band includes a 20 piece showband with lead vocalists and a rhythm section, a world-class brass quintet, a swinging big band, a pipes and drums ensemble, and full-cast ensemble parade band. Thirty-five professional musicians play at military and public parades, ceremonial occasions, tattoos, public and school concerts, and official dinners, dances and receptions in Canada and around the world. In July 2018, as part of the first-ever RCAF contingent to perform public duties for Her Majesty Queen Elizabeth II, the RCAF Band was honoured to attend Queen Elizabeth II and play during the changing of the guards at Buckingham Palace (seen above).

The band's playlist includes such favourites such as "Oh Canada," "Hockey Night in Canada," as well as the iconic "Star Wars" theme. You can enjoy their versatile talents on their latest CD, *Above and Beyond*.

Innovation in the RCAF

From the beginning of flight in Canada in 1909 when the Silver Dart lifted off the ice of Baddeck Bay and flew 800 m, innovation has always been central to Canadian success in the air. Those earliest pioneers were followed by the aces of the First World War, who brought home an interest and energy that ignited aviation. From mail delivery, medical evacuation, to mapping the North, aviation was especially important to a young country as large as Canada.

The RCAF was the fourth-largest air force in the world by the end of the Second World War, paving the way for many of the innovators and innovations highlighted earlier in this book: the G-suit, aircraft de-icing systems, crash position indicators, short take off, and landing aircraft design to name but a few. And when Canada launched the Alouette satellite in 1962, it became only the third space-faring nation in the world—the RCAF standing up 3 Canadian Space Division in 2022 builds upon those early innovations.

Innovation is alive and well in today's RCAF with no better example than the RCAF Flight Deck at Communitech in Waterloo, Ontario. In 2016, then RCAF Commander Michael Hood called his good friend Tom Jenkins to discuss how to continue to stimulate the innovative spirit in the force. Tom set up a tour for the entire Air Board (all General Officers of the RCAF and a small civilian advisory committee) to Waterloo. Quantum computing and artificial intelligence figured largely but the key tour was of the innovation supercluster at Communitech (Tom was one of the founders). In the days that followed, Air Force consensus settled on ensuring that the RCAF was part of this incredible ecosystem, and the Flight Deck at Communitech was born. Since then, numerous groups of RCAF personnel have participated in "base camps" at the Flight Deck, exposing them to young entrepreneurs and start-ups, some of whom have gone on to create pioneering technology for the air force.

Looking to the future, the RCAF Foundation's Student Scholarship program is offered to Canada's next generation of aviation and aerospace leaders. These scholarships are designed to assist post-secondary students in STEM (Science, Technology, Engineering, and Math) areas of study who are planning future careers in the fields of either aviation or aerospace. The foundation expects these student scholarships to help encourage more young people to consider careers in these fields as the demand for skilled people grows in both the private and defence sectors. The hope as well is that many find themselves in the RCAF of tomorrow and continue to foster the spirit of innovation.

Cyber Operator

Cyber Operators conduct defensive cyber operations, and when required and where feasible, active cyber operations. They monitor CAF communication networks to detect and respond to unauthorized network access attempts and provide cyber support to meet the operational requirements of the Navy, Army, Air Force, and special operations.

"I'm Sergeant Amy Lauritzen from Alliston, Ontario, a Cyber Operator currently posted to the Canadian Forces Network Operations Centre in Ottawa, Ontario. Cyber Operators defend Canadian information systems from hostile threat actors by implementing security procedures and hunting for malicious activity on the network. At the Canadian Forces Network Operations Centre, we are the first and last line of defence for military networks. We're the pointy end in the cyber domain, so we're analogous to the Army who's out on the battlefield fighting—we're the ones in the trenches fighting in the cyber domain. It's going to be even more important as time goes on because we're constantly under attack in the cyber domain and when you find something and you've been looking for it for a while, it's pretty exciting."

A CC-138 Twin Otter from 440 (Transport) Squadron.

CC-138 Twin Otter: Built for the Great White North

The de Havilland CC-138 Twin Otter is a Canadian STOL (Short Takeoff and Landing) utility aircraft used for RCAF transport and support roles in northern operations, as well as for medical evacuation and search and rescue missions. Ideal for Canada's northern climate, the Twin Otter can be alternately fitted with " tundra tires" or skis for landing on rugged terrain, ice, or snow. Canada's four Twin Otters are stationed in Yellowknife, in the Northwest Territories, and used in the RCAF's northern operations. You can find the Twin Otter in Appendix 3: List of Aircraft (Current and Historical).

CHAPTER 8
REFLECTING ON THE IMPACT OF THE RCAF
Canada and the World

Opposite: Lockheed Martin F-35A.

REFLECTING ON THE IMPACT OF THE RCAF
CANADA AND THE WORLD

Pathway to the Stars: 100 Years of the Royal Canadian Air Force is a celebration of the visionary people, marvellous machines, and global events that shaped the Royal Canadian Air Force from 1924 to 2024. The book is a collection of stories about great courage, devotion to duty, and service to humanity in Canada and throughout the world. The Government of Canada's official motto for the RCAF Centennial is "Your Air Force" and this is true—the Air Force belongs to all of us. Its stories of tremendous achievement and sacrifice have influenced Canadian lives in so many ways.

By any performance measure, the RCAF has set the standard for the enormous impact that a small group of people can achieve on the world stage. Over the span of 100 years, the RCAF has consistently played a prominent role in history. From fighting in the world wars when called upon by the government to providing critical relief to people both within and outside of Canada to setting the stage for Canada's future in space, the RCAF has delivered in every year of its century of existence, consistently punching above its weight. This is especially true when we consider that Canada has approximately one-half of one per cent of the world's population. The flight hours, inventions, lives saved, and victories per capita are without peer in the world.

The story of the RCAF begins during the First World War, in the context of Canada's loyalty to the British Empire as a Commonwealth country. We went to war out of principle because it was the right thing to do. Over 22,000 Canadians flew in the First World War. Without an official air force, they joined the British Royal Flying Corps (RFC) and Royal Naval Air Service (RNAS), which were later consolidated into the Royal Air Force (RAF). By 1918, 25 per cent of all RAF Officers were Canadian which is an incredible ratio given that the populations were 10–1 in size. Canadians took to combat flying so well that they earned over 800 decorations, impressing their Allied comrades and the rest of the world with their fearless flying. Aces like Billy Bishop, Alan McLeod, and William Barker became Canadian heroes, each awarded the Victoria Cross—one of the highest decorations for bravery in the world.

As illustrated in the first chapter of this book, Canada produced no fewer than 82 aces in the First

Fairchild A/C Super 71 on May 28, 1940.

World War, establishing a reputation for Canadians of great courage. A resilience had emerged that would manifest itself in all future RCAF squadrons, whether at home or abroad, in peacetime or at war. Pilots who survived the First World War returned to Canada with pride, though this was balanced by humility. There was work to be done. A modest Canadian Air Force (CAF) was stood up and made relevant as a civic air force under advisory from John Armistead Wilson, an aviation advocate and civilian secretary to the CAF's Air Board. On April 1, 1924, the designation "Royal" was added and the CAF officially became the Royal Canadian Air Force.

During the interwar years, the RCAF carried out civic duties that helped build the nation, such as mail and medical courier services to isolated outposts, and supporting the RCMP with forestry, wildfire, and mining patrols. With grit and determination, RCAF "bush pilots in uniform" flew floatplanes in sub-artic temperatures, transported prospectors and the injured, and used innovative cameras and techniques to map hundreds of thousands of square kilometres of remote territory in Canada. Some pilots who returned home from the war refined their techniques as daredevil "barnstormers," performing aeronautical stunts in exhibitions across the country. As if facing the Red Baron during the First World War was not daunting enough, bush pilot Wilfrid "Wop" May carried medicine and aid to northern locations, helped law enforcement in manhunts, and

managed to invent pararescue. Opening up the North laid the groundwork for establishing Canadian sovereignty in air defence. Pioneering flights in the backcountry formed the basis of the RCAF's search and rescue capability, one that would become a lifeline for Canadians.

The Second World War launched the "Canadianization" of the RCAF, as described in Chapter 2, "The Crucible of War." Some Canadians who had flown with the RFC or RNAS during the First World War stayed on in Britain to serve in the RAF. As a Commonwealth military air force, the RCAF had strong ties to the RAF's British customs and traditions. However, it would be during the Second World War that Canada's Air Force would distinguish itself, drawing from aspects of its heritage that were uniquely Canadian: a nation of three oceans that was young, geographically expansive, and rich with freedom and opportunity.

A much more concerted effort was made to identify Canadian RCAF pilots, aircrew, and groundcrew in the Second World War. After war broke out, Commonwealth countries sent their air forces to England under their own numbered squadrons. To avoid duplication, the RAF assigned blocks of numbers to each air force. The RCAF was assigned 400 to 449, and eventually created 44 squadrons on overseas service in the "400 series." To this day, the RCAF retains those numbers for all but one of its flying squadrons. Lesser known are the 39 home-based RCAF squadrons who defended our coasts during the war and retained their original numbers.

Flight Lieutenant Ian Keltie, 402 Squadron RCAF, prepares for take off.

F-86 Sabres from 439 Squadron lined up on the tarmac at RCAF Station Uplands in Ottawa, Ontario.

The sole remaining flying squadron in service today that is not from the 400 series is 103 Squadron in Gander, Newfoundland and Labrador.

In 1942, the Canadianization policy consolidated RCAF bomber squadrons from ten bases into the legendary No. 6 (Bomber) Group. Entirely manned by Canadians and eventually commanded by the famous Canadian Air Vice-Marshall Clifford "Black Mike" McEwen, No. 6 Group flew Wellington, Halifax, and Lancaster heavy bombers in the Allied bomber offensive. By the end of the war, it had grown to 14 squadrons, flown over 40,000 sorties, and destroyed key enemy targets and assets. A total of 8,000 decorations for bravery were awarded to No. 6 Group's pilots, aircrew, and groundcrew. This was a remarkable achievement for such a small country. At the time, Canada only had a population of 11 million people.

The RCAF played a decisive role in Allied victory in the Second World War. Along with No. 6 Group, RCAF fighter squadrons were also concentrated into No. 83 Group. Commanded by a British officer, No. 83 Group was made up of 15 RCAF squadrons and flew Spitfires, Mosquitos, and Typhoons in support of D-Day and the North West Europe campaign. On June 6, 1944, hundreds of Canadian aircraft were in the air, and thousands of RCAF men and women served in Canadian or other Commonwealth units. Of the 23 Canadian airmen who lost their lives on D-Day, paying the ultimate sacrifice in a pivotal battle, seven flew in RCAF squadrons.

Possibly the greatest contribution Canada made to the Second World War effort was the British Commonwealth Air Training Program (BCATP), one of the largest ever aviation training programs in the world. Heralded as the "aerodrome of democracy" by U.S. President Franklin Roosevelt, the BCATP trained 131,000 pilots and aircrew for the Allied war effort. It was fundamental in evolving air combat training, as well as establishing an infrastructure for aviation in Canada. Hundreds of airports were built across the country, building the nation by connecting Canadians across its vast territory.

With a standout training school at its core during the war and a Women's Division that was quickly gaining traction, the RCAF finished the war as a well-managed and effective military organization. As the fourth-largest air force in the world, its reach extended well beyond the modest population it represented. From 1948 to 1957, the RCAF reached the apex of its development—its so-called "Golden Age." It played a world-class leadership role in the Cold War years supporting the North Atlantic Treaty Organization (NATO) and as a joint partner in NORAD, the continental air defence of North America. In 1950, with Cold War tensions rising, Canada stationed forces in Europe with a substantial presence of air power. The RCAF contributed four wings made up of 12 squadrons of Canadair Sabre jets, collectively designated No. 1 Air Division—a formation perpetuated today as 1 Canadian Air Division. This was also the Sabre Era, when RCAF pilots amazed their NATO allies, flying Sabres in tight formation and then, the low-altitude, high-speed CF-104 Starfighters in

Captain Jeff Baldwin (left) and Captain Pat O'Dwyer (right), pilots with 429 Squadron, in the cockpit of a CC-177 Globemaster.

the fog-veiled valleys of the Rhine in Europe.

At the same time as it was building up an Air Division in Europe, the RCAF, equipped first with Vampires and then both Sabre jets and CF-100 Canucks, was defending the skies over Canada as the Cold War Deterrent Force. To face the growing Soviet bomber threat, Canada and the United States formed the North American Air Defense Command (NORAD) in 1958. It ran a combined system of fighter interceptors, detection through a series of radar lines and unmanned vehicles, and nuclear weapons such as strategically placed BOMARC missiles to maintain air supremacy in the North. Security in the North remains a significant priority under the RCAF's jurisdiction today, supported by the government's announcement of a renewed investment in modernizing NORAD to counter a renewed threat to Canadian sovereignty.

On a global scale, Canada is also respected as a diplomatic peacekeeper. Over the span of 100 years, the RCAF has operated as an extension of this effort around the world. Today, the RCAF is a major global expeditionary force, operating a complex system of peacekeeping and humanitarian missions. Many are described in Chapter 5 of this book. Beyond the world wars, the Cold War, and the Korean War, the RCAF has provided critical airlift and combat support to the War on Terror and the rising second Cold War with Russia's invasion of Ukraine. It has been fundamentally involved in supporting peace in Egypt, Cyprus, Golan Heights, Rwanda, Afghanistan, Romania, and Mali. Along with

peacekeeping efforts, the RCAF has provided humanitarian aid during natural disasters such as the Indian Ocean tsunami, the earthquakes in Haiti and Nicaragua, and the famine in Africa.

Few organizations in history have retained the RCAF's non-stop tempo of operations to impact countless lives around the world. In Canada, the RCAF provides continual search and rescue support and humanitarian aid during ice storms, wildfires, hurricanes, snowstorms, and floods. From the Oka Crisis to the Winter Olympics to the coronavirus pandemic, throughout Canada's history, the RCAF has remained steadfast its dedication to protecting and serving Canadians.

Those who serve in the RCAF are known to get the job done in very tough conditions. This resolve is demonstrated throughout the RCAF's history, from the First World War aces to the outstanding squadrons of No. 6 (Bomber) Group in the Second World War to the Cold War's "Sabre Jockeys" and the "Crazy Canucks" flying the Starfighter. Whatever the mission, RCAF personnel are adaptable and undeterred—able to shift from airlifting supplies to CFS Alert in −40°C weather to supporting Operation IMPACT in the middle of the sweltering desert heat in Iraq. The RCAF embodies a can-do attitude that is a part of Canada's DNA. It has its roots in the history of those Indigenous Peoples and early pioneers who tamed Canada's immense waterways, varied typographies, and harsh climates. Uniquely shaped by their environment, Canadians have learned to be intrepid survivors.

A CC-130J Hercules aircraft from 436 Transportation Squadron, 8 Wing Trenton, Ontario, transports firefighters from Edmonton, Yellowhead, Hinton, and Coledale to relieve the firefighters currently on location at Fort McMurray, Alberta on May 9, 2016.

Flight Engineers unload supplies from a CH-147 Chinook helicopter in a cut off community during Operation LENTUS 17–04 in British Columbia on July 18, 2017.

To survive and grow as a nation, Canadians had to continuously innovate to overcome these challenges. The RCAF is a Canadian success story of innovation and ingenuity against unbelievable odds. More than 100 years ago, the Silver Dart/Burgess Dunne, Canada's first military plane, took off from a frozen lake in Nova Scotia. Ever since that first heavier-than-air flight, the RCAF has been at the forefront of the aviation industry, breaking new ground with black boxes, the G-suit, the Avro CF-105 Arrow, satellites, simulated training, and space technology. Throughout Canada's history, the RCAF has been consistently innovating at the forefront of technology. It has pioneered new tactics for dogfighting and bombing in the world wars, refined barnstorming techniques over thousands of lakes in Canada, developed a safety program that is emulated worldwide, formalized tactics for helicopters in lethal environments, and integrated bilateral systems of defence. For over a century, the RCAF has consistently kept pace with innovation and the demands made upon it by world events.

Today, the changing nature of defence is based on revolutionary new technologies. With the influx of new aircraft and young, technologically savvy people, the RCAF is transitioning to future platforms and technology. It will continue to nurture a culture of innovation and work with Canadian industry to remain on the leading edge of aerospace defence. In 2016, the RCAF became responsible for the defence space program with ambitious goals for future investments in space-based capabilities. These capabilities impact our daily life in aspects of communications, navigation, remote sensing, weather services, and even financial transactions. In 2022, the RCAF established 3 Canadian Space Division to maintain these capabilities and protect Canada's interests in space.

Technological advances are requiring greater diversity in the RCAF. Diversity requires an environment that values and respects individuals for their skills and abilities to contribute to a collective whole. Canada is a multicultural nation with a diverse population. According to the 2021 consensus, one-quarter of Canadians have a first language that is neither English nor French. The RCAF strives to reflect this diversity with tolerance and inclusivity. In an organizational context, diversity is an operational asset that is linked to stronger performance and higher levels of innovation. This includes the participation of women, Indigenous

Canada has always been a leader in space. In 1962, Canada launched a satellite into orbit, only the third country to do so. Pictured here is the innovative, Canadian-designed Canadarm.

The RCAF Today and Tomorrow: Simulation will continue to play a critical role in the modern RCAF.

Peoples, visible minorities, and members of the LGBTQ2+ community in the Canadian Armed Forces (CAF). As portrayed in this book, Indigenous Peoples (First Nations, Inuit, and Métis), along with Black, Chinese, and Japanese Canadians have a long and celebrated history of serving in Canada's military that reaches back to the War of 1812, with contributions to the First and Second World Wars, the Korean War, and the war in Afghanistan.

For more than 100 years, women have also played a significant role in defending Canada. Our nation is a world leader in terms of the proportion of women serving in its military. The RCAF is outpacing its allies in women involved in UN missions, for example, with 30 per cent representation on each mission's Air Detachment. As part of Operation PRESENCE based in Goma, Democratic Republic of Congo, RCAF women aviators and support personnel ranged from the rank of Corporal to Major and filled the roles of technicians, commanding officers, operations officer, pilot, and Deputy Task Force Commander. Notably, five of the eight key commanding and advisory positions were filled by experienced women officers and a senior non-commissioned member.

The people who serve in the RCAF are its greatest strength and the foundation on which its future is built. Extraordinary and professional, they are capable of accomplishing great things and setting standards of quality that are respected around the world. Day after day, RCAF personnel contribute to the delivery of air and space power for our nation. As we have learned from Bishop to Barker to Billie Flynn, the RCAF's story is based on devotion to duty and service to humanity. Though the early years of unification provided its challenges, the RCAF regrouped and restored its traditions, infusing them with its own customs. We celebrate the heritage of the RCAF because as Canadians, it is intertwined with our own. It tells us where we have been, what we have accomplished, and what standards we must strive to achieve in the future.

This book is both a homage to the past and an excited overture for the RCAF's future. The arrival of new fleets of aircraft, such as the F-35 stealth multi-role fighter jet, will advance the RCAF's war-fighting capabilities, training capacity, and future operations. As much as technology is an enabler, it also poses a threat to mission success. Cyberspace is enmeshed into all levels of the RCAF's aircrafts, weapons, systems, and networks. As new and complex threats emerge, the RCAF will continue to guarantee Canadian sovereignty along the spectrum of cyber operations. The establishment of 3 Canadian Space Division will extend the RCAF's proud heritage into its second 100 years, to meet the expanding need to protect and serve Canada and the rest of the world in the skies, in cyberspace, and beyond—on a pathway to the stars.

HM QUEEN ELIZABETH II
UNVEILED THIS MEMORIAL
28 JUNE
IN THE YEAR OF HER DIAMOND JUBILEE
2012

Remembering the Cost

Canadian aircrews have suffered greatly to achieve the mission success that the RCAF has demonstrated. From dogfights in the First World War to bomber crews over Europe in the Second World War to dangerous peacekeeping missions and search and rescue in extreme conditions, the men and women of the RCAF have carried our nation's burden over the past century, answering every call to duty no matter what the risk or cost. The RCAF continues to honour their sacrifices in memorials throughout the world.

There are over 6,000 war memorials across Canada commemorating those who sacrificed their lives or were injured in conflicts or on peacekeeping missions. There are also many war memorials located around the world, honouring Canadians for their outstanding service and sacrifice abroad. We've elected to include here a few specific to the RCAF and its members' impressive contributions in the service of Canada. The following pages contain just some of these locations where Canada and the world remembers their sacrifice.

In addition to these memorials, there are thousands of smaller RCAF memorials scattered around the world dedicated to the RCAF crew who perished there. An example of this can be found in a Dutch farmers field that contains the remains of Les Sutherland who was buried where his aircraft went down on the way home from a sortie during the Second World War. His story can be found at the end of the chapter.

Canadian National Vimy Memorial

The Canadian National Vimy Memorial was unveiled in 1936 near Arras in northern France as a tribute to those who fought and gave their lives in the First World War. The majestic memorial overlooks the Douai Plain from the highest point of Vimy Ridge. It is the centrepiece of a preserved battlefield park that encompasses the ground over which the Canadian Corps made their assault during the Battle of Vimy Ridge in April 1917. The ground still contains wartime tunnels, trenches, craters, and unexploded munitions. The Canadian symbol of sacrifice took designer Walter Seymour Allward eleven years to build and was unveiled by King Edward VIII in July 1936.

In 2017, a ceremony at the memorial commemorated the 100th anniversary of the Battle of Vimy Ridge and was attended by Canadian Governor General David Johnston, King Charles III (then The Prince of Wales), Prince William, Prince Harry, Canadian Prime Minister Justin Trudeau, and French President François Hollande. The ceremony also featured a flypast by replica aircraft: four Nieuport XIs and one SE5. Along with two Sopwith Pups, the aircraft were shipped to France aboard an RCAF CC-177 Globemaster to form a five-aircraft formation. One of the Nieuports, owned by retired RCAF Sea King pilot, J. Paul O'Reilly, was flown by Captain Brent Handy, a former Snowbird and CF-18 pilot. Allan Snowie flew the SE5, while the three Nieuport XI replica biplanes were flown by Dale Erhart, Peter Thornton, and Larry Ricker, who along with O'Reilly, belong to the Vimy Flight project and were all former RCAF pilots. The Sopwith Pup replicas, used as static displays, were built by volunteers from the Canadian Museum of Flight and Air Cadets from 746 Lightening Hawk Squadron.

Arras Flying Services Memorial

Located in Arras, France, the Flying Service Memorial commemorates nearly 1,000 airmen of the First World War who were lost with no known grave. Since Canadian airmen served with the Royal Flying Corps (RFC) there are many Canadians listed there. Designed by Edwin Lutyens and sculpted by William Reid Dick, the memorial was unveiled on July 13, 1932 by Hugh Trenchard, 1st Viscount Trenchard, Marshal of the Royal Air Force. The names of the missing are inscribed on the memorial, those who served with the Royal Naval Air Service, the RFC, the Australian Flying Corps, and the Royal Air Force.

National War Memorial

The National War Memorial, a tall marble arch in Ottawa, Ontario, is the pre-eminent war memorial of over 70 cenotaphs in Canada. It was designed by Vernon March and dedicated by King George VI in 1939. Originally built to honour the Canadians who died in the First World War, in 1982 the memorial was rededicated to those who had lost their lives in both the Second World War and the Korean War, and again in 2014 to include those who fell in the Second Boer War and the war in Afghanistan, along with all Canadians killed in combat. The Tomb of the Unknown Soldier was added in 2000 to symbolize any Canadian who has, or is willing to, make the ultimate sacrifice for their country.

Major-General (Retired) Richard H. Rohmer escorts Her Majesty Queen Elizabeth II on a walkabout to meet veterans at the first commemoration of D-Day at the new Juno Beach Centre in France, June 6, 2004.

The Juno Beach Centre

The Juno Beach Centre, Canada's Second World War museum located in Normandy, France, honours the 45,000 Canadians who lost their lives during the war, of which 5,500 were killed during the Battle of Normandy and 381 on D-Day. Opened in 2003 by veterans and volunteers with a vision to create a permanent memorial to all Canadians who served during the Second World War, the Centre's mandate is to preserve this legacy for future generations through education and remembrance.

RAF Bomber Command Memorial

The Royal Air Force Bomber Command Memorial is located in The Green Park, London, England, and honours the crews of RAF Bomber Command who carried out bombing raids during the Second World War. Specifically, it marks the sacrifice of 55,573 Allied aircrew from the United Kingdom, Canada, Australia, New Zealand, the Czech Republic, Poland and other countries, along with civilians of nations that were killed during the raids.

Designed by Liam O'Connor and sculptor, Philip Jackson, the memorial features a bronze sculpture of seven aircrew returning from a mission. Aluminium from an RCAF 426 Squadron Handley Page Halifax that crashed in 1944 was used to construct the roof of the memorial, which was designed to imitate the interior of a Vickers Wellington bomber, the first bomber used by the RCAF in the war. Some of the metal was also used to restore a Halifax in Trenton, Ontario, and the rest was melted down by the Bomber Command Museum of Canada in Nanton, Alberta to be used as ingots for the memorial to commemorate the 10,659 Canadians of Bomber Command that were killed during the Second World War. The aluminum even found its way into the new RCAF silver metal wings.

Bomber Command Memorial ceiling, a nod to the Vickers Wellington.

Ottawa Memorial

At the outbreak of the Second World War, there was a shortage of aircraft and trained pilots. Bases in North America trained over 137,000 Commonwealth aircrew. The memorial, unveiled by Queen Elizabeth II in 1959, honours by name the more than 800 men and women serving or training with the Air Forces of the British Commonwealth and Empire who gave their lives in Canada, the United States, and the neighbouring lands and seas and who have no known grave.

Dieppe Gardens

The Dieppe Gardens in Windsor, Ontario, pays tribute to those who fought in the Second World War. Created by local sculptors, the monument includes etchings of pilots with a model of one of the planes used in battle: a Hurricane, a Spitfire, and a Lancaster. A bronze inscription reads: "Windsor Memorial to our glorious dead of the Royal Canadian Air Force who represented this area in the Second World War."

RCAF Memorial at 16 Wing Borden

The 16 Wing/CFB Borden Memorial pays tribute to the base as the official birthplace of the RCAF, along with its history and personnel. A plaque at the site is dedicated to RCAF officers and aircrew who died in service to their country as members of the Royal Flying Corps (1917), the Royal Air Force (1918), the Canadian Air Force (1920), and the RCAF (from 1924 onward).

Malta Memorial

The Malta Memorial is a war monument dedicated to the 2,297 Commonwealth aircrew who lost their lives in Second World War operations in the Mediterranean and have no known grave. This includes 285 men from the RCAF whose names are listed on the memorial. The location was chosen due to its decisive contribution to the air war in keeping vital shipping routes open. The column, topped by a gilded bronze eagle, commemorates those who, in gaining mastery in the air, sacrificed their lives. It stands close to the City Gate entrance of Malta's capital city, Valetta, and was unveiled by Queen Elizabeth II in May 1954.

Les Sutherland: Overseas Respect for the Greatest Sacrifice

Warrant Officer Leslie Sutherland

Warrant Officer II Pilot Leslie Gordon Sutherland.

Royal Canadian Legion Leslie Sutherland Branch 447 in Corunna, Ontario, is named after Leslie Sutherland, a local serviceman who perished in the Second World War. Les's story is not only one of great bravery and sacrifice; it is also a testament to the humanity of overseas Allies in Europe and the deep respect they showed for fallen Canadians during the war.

Leslie "Les" Sutherland was born in London, Ontario on November 26, 1918. He enlisted in the Royal Canadian Air Force on May 15, 1941 and, after being trained and posted in Toronto, Trenton, Windsor, and Service Flying Schools at Aylmer and Halifax, Les graduated as a Sergeant Pilot on February 27, 1942.

At the outbreak of war, Sutherland was posted overseas. He became a skilled bomber pilot, serving with 426 Thunderbird Squadron as a Warrant Officer. On his fateful flight in May 1943, with his tour of operations almost complete, Sutherland's Wellington was shot down over the Netherlands. As Les flew the plane home after a successful raid in Dortmund, Germany, a Messerschmitt strafed the bomber and it crashed in Haaksbergen, Netherlands.

All five crewmembers of the Wellington perished. Les, at the age of 24, was reported missing and his remains left unidentified because several dog tags of his crew were lost in the wreckage. The crash site would be visited by Les's family years later, but only after his mother learned of its whereabouts from a woman who cleaned her house—and also happened to be from Haaksbergen, having emigrated with her family from the Netherlands to Canada.

But the coincidences didn't stop there. As there was no longstanding care of graves at the time, this same family had taken on the responsibility for identifying Sutherland and his crew and maintaining their graves. When Les's family made the trek to Haaksbergen, they were impressed at the care the family had taken to maintain Les's grave. They also visited the site of the plane crash, preserved in a small copse of trees, where the farmer left the debris untouched as a memorial to those who died there many years ago, fighting for freedom during the Second World War.

Leslie Sutherland was buried in Haaksbergen General Cemetery, Netherlands. Back home in Canada, his name is inscribed on two memorial plaques in Corunna: one in the entrance foyer of Branch 447 of the Royal Canadian Legion and one on a brass altar in Christ Anglican Church in Corunna. He is also commemorated on the Bomber Command Memorial Wall in Nanton, Alberta.

Opposite: A CC-130J Hercules stationed on the airfield in support of Air Task Force Prestwick prior to flight on January 31, 2023, in Scotland, United Kingdom.

APPENDICES

Appendix 1: List of RCAF Commanders and Command Chiefs

Provisional Commander
Captain E.L. Janney — 1914–1915

Officer Commanding
Lieutenant-Colonel W.A. Bishop — 1918

Air Officer Commanding
Air Commodore A.K. Tylee — 1920–1921

Officer Commanding
Wing Commander R.F. Redpath — 1921

Wing Commander J.S. Scott — 1921–1922

Director
Wing Commander J.L. Gordon — 1922–1924

Wing Commander W.G. Barker — 1924

Group Captain J.S. Scott — 1924–1928

Wing Commander L.S. Breadner — 1928–1932

Squadron Leader A.A.L. Cuffe — 1932

Senior Air Officer
Group Captain J.L. Gordon — 1932–1933

Wing Commander G.O. Johnson — 1933

Air Vice Marshal G.M. Croil — 1934–1938

Chief of the Air Staff
Air Vice Marshal G.M. Croil — 1938–1940

Air Marshal L.S. Breadner — 1940–1943

Air Marshal R. Leckie — 1944–1947

Air Marshal W.A. Curtis — 1947–1953

Air Marshal C.R. Slemon — 1953–1957

Air Marshal H.L. Campbell — 1957–1962

Air Marshal C.R. Dunlap — 1962–1964

Commander of Air Command
Lieutenant-General W.K. Carr — 1975–1978

Lieutenant-General G.A. MacKenzie — 1978–1980

Lieutenant-General K.E. Lewis — 1980–1983

Lieutenant-General P.D. Manson — 1983–1985

Lieutenant-General D.M. McNaughton — 1985–1986

Lieutenant-General L.A. Ashley — 1986–1988

Lieutenant-General F.R. Sutherland — 1989–1991

Lieutenant-General D. Huddleston — 1991–1993

Lieutenant-General G.S. Clements — 1993–1995

Lieutenant-General A.M. DeQuetteville — 1995–1997

Chief of the Air Staff
Lieutenant-General D.N. Kinsman — 1997–2000

Lieutenant-General L.C. Campbell — 2000–2003

Lieutenant-General K.R. Pennie — 2003–2005

Lieutenant-General J.S. Lucas — 2005–2007

Lieutenant-General A. Watt — 2007–2009

Lieutenant-General A. Deschamps — 2009–2011

Commander of the Royal Canadian Air Force
Lieutenant-General J.P.A. Deschamps — 2011–2012

Lieutenant-General Y. Blondin — 2012–2015

Lieutenant-General M.J. Hood — 2015–2018

Lieutenant-General A.D. Meinzinger — 2018–2022

Lieutenant-General E.J. Kenny — 2022–present (at time of writing)

Command Chief Warrant Officers

A.G. Moran	*1975–1977*
J.M.A. Blais	*1977–1980*
W.J. Neve	*1980–1982*
P.E. Delaney	*1982–1984*
R. Ouellette	*1984–1987*
D.J. Lloyd	*1987–1989*
P.J. Sarty	*1989–1992*
J.L.G.G. Parent	*1992–1995*
R.N. Elphick	*1995–1997*
J.G. Guilbault	*1997–2001*
D. Gilbert	*2001–2004*
R. Bouchard	*2004–2007*
J.J.G.R. Couturier	*2007–2010*
M.L. Barham	*2010–2012*
K.C. West	*2012–2013*
J.C.P. Young	*2013–2015*
E.G.J. Poitras	*2015–2018*
J.R.D. Gaudreault	*2018–2021*
W.J. Hall	*2021–present (at time of writing)*

Appendix 2: RCAF Victoria Cross Recipients

The Victoria Cross (VC) is awarded for the most conspicuous bravery, a daring or pre-eminent act of valour, or self-sacrifice or extreme devotion to duty in the presence of the enemy.

For more information about honours and awards, visit the Department of National Defence website at https://www.forces.gc.ca and Veterans Affairs Canada at https://www.veterans.gc.ca/.

First World War:

William George Barker

Citation: "On the morning of the 27th October, 1918, this officer observed an enemy two-seater over the Fôret de Mormal. He attacked this machine, and after a short burst it broke up in the air. At the same time a Fokker biplane attacked him, and he was wounded in the right thigh, but managed, despite this, to shoot down the enemy aeroplane in flames. He then found himself in the middle of a large formation of Fokkers, who attacked him from all directions; and was again severely wounded in the left thigh; but succeeded in driving down two of the enemy in a spin. He lost consciousness after this, and his machine fell out of control. On recovery he found himself being again attacked heavily by a large formation, and singling out one machine, he deliberately charged and drove it down in flames... This combat, in which Major Barker destroyed four enemy machines (three of them in flames), brought his total successes up to fifty enemy machines destroyed, and is a notable example of the exceptional bravery and disregard which this very gallant officer has always displayed throughout his distinguished career.

Major Barker was awarded the Military Cross on 10th January, 1917; first Bar on 18th July, 1917; the Distinguished Service Order on 18th February, 1918; second Bar to Military Cross on 16th September, 1918; and Bar to Distinguished Service Order on 2nd November, 1918."

(London Gazette, no. 31042, November 30, 1918)

William Avery Bishop

Citation: "For most conspicuous bravery, determination and skill. Captain Bishop, who had been sent out to work independently, flew first of all to an enemy aerodrome; finding no machine about, he flew on to another aerodrome about three miles southeast, which was at least twelve miles the other side of the line. Seven machines, some with their engines running, were on the ground. He attacked these from about fifty feet, and a mechanic, who was starting one of the engines, was seen to fall. One of the machines got off the ground, but at a height of sixty feet Captain Bishop fired fifteen rounds into it at very close range, and it crashed to the ground. A second machine got off the ground, into which he fired thirty rounds at 150 yards range, and it fell into a tree. Two more machines then rose from the aerodrome. One of these he engaged at the height of 1,000 feet, emptying the rest of his drum of ammunition. This machine crashed 300 yards from the aerodrome, after which Captain Bishop emptied a whole drum into the fourth hostile machine, and then flew back to his station.

Four hostile scouts were about 1,000 feet above him for about a mile of his return journey, but they would not attack. His machine was very badly shot about by machine gun fire from the ground."

(London Gazette, no. 30228, August 11, 1917)

Alan Arnett McLeod

Citation: "Whilst flying with his observer (Lt. A.W. Hammond, M.C.), attacking hostile formations by bombs and machine-gun fire, he was assailed at a height of 5,000 feet by eight enemy triplanes, which dived at him from all directions, firing from their front guns. By skilful manoeuvring he enabled his observer to fire bursts at each machine in turn, shooting three of them down out of control. By this time Lt. McLeod had received five wounds, and whilst continuing the engagement a bullet penetrated his petrol tank and set the machine on fire. He then climbed out on to the left bottom plane, controlling his machine from the side of the fuselage, and by side-slipping steeply kept the flames to one side, thus enabling the observer to continue firing until the ground was reached. The observer had been wounded six times when the machine crashed in "No Man's Land," and 2nd Lt. McLeod, not withstanding his own wounds, dragged him away from the burning wreckage at great personal risk from heavy machine-gun fire from the enemy's lines. This very gallant pilot was again wounded by a bomb whilst engaged in this act of rescue, but he persevered until he had placed Lt. Hammond in comparative safety, before falling himself from exhaustion and loss of blood."

(London Gazette, May 1, 1918)

Second World War

Robert Hampton Gray

Citation: "...for great valour in leading an attack on a Japanese destroyer in Onagawa Wan on 9th August, 1945. In the face of fire from shore batteries and a heavy concentration of fire from some five warships Lieutenant Gray pressed home his attack, flying very low in order to ensure success, and, although he was hit and his aircraft was in flames, he obtained at least one direct hit, sinking the destroyer. Lieutenant Gray has consistently shown a brilliant fighting spirit and most inspiring leadership."

(London Gazette, no. 37346, November 13, 1945)

David Ernest Hornell

Citation: "Flt. Lt. Hornell was captain and first pilot of a twin engined amphibian aircraft engaged in an anti-submarine patrol in northern waters. A fully surfaced U-boat was sighted travelling at high speed on the port beam, and Flt. Lt. Hornell at once attacked. His aircraft had been seen and there could be no surprise. The U-boat altered course and opened up with fire which became increasingly fierce and accurate. At a range of 1,300 metres the guns of the aircraft replied and hits were obtained, but the aircraft itself was hit and badly damaged, and its starboard gun jammed. Ignoring the fire Flt. Lt. Hornell carefully manoeuvred for attack. Holed in many places, oil pouring from the starboard engine which with the starboard wing was on fire, and with petrol tanks endangered, the aircraft was very difficult to control. Nevertheless the captain decided to press his attack, and bringing his aircraft down low released his depth charges in a perfect straddle. The bows of the U-boat were lifted out of the sea; it sank, and the crew were seen in the water. The plight of the aircraft and crew was now desperate. With the utmost coolness, Flt. Lt. Hornell took his badly damaged, blazing aircraft into the wind and brought it safely on to the heavy swell where it rapidly settled down. After ordeal by fire came ordeal by water. Two of the crew succumbed from exposure, and the survivors were finally rescued after 21 hours in the water. Blinded and completely exhausted, Flt. Lt. Hornell died shortly after being picked up. By pressing home a skillful and successful attack against fierce opposition, with his aircraft in a precarious condition, and by fortifying and encouraging his comrades in the subsequent ordeal, this officer displayed valour and devotion to duty of the highest order."

(London Gazette, no. 36630, July 28, 1944)

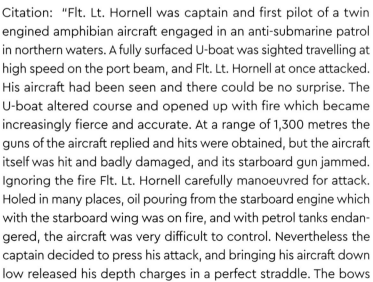

Andrew Charles Mynarski

Citation: "Pilot Officer Mynarski was the mid-upper gunner of a Lancaster aircraft, detailed to attack a target at Cambrai in France, on the night of 12th June, 1944. The aircraft was attacked from below and astern by an enemy fighter and ultimately came down in flames.

As an immediate result of the attack, both port engines failed. Fire broke out between the mid-upper turret and the rear turret, as well as in the port wing. The flames soon became fierce and the captain ordered the crew to abandon the aircraft. Pilot Officer Mynarski left his turret and went towards the escape hatch. He then saw that the rear gunner was still in his turret and apparently unable to leave it. Without hesitation, Pilot Officer Mynarski made his way through the flames in an endeavour to reach the rear turret and release the gunner. Whilst so doing, his parachute and his clothing, up to the waist, were set on fire. Eventually the rear gunner clearly indicated to him that there was nothing more he could do and that he should try to save his own life. Pilot Officer Mynarski reluctantly went back through the flames to the escape hatch. There, as a last gesture to the trapper gunner, he turned towards him, stood to attention in his flaming clothing and saluted before he jumped out of the aircraft. Pilot Officer Mynarski's descent was seen by French people on the ground. Both his parachute and clothing were on fire. He was found eventually by the French, but was so severely burnt that he died from his injuries.

The rear gunner had a miraculous escape when the aircraft crashed. He subsequently testified that, had Pilot Officer Mynarski not attempted to save his comrade's life, he could have left the aircraft in safety and would, doubtless, have escaped death. Willingly accepting the danger, Pilot Officer Mynarski lost his life by a most conspicuous act of heroism which called for valour of the highest order."

(London Gazette, no. 37754, October 11, 1946)

Ian Willoughby Bazalgette

On 4th August 1944 Squadron Leader Bazalgette was "Master bomber" of a Pathfinder Squadron detailed to mark an important target for the main bomber force. When nearing the target his Lancaster came under heavy anti-aircraft fire. Both starboard engines were put out of action and serious fire broke out in the fuselage and the starboard main-plane. The bomb aimer was badly wounded. As the deputy "master bomber" had already been shot down, the success of the attack depended on Squadron Leader Bazalgette and this he knew. Despite appalling conditions in his burning aircraft, he pressed on gallantly, marking and bombing it accurately. That the attack was successful was due to his magnificent effort.

After the bombs had been dropped, the Lancaster dived, practically out of control. By expert airmanship and great exertion Squadron Leader Bazalgette regained control. He then ordered those of his crew who were able to leave by parachute to do so. He remained at the controls and attempted the almost hopeless task of landing the crippled and blazing aircraft in a last effort to save the wounded bomb aimer and helpless air gunner. With superb skill and taking great care to avoid a French village, he brought the aircraft safely down. Unfortunately, it then exploded and this gallant officer and his two comrades perished.

His heroic sacrifice marked the climax of a long career of operations against the enemy. He always chose the more dangerous and exacting roles. His courage and devotion to duty were beyond praise.

(London Gazette, August 14, 1945)

Appendix 3: List of Aircraft (Current and Historical)

A-17 Nomad, Northrop

AS 5 Firefly, Fairey

Albacore, Fairey

Anson (652A/AT-20), Avro

Argus (Fairchild 24H/R), Fairchild

Atlas, Armstrong Whitworth

Audax, Hawker

Auster AOP, Auster

Avenger, Grumman

Avro 504, Avro Canada

Avro 616, Avro Canada

B-17 E/F Flying Fortress, Boeing

B-25 Mitchell, North American Aviation, Inc.

B-47 Stratojet, Boeing

B.A. Eagle, British Aircraft Manufacturing Co.

Baltimore (Martin 187), Martin

Banshee (F2H-3), McDonnell

Barkley Grow T8P-1, Barkley Grow

Battle, Fairey

BE-350 King Air, Beechcraft

Beaufighter, Bristol

Beaufort (Bristol 152), Bristol

Beechcraft D-17DS, Beechcraft

Bell 412CF, Bell

Bellanca Pacemaker, Bellanca Aircraft Company

Bermuda (Brewster 340), Brewster

Bestmann, Brewster

Bird Dog CO-119, Cessna

Blenheim, Bristol

Boeing 247D, Boeing

Bolingbroke (Bristol 142M), Bristol

Boston DB-7B/A-20G), Douglas

C-47 Dakota, Douglas

C-90B King Air, Beechcraft

C-119F Flying Boxcar, Fairchild

Canso, Consolidated

Catalina, Consolidated

CC-106 Yukon, Canadair

CC-108 Caribou, de Havilland Canada

CC-109 Cosmopolitan, Canadair

CC-115 Buffalo, de Havilland Canada

CC-117 Falcon, Dassault

CC-295 Kingfisher, Airbus

CC-130 B/E/H/J Hercules, Lockheed Martin

CC-138 Twin Otter, de Havilland Canada

CC-132/142 Dash-7/Dash-8, de Havilland Canada

CC-137 Stratoliner (Boeing 707–347C), Boeing

CC-144 Challenger, Bombardier

CC-150 Polaris, Airbus

CC-177 Globemaster III, Boeing

CF-100 Canuck, Avro Canada

CF-101 Voodoo, McDonnell

CF-104 Starfighter, Canadair

CF-105 Arrow, Avro Canada

CF-116 Freedom Fighter

CF-188 Hornet, McDonnell Douglas

CG-4A Hadrian II, Waco

CH-112 Nomad, Hiller

CH-113 Labrador/Voyageur, Boeing Vertol

CH-118 Iroquois, Bell

CH-124 Sea King, Sikorsky

CH-125 Workhorse, Vertol

CH-126 Choctaw, Sikorsky

CH-135 Twin Huey, Bell

CH-136 Kiowa, Bell

CH-139 Jet Ranger, Bell

CH-143, MBB

CH-146 Griffon, Bell

CH-148 Cyclone, Sikorsky

CH-147C/D/F Chinook, Boeing

CH-149 Cormorant, AgustaWestland

CH-178 Hip, Mil

CH-300/30/31 Pacemaker, Bellanca

Chickasaw (S-55/RCAF H-19/RCN HO4S-3), Sikorsky

Cirrus Moth, de Havilland Canada

CL-219/CL-226 Freedom Fighter, Canadair

Courier 0–17, Consolidated

CP-107 Argus, Canadair

CP-122 Neptune, Lockheed Martin

CP-140 Aurora, Lockheed Martin

CP-140A Arcturus, Lockheed Martin

CP-121 Tracker (Grumman G-89/CS2F), de Havilland Canada

Crane T-50, Cessna

CSR-110 Albatross, Grumman

CT-102 Astra, Grob

CT-111 Firefly, Slingsby

CT-114 Tutor, Canadair

CT-120 Chipmunk, de Havilland Canada

CT-133 Silver Star, Canadair

CT-134 Musketeer, Beechcraft

CT-142 Dash-8, de Havilland Canada

CT-155 Hawk, BAE

CT-156 Harvard II, Beechcraft

Cub Coupe J4A, Piper

Curtiss H-16/ HS-2L, Curtiss

Cygnet, General Aircraft Ltd.

DH-103 Sea Hornet, de Havilland Canada

DH-106 Comet, de Havilland Canada

DH-4/DH-9, de Havilland Canada

DH-60 Moth, de Havilland Canada

DH-75 Hawk Moth, de Havilland Canada
DH-80A Puss Moth, de Havilland Canada
DH-82 Tiger Moth, de Havilland Canada
DH-83 Fox Moth, de Havilland Canada
DH-87 Hornet Moth, de Havilland Canada
DH-90 Dragonfly, de Havilland Canada
DH-98 Mosquito, de Havilland Canada
Digby DB-1/B-18A, Douglas
Dolphin Sopwith 5F.1, Sopwith
Dynavert, Canadair
Empire Flying Boat S-23M, Short
Expeditor 18 D-18S/C-45, Beechcraft
F.2B Fighter, Bristol
F.3, Felixstowe
Fairchild FC-2, Fairchild
Fairchild KR-34, Fairchild
Fawn, Fleet
Finch, Fleet
Fort, Fleet
Freighter, Bristol 170
Freighter, Fleet 50K
Fw-190, Focke Wulf
G-21A Goose, Grumman
G-23 Goblin, Grumman
Grob-G120A, Grob
Gypsy Moth, de Havilland Canada
H-5 Dragonfly, Sikorsky
Halifax, Handley Page
Hampden, Handley Page
Harvard (NA 49/61/66/75/76/81),
	North American
Hawker, Hart
Hind, Hawker
Horsa, Airspeed
Hotspur, General Aircraft
HP-54 Harrow, Handley Page

Hurricane, Hawker
JN-4 Canuck, Curtiss
Ju-87 Stuka, Junkers
Ju-88H-1, Junkers
KH-32 Helix, Kamov
Kittyhawk, Curtiss
L-214/L-414 Hudson, Lockheed Martin
Lancaster, Avro
Lerwick Mk. I, Saunders-Roe
Liberator (B-24D/G/J), Consolidated
Lincoln, Avro
Lockheed 10A/B, 12A, 212, Lockheed
Lodestar, Lockheed Martin
Lysander, Westland
Nieuport 17, Société Anonyme des Établissement
	Nieuport
Macchi C.202, Macchi
Magister, Miles
Mailwing (Pitcairn PA-5), Pitcairn
Manchester, Avro
Martinet, Miles
Martinsyde F6, Martinsyde
Master, Miles
Menasco Moth, de Havilland Canada
Messerschmitt BF-108/Me-109, Messerschmitt
Meteor, Gloster
Mitchell, North American
MO-2B, Douglas
Mustang (Mk. 1, Mk. 3, Mk. 4, P-51D), North American
Norseman, Noorduyn
North Star, Canadair
Otter, de Havilland Canada
Oxford, Airspeed
P-39 Airacobra, Bell
PT-26 Cornell, Fairchild
PT-27 Stearman, Stearman

Phoenix, Heston
Prefect, Avro 262, Avro
Prentice (Percival P. 40), Percival
Privateer Consolidated 32/RY-3), Consolidated
Proctor Mk. III, Percival
Puffer, Keystone
Rambler, Curtiss-Reid
Reliant (Stinson SR-7B), Stinson
Retriever (HUP-3), Piasecki
Roc, Blackburn
Sabre (CL-13), Canadair
Schweizer SGS 2–12 / TG-3, Schweizer
Scout (Bellanca 8GCBC), Bellanca
S.E. 5a, Royal Aircraft Factory
Seafire (Supermarine 377), Supermarine
Seafury, Hawker
Sea Hurricane, Hawker
Seamew (Mk. 1), Curtiss
Shark, Blackburn
Silverstar, Lockheed/Canadair
Sioux (Bell 47/ H-13B, HTL-4,6), Bell
Siskin, Armstrong Whitworth
Sopwith Camel, Sopwith
Snipe, Sopwith
Spitfire, Supermarine
Stinson HW-75, Stinson
Storch Fi-156, Fieseler
Stranraer, Supermarine
Sunderland, Shorts
Super 71P, Fairchild
Super Universal, Fleet
Swordfish, Fairey
T-34 Mentor, Beechcraft
Tempest, Hawker
Texan, North American
Tomahawk (P-40), Curtiss

Tomtit, Hawker
Transatlantic (Fairey IIIC/IIIF), Fairey
Trimotor, Ford
Tutor (Avro 621), Avro
Typhoon, Hawker
Valetta C.1, Vickers
Vampire, de Havilland Canada
Vancouver, Canadian Vickers
Vanessa, Canadian Vickers
Varuna, Canadian Vickers
Vedette, Canadian Vickers
Vegal Gull, Percival
Velos, Canadian Vickers
Ventura, Lockheed-Vega
Vertol CH-127, Boeing
Vigil, Canadian Vickers
Viking, Vickers
Viper (Avro 552A), Avro
Vista, Canadian Vickers
Waco AQC-6, Waco
Waco CG-15A, Waco
Waco PG-2A, Waco
Waco ZQC-6, Waco
Walrus, Supermarine
Wapiti, Westland
Warhawk (P-40), Curtiss
Wellington, Vickers
Westwind 1124, IAI
Whitley, Armstrong
Wright (Avro 504), Avro
Yale (NA-64), North American

Appendix 4: RCAF Organization and Ceremonies

RCAF Headquarters: Ottawa, Ontario

Located in Ottawa, Ontario, the Commander of the RCAF is the Senior Air Force Officer in the Canadian Armed Forces. The RCAF Command Chief Warrant Officer (CCWO) is the senior non-commissioned member of the Air Force who acts as an advisor to the Commander of the RCAF.

Under the Commander and CCWO, the RCAF is organized into three Divisions, along with the RCAF Aerospace Warfare Centre:

1. Canadian Air Division: Air Power Generation and Delivery
2. Canadian Air Division: Personnel Training
3. Canadian Space Division: Space Power Generation and Delivery

Below these Divisions, the RCAF is formed by Wings consisting of Squadrons. For more details on the Wings and Squadrons of the RCAF today, please consult the back page of the book for the complete diagram of where these units are located. You can also find them online: https://www.canada.ca/en/air-force/corporate/wings-squadrons.html.

Air Force Ranks

Original RCAF	Present-Day RCAF
Air Chief Marshal (A/C/M)	General (Gen)
Air Marshal (A/M)	Lieutenant-General (LGen)
Air Vice-Marshal (A/V/M)	Major-General (MGen)
Air Commodore (A/C)	Brigadier-General (BGen)
Group Captain (G/C)	Colonel (Col)
Wing Commander (W/C)	Lieutenant-Colonel (LCol)
Squadron Leader (S/L)	Major (Maj)
Flight Lieutenant (F/L)	Captain (Capt)
Flying Officer (F/O)	Lieutenant (Lt)
Pilot Officer (P/O)	Second Lieutenant (2Lt)
Officer Cadet (O/C)	Officer Cadet (OCdt)
Warrant Officer Class 1 (WO1)	Chief Warrant Officer (CWO)
Warrant Officer Class 2 (WO2)	Master Warrant Officer (MWO)
Flight Sergeant (F/S)	Warrant Officer (WO)
Sergeant (Sgt)	Sergeant (Sgt)
Corporal (Cpl)	Master Corporal (MCpl)
Leading Aircraftman (LAC)	Corporal (Cpl)
Aircraftman First Class (AC1)	Aviator (Trained) (Avr (T))
Aircraftman Second Class (AC2)	Aviator (Basic) (Avr (B))

Honorary Colonels

Noted Canadians, such as eminent business people, opinion leaders, and even retired RCAF members may be appointed as Honorary Colonels of wings, squadrons or other formations.

Annual Ceremonies and Celebrations

Battle of Britain

Held every year on the third Sunday of September, the Battle of Britain honours the heroic feat of pilots, aircrew, and groundcrew from Britain, Canada, the Commonwealth and Allies to celebrate their defeat of the German Luftwaffe. Battle of Britain Day is the most honoured day of the year for the RCAF with parades and ceremonies at RCAF locations across the country.

Birthday of the RCAF

April 1 is recognized as the Royal Canadian Air Force's birthday and the day is celebrated often by formal mess dinners or dinings-in.

Remembrance Day

Every November 11, the RCAF joins the Canadian Army and Royal Canadian Navy to pay homage to the fallen at Remembrance Day ceremonies across the country. The date celebrates the Armistice signed in 1918 that ended the First World War. The National Remembrance Day ceremony is held at the National War Memorial in Ottawa, with sentries posted, one of whom is an RCAF sentry chosen to represent the Air Force based on exemplary performance of duty.

Appendix 5: Timeline of the RCAF

1909 Flight of the "Silver Dart" is the first heavier-than-air flight in Canada in Baddeck, Nova Scotia. Its first military flight occurred later at Camp Petawawa, Ontario.

1914 First World War begins; Canadian Aviation Corps founded; Canadians fly with Britain's Royal Flying Corps.

1918 First World War ends; Nos. 1 and 2 Squadrons Canadian Air Force (CAF) created in England.

1919 No. 1 Canadian Wing, CAF formed in Britain.

1920 CAF Squadrons and Wing disbanded in England. Formation of CAF in Canada authorized by Order in Council.

1922 *National Defence Act* (NDA) passed. Consolidation of CAF and Civil Operations Branch.

1923 NDA takes effect. Air Board is no longer a separate government department.

1924 Royal Canadian Air Force (RCAF) becomes a permanent component of Canada's defence forces.

1926 First RCAF-trained pilots receive wings.

1938 RCAF Senior Air Officer reports directly to Minister of National Defence.

1939 The Second World War begins: RCAF defends Canadian airspace, operates the British Commonwealth Air Training Plan (BCATP) and fights overseas with Britain's Fighter Command, Bomber Command, and Coastal Command.

1940 The Battle of Britain; first time for RCAF in combat.
RCAF Ensign approved by His Majesty King George VI.
The first intake of BCATP pupils for service flying training reported to No. 1 Service Flying Training School at Camp Borden.

1941 400 Squadron series introduced.
Canada declares war on Japan; RCAF participates in missions in Alaska, Ceylon, India, and Burma.

1942 Canadian Women's Auxiliary Air Force renamed RCAF Women's Division.
Six RCAF fighter and two army-cooperation squadrons provide air support for ill-fated Dieppe raid.

1943 No. 6 RCAF Group becomes operational in Bomber Command.

1944 D-Day, the invasion of Normandy, and liberation of Europe begins; Canadians contribute to aerial cover for invasion fleet.

1945 Victory in Europe (VE) and Victory in Japan (VJ) bring an end to the Second World War. Canada has the fourth-largest air force in the world.

1946 Authorization given for RCAF aircraft to be marked with a roundel bearing a red maple leaf in the centre.

1948 RCAF participates in the Berlin Airlift, providing West Berlin with food, medicine, and essential goods.

1950 Korean War begins. No. 426 (Transport) Squadron begins Operation HAWK. Twenty-two RCAF pilots seconded to the United States Air Force for air combat operations.

1951 Operation LEAP FROG (Phase 1); RCAF begins deploying F-86 Sabre squadrons to No. 1 Air Division (headquartered at Metz, France) as part of its North Atlantic Treaty Organization (NATO) commitment.

1953 Korean War ends; RCAF continues to focus on European NATO commitments.

1958 CF-105 Arrow makes it maiden flight at Malton, Ontario. North American Aerospace Defense Command (NORAD) Agreement signed.

1959 CF-105 Avro Arrow cancelled.

1967 *Canadian Forces Reorganization Act* given Royal Assent.

1968 The three arms of the Canadian Forces are unified into a single organization, the Canadian Armed Forces (CAF). RCAF ceases to exist.

1974 A CC-115 Buffalo aircraft was shot down over Syria, killing nine crew and passengers.

1975 Air Command formed.

1985 Air Force returns to its light blue distinctive environmental uniform.

1991 First Gulf War begins (and ends); Air Force conducts sweep and escort missions with CF-18s to support ground forces while CH-124 Sea Kings support the naval embargo of Iraq. CC-137 and CC130s provide vital airlift support.

1992 Canadian Forces closes bases in Europe; 1 Canadian Air Group's fighter operations end in Baden–Soellingen, Germany.
Canadian Forces deploy on UN mission to Somalia. Sea King helicopters provide intelligence, reconnaissance, and airborne transport services.

1993 Air Force bases designated as Wings.

1997 1 Canadian Air Division created, Air Command moves to Ottawa, Ontario, and office of Chief of the Air Staff recreated. Group Headquarters disappear and 1 Canadian Air Division assumes responsibility for their functions.

1998 Deployment of CH-146 Griffon helicopters to Bosnia in support of NATO-led mission.

1999 RCAF CF-18s participate in NATO-led bombing of Kosovo. The contribution eventually grows to 18 CF-18s and 300 personnel; the mission is dubbed Operation ECHO. On June 20, the NATO Secretary General formally ends the air campaign.

2001 Chris Hadfield, a former CF-18 pilot, becomes the first Canadian to walk in space during his second space shuttle mission aboard *Endeavour*.
Terrorist attacks are carried out against the United States. Canada's airports accept 224 diverted planes and more than 33,000 displaced passengers. All NORAD forces, including Canadian NORAD Region CF-18 Hornets, go on heightened state of alert in preparation for further attacks.
The first air force deployment as part of the Afghanistan campaign begins in the form of the airlift detachment of CC-130s. Two CP-140 Auroras deploy to the Afghanistan region to support the Canadian Naval Task Group as part of Operation APOLLO.

2002 RCAF begins contribution to war in Afghanistan.
The CAF begin working out of Camp Mirage in the United Arab Emirates; the unit working there is eventually named the Theatre Support Element. Camp Mirage is assigned to Operation ATHENA (established in July 2003) on August 16, 2003.

2008 Joint Task Force Air Wing deployed to Afghanistan as part of Operation ATHENA; the first time Canada dispatched an air formation to participate in an armed conflict since the Second World War.

2009 2 Canadian Air Division/Air Force Doctrine and Training Division is established in Winnipeg.
The NATO Training Mission in Afghanistan is activated. The Canadian contribution is called Operation ATTENTION

and the mission includes members of the Navy, Army, and Air Force.

2010 Camp Mirage closes.

Operation PODIUM: RCAF lends support to RCMP-led security for Vancouver Olympic and Paralympic Games.

Support to RCMP-led security operations surrounding the G8 and G20 summits in Ontario.

2011 Task Force Malta, the first phase of Operation MOBILE, begins. Over 11 days, the Air Force assists in the evacuation of Canadian and foreign nationals from Libya.

The second phase of Operation MOBILE begins. Dubbed Task Force Libeccio, it is the Forces' combat mission to the NATO-led Operation UNIFIED PROTECTOR in the seas near and skies over Libya.

The CAF combat mission in Afghanistan ends. The final RCAF flying unit returns home in November and Operation ATHENA ends on December 1.

The titles Royal Canadian Navy, Canadian Army, and Royal Canadian Air Force are restored, replacing Maritime Command, Land Force Command, and Air Command.

Operation MOBILE ends.

Operation FORGE: Airlift of 3,600 civilians from communities in northern Ontario threatened by wildfires.

2013 Operation RENAISSANCE, the CAF's contribution to humanitarian aid in the Philippines in the wake of Typhoon Haiyan, begins.

2014 The last Canadian troops return home from Afghanistan.

Operation IMPACT begins with the deployment of CF-18s to Kuwait to participate in Allied bombing operations against ISIL in Iraq and Syria. CC-150 Polaris tanker, CC-130 Hercules, CP-140 Auroras, and CH-146 Griffons are all deployed to theatre to support operations.

Operation REASSURANCE begins to provide Canadian support to NATO in the face of Russian incursions into Ukraine. Air Task Force Romania is stood up with the deployment of 6 CF-18s to Constanta, Romania.

2018 As part of MINUSMA, Task Force-Mali is stood up with the deployment of CH-147 Chinooks and CH-146 Griffons.

2022 On September 15, 2022, Air Task Force Prestwick (ATF-P) was created as part of the expansion of the tactical airlift detachment that previously supported Operation REASSURANCE.

Royal Canadian Air Force CC-130J Hercules, CC-150 Polaris, and CC-177 Globemaster aircraft, aircrew, and support staff help transport Afghan evacuees following the return of the Taliban.

2024 April 1, 2024 is the 100th Anniversary of the RCAF.

BIBLIOGRAPHY

Opposite: Members of the Helicopter Air Detachment aboard HMCS *Montréal* conduct helicopter hoist drills with a CH-148 Cyclone helicopter, call sign Strider, during Operation REASSURANCE on February 13, 2022.

"408 Goose" Squadron Association. "408 Squadron: SHORAN Operations 1949–1957." Accessed August 2, 2023. https://www.forfreedom. ca/?page_id=725.

Adams, Sharon. "Canadian Pilots Respond to Crisis in Kosovo." *Legion Magazine*, June 3, 2020. https://legionmagazine.com/en/2020/06/ canadian-pilots-respond-to-crisis-in-kosovo/.

Adams, Sharon. "A Gruelling Rescue Effort." *Legion Magazine*, October 28, 2020. https://legionmagazine.com/en/2020/10/a-gruelling-rescue-effort/.

Air Cadet League of Canada. "History." Accessed August 2, 2023. https://aircadetleague.com/history/.

Air Force Museum of Alberta. "RCAF History." Accessed August 2, 2023. https://www.rcaf.museum/history.

Alberta Aviation Museum. Accessed August 2, 2023. https://albertaaviationmuseum.com/.

Barris, Ted. *Dam Busters: Canadian Airmen and the Secret Raid against Nazi Germany*. Toronto: Patrick Crean Editions, 2018.

Barris, Ted. *The Great Escape: The Untold Story*. Toronto: Dundurn Press, 2014.

Bashow, David L. "The Incomparable Billy Bishop: The Man and the Myths." *Canadian Military Journal* 3, no. 3 (Autumn 2002): 55–60.

Bashow, David L., Dwight Davies, André Viens, John Rotteau, Norman Balfe, Ray Stouffer, Captain James Pickett, and Steve Harris. "Mission Ready: Canada's Role in the Kosovo Air Campaign." *Canada Military Journal* 1, no. 1 (Spring 2000): 55–61.

Beckwith, Mark. "The RCAF's No. 404 "Buffalo" Squadron." *Making History*, November 28, 2019. https://making-history.ca/2019/11/28/ royal-canadian-air-force-no-404-buffalo-squadron/.

Bishop, William Avery. *Winged Warfare*. New York: George H. Doran, 1918.

Bomber Command Museum of Canada. Accessed August 2, 2023. https:// www.bombercommandmuseum.ca/.

Brickhill, Paul. *The Great Escape*. New York: W.W. Norton, 2004.

Brown, Edward. "Duty and Danger: The Remarkable Story of the Carty Family's Commitment to Defending Canada." *Toronto Star*, Special to the *Star Sun*, February 6, 2022. https://www.thestar.com/news/canada/2022/02/06/ duty-and-danger-the-remarkable-story-of-the-carty-familys-commitment-to-defending-canada.html.

Bryce, Gladysann. *First in, Last Out: The RCAF, Women's Division and Nursing Sisters in World War II*. Toronto: University Women's Club of Toronto, 2010.

Buffalo 461. Accessed August 2, 2023. https://www.buffalo461.ca/.

Calder, Joanna. "Toronto 'Goes Blue' for Presentation of RCAF Colours." Government of Canada, Department of National Defence, September 21, 2017. https://www.canada.ca/en/ department-national-defence/maple-leaf/rcaf/migration/2017/ toronto-goes-blue-for-presentation-of-rcaf-colours.html.

Canada. *60th Anniversary: The British Commonwealth Air Training Plan*. Ottawa: Veterans Affairs, 2000.

Canada, Canadian Armed Forces. "Wars and Operations." Last modified February 10, 2023; accessed August 2, 2023. https://www.canada.ca/en/ services/defence/caf/militaryhistory/wars-operations.html.

Canada, Canadian Space Agency. Accessed August 2, 2023. https://www. asc-csa.gc.ca/eng/.

Canada, Department of National Defence. Last modified March 8, 2023; accessed August 2, 2023. https://www.canada.ca/en/department-national-defence.html.

Canada, Department of National Defence. "Establishment of 3 Canadian Space Division." News Release, July 22, 2022. https://www.canada.ca/en/ department-national-defence/news/2022/07/establishment-of-3-canadian-space-division.html.

Canada, Independent Panel on Canada's Future Role in Afghanistan. *Report of the Independent Panel on Canada's Future Role in Afghanistan* [Manley parliamentary report], January 2008. https://publications.gc.ca/ collections/collection_2008/dfait-maeci/FR5–20–1–2008E.pdf.

Canada, Library and Archives Canada. "William Avery 'Billy' Bishop." Last modified August 31, 2022; accessed September 18, 2022. https://web.archive. org/web/20220918072529/https://www.bac-lac.gc.ca/eng/discover/ military-heritage/first-world-war/100-stories/Pages/bishop.aspx.

Canada, Ministry of Industry, Trade and Commerce. *Aviation in Canada 1971: A Statistical Handbook of Canadian Aviation*. Catalogue no. 51–501. Ottawa: Statistics Canada, Transportation and Public Utilities Division, Aviation Statistics Centre, 1972.

Canada, National Research Council of Canada. "Aerospace Research Centre." Last modified April 6, 2023; accessed August 2, 2023. https://nrc.canada. ca/en/research-development/research-collaboration/research-centres/ aerospace-research-centre.

Canada, National Research Council of Canada. "The Flight Research Laboratory Celebrates 75 Years of Contributions to Global Aerospace Research." December 21, 2021. https://nrc.canada.ca/en/stories/flight-research-laboratory-celebrates-75-years-contributions-global-aerospace-research.

Canada, National Research Council of Canada. "Picture Perfect: Aerial Surveying with Bush Planes." In "History: 1916–1945." Last modified March 13, 2019; accessed August 2, 2023. https://nrc.canada.ca/en/corporate/ history/1916–1945#3.

Canada, National Research Council of Canada. "Reinforcing Canada's Defence and Security Industry with New Memorandum of Understanding between the NRC and DND." Article published April 21, 2022; last modified February

24, 2023. https://nrc.canada.ca/en/stories/reinforcing-canadas-defence-security-industry-new-memorandum-understanding-between-nrc-dnd.

Canada, National Research Council of Canada. "Saving Survivors by Finding Fallen Aircrafts." Last modified March 5, 2008; accessed October 2, 2013. https://web.archive.org/web/20131002141527/http://www.nrc-cnrc.gc.ca/eng/education/innovations/discoveries/fallen_aircraft.html.

Canada, National Research Council of Canada. *Science at Work for the New Age of Aerospace Innovation.* June 2018. Catalogue no. NR16-233/2018E-PDF. https://publications.gc.ca/collections/collection_2019/cnrc-nrc/NR16–233–2018-eng.pdf.

Canada, Royal Canadian Air Force. Last modified May 29, 2023; accessed August 2, 2023. https://www.canada.ca/en/air-force.html.

Canada, Royal Canadian Air Force. "3 Canadian Space Division." Last modified October 11, 2022; accessed August 2, 2023. https://www.canada.ca/en/air-force/corporate/3-canadian-space-division.html.

Canada, Royal Canadian Air Force. "British Commonwealth Air Training Plan 1940–1945." Last modified June 5, 2017; accessed August 2, 2023. https://www.canada.ca/en/air-force/services/history-heritage/british-commonwealth-air-training-plan.html.

Canada, Royal Canadian Air Force. "Canadian Forces Snowbirds." Last modified July 27, 2021; accessed August 2, 2023. https://www.canada.ca/en/air-force/services/showcasing/snowbirds.html.

Canada, Veterans Affairs Canada. *Canada Remembers Times, Veterans' Week Special Edition.* Accessed August 2, 2023. https://publications.gc.ca/site/eng/9.506381/publication.html.

Canada, Veterans Affairs Canada. "The Nursing Sisters of Canada." Catalogue no. V32–146/2005. Accessed August 2, 2023. https://www.veterans.gc.ca/eng/remembrance/those-who-served/women-veterans/nursing-sisters. Also published as *Canada's Nursing Sisters* (Ottawa: Veterans Affairs Canada, 2005).

Canada Aviation and Space Museum. "Canada's Jet-Age Dream: The Avro Arrow." Created in 2016; accessed August 2, 2023 from Google Arts & Culture. https://artsandculture.google.com/story/RgWh1ZCGfwg4IQ.

Canada Aviation and Space Museum. Ingenium. Accessed August 2, 2023. https://ingeniumcanada.org/aviation.

Canada's Aviation Hall of Fame. Accessed August 2, 2023. https://cahf.ca/.

Canada's Aviation Hall of Fame. "William George Barker." Accessed August 2, 2023. https://cahf.ca/william-george-barker/.

Canada's Sports Hall of Fame. "The RCAF Flyers." Accessed August 2, 2023. http://canadasports150.ca/en/military-teams/the-rcaf-flyers/98.

The Canadian Museum of Flight. Accessed August 2, 2023. http://www.canadianflight.org/.

Canadian Warplane Heritage Museum. Accessed August 2, 2023. https://www.warplane.com/.

Carr, W.K. Bill. "Canadian Forces Air Command: Evolution to Founding." *The Royal Canadian Air Force Journal* 1, no. 1 (Winter 2012): 13–23.

CFB Baden Remembered. Accessed August 2, 2023. http://www.badenremembered.com/.

Chinese Canadian Military Museum Society. Accessed August 2, 2023. https://www.ccmms.ca/.

Clinton, Jared. "The Incredible 1948 RCAF Flyers, Who Went from Being Booed off the Ice to Capturing Olympic Gold." *The Hockey News*, November 11, 2015. https://thehockeynews.com/news/the-incredible-1948-rcaf-flyers-who-went-from-being-booed-off-the-ice-to-capturing-olympic-gold.

Connolly, Amanda. "Canada Will Spend $40B over 20 Years to Upgrade NORAD Defences amid 'New Threats.'" *Global News*, June 20, 2022. https://globalnews.ca/news/8933288/nada-upgrading-norad-amid-new-threats/.

Connolly, Amanda. "Canadian Military Boosts Air Support to Help B.C. Flood Evacuations, Supply Chain Chaos." *Global News*, November 17, 2021. https://globalnews.ca/news/8380049/canadian-military-bc-floods-2021/.

Cothliff, Kenneth B. *Canadian Pathfinder: The Life of a Canadian Bomber Ace.* Biography of Lt. General Reg Lane. N.p.: Air Supply Publications, 2021.

Cuggy, Emily. "Korea: 1951." *Canada's History*, October 20, 2011. https://www.canadashistory.ca/explore/military-war/korea-1951.

Da Silva, Susana, and The Canadian Press. "Rescuers Lift Hundreds of Motorists Trapped on B.C. Highway to Safety." *CBC News*, November 15, 2021: https://www.cbc.ca/news/canada/british-columbia/bc-landslide-weather-road-debris-nov15–1.6249085.

Daubs, Katie. "The Flying Ace You've Never Heard of." *Toronto Star*, September 19, 2011. https://www.thestar.com/news/gta/2011/09/19/the_flying_ace_youve_never_heard_of.html.

Day, Adam. "Afghanistan Air Wing Stands Up." *Legion Magazine*, March 21, 2009. https://legionmagazine.com/en/2009/03/afghanistan-air-wing-stands-up/.

Dempsey, Dan. *A Tradition of Excellence: Canada's Airshow Team Heritage.* Victoria: Vanwell Publishing, 2004.

Dedyna, Katherine. "Daring Pilots of Cold War Gather for Victoria Reunion." *Times Colonist*, September 13, 2014.

Douglas, W.A.B. The Creation of a National Air Force: *The Official History of the Royal Canadian Air Force.* Vol. 2. Toronto: University of Toronto Press, 1986.

Dow, James. *The Arrow.* Toronto: J. Lorimer, 1979.

Duhamel, Roger. *The Royal Canadian Air Force: 5 BX Exercise Plan*, 2nd ed. RCAF Pamphlet 30/1. Catalogue no. DC72–162. Ottawa: RCAF, 1962.

Available from the National Air Force Museum of Canada. http://airforcemuseum.ca/eng/?page_id=3952.

Eskritt, Jodi Ann. "Remembering... The Para-Belles: First Para Rescue Nurses." *The Contact*, 44, no. 12, March 27, 2009, 12. http://thecontactnewspaper. cfbtrenton.com/archives/2009/10_March_2009/mar_27_2009/thecontact_ mar_27_2009.pdf.

Fawcett, Michael T. "The Politics of Sovereignty – Continental Defence and the Creation of NORAD." *Canadian Military Journal* 10, no. 2 (2010): 33–40.

Flynn, Billie. "Billie Flynn." Accessed August 2, 2023. https://billieflynn.com/.

Forbes, David W. "Soldier, Aviator, or Both: Analyzing the Impacts of Canada's Unified Air Powers Structure on Tactical Aviation." Master's thesis, Canadian Forces College, 2019 (JCSP 42).

Gillis, Charlie. "Chris Hadfield on the View from Above and His Fear of Heights." *Maclean's Magazine*, October 8, 2013. https://macleans.ca/general/ chris-hadfield-on-the-view-from-above-and-his-fear-of-heights/.

Goette, Richard, and P. Whitney Lackenbauer. *Northern Skytrails: Perspectives on the Royal Canadian Air Force in the Arctic from the Pages of* The Roundel, *1949–65.* DCASS Number 10, 2017.

Gonzalez, Robbie. "Astronaut Life Is Much More than a Spacewalk." *Wired*, February 27, 2019. https://www.wired.com/story/ chris-hadfield-astronaut-life-is-much-more-than-a-spacewalk/.

The Great War Flying Museum. Accessed August 2, 2023. https://greatwarflyingmuseum.org/.

Greenhous, Brereton, Steven J. Harris, William C. Johnston, and William G.P. Rawling. *The Crucible of War, 1939–1945: The Official History of the Royal Canadian Air Force.* Vol. 3. Toronto: University of Toronto Press, 1994.

Hadfield, Chris. *An Astronaut's Guide to Life on Earth.* Rev. ed. Toronto: Vintage Canada, 2015.

Hadfield, Chris. "Colonel Chris Hadfield." Accessed August 2, 2023. https:// chrishadfield.ca/.

Halliday, Hugh A. "Canada's Air Force in War and Peace." Canadian War Museum. Accessed August 2, 2023. https://www.warmuseum.ca/learn/ dispatches/canadas-air-force-in-war-and-peace/.

Harvey, J. Douglas. *The Tumbling Mirth: Remembering the Air Force.* Toronto: McClelland and Stewart, 1983.

Harvey, J. Douglas. *Laughter Silvered Wings: Remembering the Air Force II.* Toronto: McClelland and Stewart, 1988.

"A History of the Institute for Aerospace Research." *Canadian Aeronautics and Space Journal* 47, no. 3 (September 2001): 111–116.

Hitchins, F.H. *Air Board, Canadian Air Force and Royal Canadian Air Force.* Mercury Series No. 2. Ottawa: Canadian War Museum, 1972.

Hurdis, Blake. "Flying High with Test Pilot Billie Flynn." *The Free Library*, April 1, 2012. https://www.thefreelibrary.com/ Flying+high+with+test+pilot+Billie+Flynn.-a0287517654.

Joost, Mathias. "Racism and Enlistment the Second World War Policies of the Royal Canadian Air Force." *Canadian Military History* 21, no. 1 (Winter 2015): 17–34.

Krayden, David. *On Windswept Heights: Historical Highlights of Canada's Air Force.* Edited by Joanna Calder and John Blakeley. Catalogue no. D2–241/2009E-PDF. Ottawa: Government of Canada, Department of National Defence, 2009.

Leversedge, Terry. "Royal Canadian Air Force F-86 Sabre Pilots in the Korean War." Extracts originally published in T.F.J. Leversedge, *Canadian Eagles in Crimson Skies* (Ottawa: Kestrel Aerospace Publications, 2020). Available from the New Brunswick Aviation Museum. Accessed August 2, 2023. https://nbaviationmuseum.com/korea.

Lindahl, Emily. "Move over Maverick! Canadian Pilot Graduates TOPGUN Program." Government of Canada, Department of National Defence, December 21, 2020. https://www.canada.ca/en/department-national-de- fence/maple-leaf/rcaf/2020/12/move-over-maverick-canadian-pilot-grad- uates-topgun-program.html.

Manson, Paul. "1977–80 Fighter Aircraft Project." *FrontLine Defence Magazine*, no. 1, 2021. https://frontline.online/ defence/2021/1/6211–1977–80-fighter-aircraft-project.

March, William. "Royal Canadian Air Force (RCAF)." In *The Canadian Encyclopedia*. Historica Canada, 1985–. Article published March 5, 2015; last modified September 16, 2021. https://www.thecanadianencyclopedia. ca/en/article/royal-canadian-air-force.

Marsh, James H. "The Silver Dart and the Dawn of Flight in Canada." In *The Canadian Encyclopedia*. Historica Canada, 1985–. Article published February 22, 2012; last modified March 4, 2015. https://www.thecanadi- anencyclopedia.ca/en/article/silver-dart-dawn-of-flight-in-canada-feature.

Mayne, Richard. "The Influence of Empire: A National Organization and the Birth of the Royal Canadian Air Force, 1918–1924." *Canadian Military Journal* 19, no. 3 (Summer 2019): 37–44.

Mayne, Richard, and William March, eds. *AIR WING: RCAF Commanders' Perspectives during the 2011 Libyan Conflict.* Catalogue no. D2–401/2018. Ottawa: Government of Canada, Department of National Defence, 2018.

Middleton, W.E. Knowles. *Mechanical Engineering at the National Research Council of Canada.* Waterloo, Ontario: Wilfrid Laurier University Press, 1984.

Milberry, Larry. *Aviation in Canada: Evolution of An Air Force.* Toronto: Canav Books, 2003.

Milberry, Larry. *Canada's Air Force: At War and Peace.* 3 vols. Toronto: Canav

Books, 2000–2001.

Milberry, Larry. *Sixty Years: The RCAF and CF Air Command 1924–1984*. Toronto: Canav Books, 1984.

National Air Force Museum of Canada. Accessed August 2, 2023. http://airforcemuseum.ca/.

Ogilvie, Keith. *The Spitfire Luck of Skeets Ogilvie: From the Battle of Britain to the Great Escape*. Victoria: Heritage House, 2017.

Parkin, J.H. "Aeronautical Research in Canada: The Organization of Aeronautical Laboratories under the National Research Council and Some of the Special Problems under Investigation." *Canadian Aeronautics and Space Journal* 47, no. 3 (September 2001): 117–124.

Payne, Stephen R. *A History of the Rockcliffe Airport Site: Home of the National Aviation Museum*. Ottawa: National Aviation Museum, 1999.

Peden, Murray. *A Thousand Shall Fall: The True Story of a Canadian Bomber Pilot in World War Two*. Canada: Dundurn Press, 2003.

Petite, Bob. "Canada's First Military Helicopter." *Skies Magazine*, March 20, 2019: https://skiesmag.com/features/canadas-first-military-helicopter/.

Pierotti, James. "A Tactical Silver Lining in a Horrifying Storm: Canadian Airlift in Rwanda, 1999." *RCAF Journal* 5, no. 1 (Winter 2016): 24–42.

Pigott, Peter. *Taming the Skies: A Celebration of Canadian Flight*. Toronto: Dundurn Press, 2003.

Pigott, Peter. "Task Force Libeccio." *FrontLine Defence Magazine*, no. 6, 2011. https://frontline.online/defence/2011/6/1805-task-force-libeccio.

Reid, Sheila. *Wings of a Hero: Canadian Pioneer Flying Ace Wilfrid Wop May*. Victoria: Vanwell Publishing, 2005.

Roblin, Sebastien. "823 People, One Jet: Flight Trackers Reveal Heroic, Desperate Effort in Chaotic Afghanistan Evacuation." *Forbes*, August 16, 2021. https://www.forbes.com/sites/sebastienroblin/2021/08/16/800-people-one-jet-flight-trackers-reveal-heroic-desperate-effort-in-chaotic-afghanistan-evacuation/.

Royal Aviation Museum of Western Canada. Accessed August 2, 2023. https://royalaviationmuseum.com/.

Royal Canadian Air Force Association. "Canadian Military Aviation Chronology 1883–1929." Accessed July 17, 2023. https://www.rcafassociation.ca/heritage/history/canadian-military-aviation-chronology/.

Sissons, Crystal. *Queen of the Hurricanes: The Fearless Elsie MacGill*. Toronto: Second Story Press, 2014.

Skaarup, Harold. A. "1 Canadian Air Division (1 CAD), 1 Canadian Air Group (1 CAG), Canadian Forces Europe (CFE), 1952–1993." SilverHawkAuthor. Accessed August 2, 2023. https://www.silverhawkauthor.com/post/1-canadian-air-division-1-cad-1-canadian-air-group-1-cag-canadian-forces-europe-cfe-1952–1993.

Skaarup, Harold. A. "Canadian Warplanes 2: Fleet Fawn and Fleet Finch Trainers." SilverHawkAuthor. Accessed August 2, 2023. https://www.silverhawkauthor.com/postcanadian-warplanes-2-fleet-fawn-and-fleet-finch-trainers.

Skies Magazine, various issues. Accessed August 2, 2023. https://skiesmag.com/issues/.

Stewart, Greig. *An Arrow through the Heart: The Life antd times of Crawford Gordon and the Avro Arrow*. Toronto: McGraw-Hill Ryerson, 1998.

Stoltz, Dean. "'We evacuated more people than I will likely see in my career': 19 Wing Comox Crews Recall Rescue Efforts in Agassiz." *CHEK News*, November 17, 2021. https://www.cheknews.ca/we-evacuated-more-people-than-i-will-likely-see-in-my-career-comox-sartech-on-monday-rescues-913477/.

Taschner, Eric. "Effort to Preserve Underground North Bay Military Complex Gains Momentum." *CTV News*, September 6, 2021. https://northernontario.ctvnews.ca/effort-to-preserve-underground-north-bay-military-complex-gains-momentum-1.5574993.

Valour Canada. "Cold War: Anti-Submarine Warfare." Accessed August 2, 2023. https://valourcanada.ca/military-history-library/anti-submarine-warfare/.

Vintage Wings of Canada. Accessed August 2, 2023. https://www.vintagewings.ca/home.

Wakelam, Randall. "The Origins of Canadian Land Aviation, Creating 'a Favourable Mobility Differential': An Air Arm for the Army." Unpublished manuscript, 2011.

Waldron, Webb. "'Buzz' Beurling." *Maclean's*, January 15, 1943.

Wilson, J.A. "The Influence of Civil Aviation in the Development of Canadian Air Power." Directorate of History and Heritage, Wilson Papers, 76/271, box 2, file 15.

Wings Magazine, various issues. Accessed August 2, 2023. https://www.wingsmagazine.com/.

Wise, S.F. *Canadian Airmen and the First World War: The Official History of the Royal Canadian Air Force*. Vol. 1. Toronto: University of Toronto Press, 1980.

The Wop May Chronicles. Accessed August 2, 2023. http://www.wopmay.com/.

Wood, Edward P. *Per Ardua Ad Arcticum: The Royal Canadian Air Force in the Arctic and Sub-Arctic*. Edited by P. Whitney Lackenbauer. Mulroney Institute of Government Arctic Operational Histories no. 2. Antigonish, Nova Scotia: Mulroney Institute, 2017.

PHOTO CREDITS

Opposite: A CP-140 Aurora aircraft flies over the Atlantic Ocean during
Exercise CUTLASS FURY on September 11, 2019.

iv Department of National Defence, PL-1531.
Department of National Defence, PCN75–681.
Department of National Defence, PL-2441.
Department of National Defence, PL-14975.
Department of National Defence, PL-7218.
Department of National Defence, PL-62311.
Photo courtesy of Jesse Bertucci.
Department of National Defence, RCAF, Corporal Dang.
Photo courtesy of Ryan Knourchid.
Photo courtesy of K.J. Allen.
Department of National Defence, RCAF, Corporal Dang.
RCAF Foundation, Scholars 2021.
Photo courtesy of Maya Cantin.
Department of National Defence, RCAF, Corporal Dang.
Photo courtesy of Kensington Hewson.
Department of National Defence, RCAF Photographer Warrant Officer Vanayan.

v   RCAF Foundation.

viii Lockheed Martin, Darin Russell, March 8, 2018, 18J00097_23.

x   Department of National Defence, Corporal Michael J. MacIsaac, SU12-2015-1640-028.

xi The Park Group, Nick Wons, November 10, 2022, Toronto in Tomorrow, Trilateral Commission North America Waterloo Trip.

xii © Government of Canada. Reproduced with the permission of Library and Archives Canada (2023). From the Library and Archives Canada, Department of National Defence fonds, e011316185.

xiii Department of National Defence, RCAF, Eric Kenny, February 3, 2023.

xvi Department of National Defence, PL-117009.

3   Department of National Defence, BellBoys.

4   Canadian Aviation and Space Museum, CAVM-06735a.

5   Canadian Aviation and Space Museum, CAVM-07113.
Canadian Aviation and Space Museum, CAVM-17378.

6   Department of National Defence, Bishop_WA-RAF-RCAF_AH-470A.

7   Department of National Defence, Bishop_WA-RFC-RCAF_AH-504.

8   Swaine/Library and Archives Canada, PA-122516.

9   Government of Canada, Department of National Defence and the Library and Archives Canada, PA-008030.
Pringle & Booth/Library and Archives Canada, C-003538.

10 J.A. Wilson and the Library and Archives Canada, PA-139754.
© Government of Canada. Reproduced with the permission of Library and Archives Canada (2023). Library and Archives Canada/Department of National Defence fonds/e011160381.

11 Canadian Aviation and Space Museum, PCN-4592.

12 Government of Canada, Department of National Defence and the Library and Archives Canada, PA-062958.

13 © Government of Canada. Reproduced with the permission of Library and Archives Canada (2023). Library and Archives Canada, Department of National Defence fonds, a066191.

14 Government of Canada, Department of National Defence and the Library and Archives Canada, PA-065127.

15 Government of Canada, Department of National Defence and the Library and Archives Canada, PA-063073.

16 Department of National Defence, Colonel (Retired) Morris D. Gates, OMM, CD, SHORAN Network.
Library and Archives Canada, PA-062588.

17 Government of Canada, Department of National Defence and the Library and Archives Canada, PA-065141.18.

18 Library and Archives Canada, PMR76-214.

20 Rainville family, Brian Rainville.

22 Library and Archives Canada, e010997489.
Rare Books and Special Collections, McGill University Library, WP2.R14.F3.

23 Department of National Defence, PL-3306.

24 Department of National Defence, PL-16961.

25 Government of Canada, Department of National Defence and the Library and Archives Canada, PA-068005.

26 Department of National Defence, National Air Force Museum of Canada.
Department of National Defence, DND65-110.

27 Department of National Defence, PL-22146.

28 Library and Archives Canada, e006611177.

29 Canadian Warplane Heritage Museum, Rick Radell, Hurricane.

30 Canadian War Museum, 20100197-001_64b.
Department of National Defence, 404 Squadron.

31 Canadian War Museum, 20100197-001_48f.
Department of National Defence, PL-5389.
Department of National Defence, PL-5388.

32 Department of National Defence, 417 Squadron.
Department of National Defence, PL 10237.

33 Department of National Defence, PL-55325.
Department of National Defence, PL-10151.

34 Department of National Defence, 412 Squadron.
Department of National Defence, PL-14940.

35 Canadian Warplane Heritage Museum, 20230106_081943.

Department of National Defence, PL 22170.

Department of National Defence, PL 32575.

36 Department of National Defence, PL-33943.

Department of National Defence, No. 6 Group RCAF badge.

37 Government of Canada, Department of National Defence Collection and the Library and Archives Canada, e005176190.

38 Department of National Defence, PL-116961.

Department of National Defence, PL-20419.

39 Canadian Warplane Heritage Museum, Doug Fisher, Lancaster.

40 Department of National Defence, 405 Squadron.

Department of National Defence, October 12, 1942, PL-11664.

41 Department of National Defence, Lane taking salute with 12 104'.

Department of National Defence, PL-19696.

Department of National Defence, PL-7096.

42 Department of National Defence, PL-8915.

43 Hockey Hall of Fame.

National Hockey League, February 10, 1942.

44 Department of National Defence, June 1, 1945, PL-36843.

45 Keith Ogilvie, June 28, 1941.

46 Department of National Defence, 435 Squadron.

Department of National Defence, 436 Squadron.

Department of National Defence, PL-60111.

47 Photo courtesy of Pierre Lapprand.

Department of National Defence, WGT85-613-12.

Elizabeth Chestney Hanson, Art Adams Memorial Kicker Cup.

48 Photo courtesy of The Collection of James Allen, Windsor Mosaic, African Canadian Community.

Department of National Defence via Royal Canadian Air Force Association.

Chinese Canadian Military Museum.

Wikimedia Commons, Jean Suey Zee Lee. Originally from the Chinese Canadian Military Museum.

49 National Research Council of Canada Archives.

50 Department of National Defence, PL-26157.

Photo courtesy of the Bolduc family, https://www.veterans.gc.ca.

51 Photo courtesy of the Carty family.

52 Department of National Defence, 413 Squadron.

Department of National Defence, PL-133463.

53 Department of National Defence, PL-7403.

Government of Canada, Department of National Defence and the Library and Archives Canada, PA-063552.

54 Photograph by Yousuf Karsh. Canadian War Museum, 19820262-001.

Department of National Defence, RCAF Women's Division.

55 Rainville family, Brian Rainville, RCAF Women's Division.

Government of Canada, Department of National Defence and the Library and Archives Canada, PA-064042.

56 Department of National Defence, Air Cadet League.

Photo courtesy of Kaden Lac.

Photo courtesy of Tom Jenkins.

57 Department of National Defence, PL-13449.

58 Department of National Defence via James Craik, PC-1311.

60 Department of National Defence, Master Corporal Carbe Orellana, ET2017-5003-01.

62 Canada's Sports Hall of Fame, OHOF993.62.3.

Library and Archives Canada, e011161364.

63 Department of National Defence; courtesy of Larry Milberry.

Department of National Defence, PL-62570.

64 Department of National Defence, 1647108147533.

Department of National Defence, 434 Squadron.

65 Department of National Defence, PL-62073.

Department of National

Defence, BNC72-2844.

66 Department of National Defence, Flying Officer Robert Mortimer, 23063.

67 Department of National Defence, via James Craik, PCN 3196.

68 Department of National Defence; courtesy Lieutenant-General (Retired) Syd Burrows.

Department of National Defence, 427 Squadron.

69 Department of National Defence, PL-121076.

Department of National Defence, Eugene Harmata, member of the RCAF 1st Air Division, 61 AC&W, metz351, January 1963.

70 Department of National Defence, FLT Ernie Glover Photo.

Library and Archives Canada, a067566-v8.

71 Department of National Defence, PL51164.

72 Department of National Defence, Corporal Andrew Wesley, Canadian Forces Support Unit (Ottawa) Imaging Services, SU2014-0229-1.

73 Lawson family.

Lawson family, 1944.

Lawson family, 2017.

Lawson family, 2013.

Lawson family.

74 © Government of Canada. Reproduced with the permission of Library and Archives Canada (2023). Library and Archives Canada, Department of National Defence fonds,

e010788105.
Department of National Defence, REC75-930.

75 © Government of Canada. Reproduced with the permission of Library and Archives Canada (2023). Library and Archives Canada, Department of National Defence fonds, a067702.
Department of National Defence, WES61-134-32.

76 Department of National Defence.

77 Department of National Defence.
Department of National Defence, 5BX Plan.

78 Reproduced with the permission of Library and Archives Canada (2023). Library and Archives Canada, Department of National Defence fonds, e010858630.
NORAD.

79 Department of National Defence, PCN70-87.
Department of National Defence, CF67-274.

80 Department of National Defence, PCN-4067.
Department of National Defence, April 30, 2023, https://forces.ca/en/careers.

81 Department of National Defence, Warrant Officer Vic Johnson, ISC87-218.
Department of National Defence, NBC72-1301.

82 Department of National Defence, PMRC 82 384.

83 National Research Council

of Canada Archives, Record Identifier 50cd9df7-63b6-4826-8219-c5996ed19175.

84 Department of National Defence, 406 Squadron.
Department of National Defence, Chief Master Sergeant Don Sutherland, REPC86-140.

85 Department of National Defence, Corporal Rick Ayer, hs2-2012-044-001.
Department of National Defence, CH-124 Sea King 425.

86 Department of National Defence via James Craik, 24102 on patrol.

87 Department of National Defence via James Craik, 20723 4.
Department of National Defence, Captain Jeffery Klassen, HMCS *Calgary*, Public Affairs Officer, 20210418PRAD0001D016.

88 Department of National Defence, Corporal Nedia Coutinho, 12 Imaging Services, Shearwater, Nova Scotia, SW2012-0698-01.

89 Department of National Defence, April 30, 2023, https://forces.ca/en/careers.

90 Department of National Defence, 4 Wing.
Department of National Defence via Steve Sauve, BAC89-360.

91 Department of National Defence, ISC86-573.
Department of National Defence, BAC93-3-10.

92 Department of National

Defence, BNA-47.

94 Department of National Defence, CKC89–3767.

96 Department of National Defence, Chief of the Defence Staff in Office.

97 Photo courtesy of Paul Manson.

98 Department of National Defence; courtesy of Lieutenant-General William Carr.

99 Photo courtesy of Lieutenant-General Allan DeQuetteville.
Department of National Defence, 410 Squadron.

101 Department of National Defence, Aviator Avery Philpott, September 29, 2021, RDAK0556D006.

102 Department of National Defence, Master Corporal Johanie Maheu, 14 Wing Imaging, GD2016-0011-32.
Department of National Defence, Corporal Gary Calvé, Bagotville Imagery Section, BN50-2018-0008-005.

103 Department of National Defence, Ordinary Seaman Erica Seymour, 4 Wing Imaging, CK02-2018-0445-067.

104 Department of National Defence, General Ron Slaunwhite.

105 Department of National Defence, November 9, 2021, 130944.
Courtesy of the Slaunwhite family, 1983ish Air Cadet family photo.
Department of National Defence, April 30, 2023,

https://forces.ca/en/careers.

106 Department of National Defence, Master Corporal Andrew Collins, 100201-F-ZZ000-001.

107 National Research Council of Canada, Wind Tunnel Testing.

108 Department of National Defence.

109 Photo courtesy of Robert Mitchell.

110 Department of National Defence.

111 Ingenium, DSC_0151.

112 Department of National Defence, Nancy Tremblay Portrait.

113 Department of National Defence, Master Corporal Steeve Picard, BFC Bagotville, Nancy Tremblay.
Department of National Defence, April 30, 2023, https://forces.ca/en/careers.

114 Department of National Defence, Canada Pride Citation logo.
Photo courtesy of Stephen Deschamps.

115 Stephen Deschamps, TACC JLC 1973.
Stephen Deschamps, Steven Deschamps.

116 Department of National Defence, CMC78-437-14.
RCAF Foundation, 36780269636_fdaa8811c7_o.

117 Department of National Defence, Private Hugo Montpetit, Canadian Forces Combat Camera, IS13-2019-0013-001.

Department of National Defence, Master Corporal Holly Swaine, 30261295_1015520532 8036237_6915327397340381184_n.

118 Department of National Defence, Roundel, 140806.
Royal Air Force, Air Force Ensign of the United Kingdom.
Department of National Defence, RCAF Type 1 Roundel.
Department of National Defence, Roundel of the Royal Canadian Air Force (1946–1965).
Department of National Defence, RCAF Centennial Roundel.
Department of National Defence, Air Force Ensign of Canada (1941–1968).
Department of National Defence, Air Force Ensign of Canada.

119 Department of National Defence, Corporal Alana Morin, Royal Canadian Air Force Public Affairs Imagery, September 1, 2017, FA03-2017-0114-171.

120 Department of National Defence, Corporal Alex Parenteau, IS22-2015-0013-026.

123 Department of National Defence, Corporal Lynette Ai Dang, Canadian Armed Forces Photo, 20210615PRAD0001D010.

124 Department of National Defence, Sergeant R. Thompson, IWC90-351.

126 Department of National Defence, Lambert Corporal, TNC94-405-15.

127 Department of National Defence, Corporal Nicolas Alonso, KW13-2020-0064-001.

128 Department of National Defence, Balkan Rats Pilots, June 1999.
Department of National Defence, Master Corporall Danielle Bernier, ckd99-2085-08.

129 Department of National Defence, CONFIRMISC00-178-26.
Department of National Defence, Corporal Roxanne Clowe, AVD00-014-003a.

130 North American Aerospace Defense Command, Rick Findlay Official Photo, NORAD.

131 Department of National Defence, April 30, 2023, https://forces.ca/en/careers.
Photo courtesy of Rick Findley.

132 North Atlantic Treaty Organization, NATO Photos, b050616ag.

133 Department of National Defence, April 30, 2023, https://forces.ca/en/careers.
Department of National Defence, MoonTNC85-749-1.

134 Photo courtesy of David Fraser.

135 Department of National Defence, Sergeant Roxanne Clowe, IS2006-1139.
Department of National Defence, April 30, 2023, https://forces.ca/en/careers.

136 Department of National Defence, Sergeant Craig Fiander, AR2007-A106-0259.

137 Department of National Defence, Sergeant Matthew McGregor, IS2011-1023-15.

138 Department of National Defence, 450 Squadron.
Michael Hood, Major-General Scott Clancy.

139 Department of National Defence, Sergeant Matthew McGregor, IS2011-1023-03.

140 Department of National Defence, Master Corporal Matthew McGregor, Image Tech, JTFK Afghanistan, Roto 8, AR2009-0055-01.

141 Department of National Defence, Corporal Tina Gillies, Image Tech, Roto 10, Task Force Kandahar, Afghanistan, AR2011-0225-004.

142 Department of National Defence, 8 Wing Imaging, Corporal Gayle Wilson, Private Kimberly Gosse, Tn2004-0592-04a.
Department of National Defence, 8 Wing Imagery, Corporal Bill Parrott, TN2003-0781-01a.

143 Department of National Defence, KW03-2016-0066-001.

144 Department of National Defence, 429 Squadron.
Department of National Defence, Master Corporall Marc-Andre Gaudreault, IS2011-6008-03.

145 Department of National Defence, Corporal Dan Strohan, 8 Wing Imaging, TN09-2015-0302-0011.

146 Department of National Defence, Corporal Ken Beliwicz, 146-448-RCAF-Mali-TM01-2018-0038-006-RCAF Photo-PM3.

147 Department of National Defence, Warrant Officer Johnson Vic, Kiowa-136234-RCAF-444 Sqn-ISC87-449-RCAF Photo.
Department of National Defence, April 30, 2023, https://forces.ca/en/careers.

148 Department of National Defence, 409 Squadron.
Department of National Defence, Corporal Eric Chaput, 20220804AF0295D020.

149 Department of National Defence, Sergeant Daren Kraus, RP14-2017-0050-06.
Department of National Defence, Sergeant Daren Kraus, October 19, 2017, RP14-2017-0083-03.
Courtesy of Tom Jenkins.

150 Department of National Defence, Aviator Randy Bross, 8 Wing Imaging, 20221027TNR0557D094.

153 Department of National Defence, Master Corporal France Morin, Imagery Section St-Jean, SJ2011-155-207.

154 University of Calgary Digital Collections, na-1258-10.

155 Department of National Defence, Corporal Gary Calvé, Imagery Technician ATF–Iceland, RP09-2017-0019-001.
University of Calgary Digital Collections, na-1821-2.
University of Calgary Digital

Collections, na-1258-101.

156 Department of National Defence, 60f72ef534f7530f-39be6e0f_para-rescue-4-w. Department of National Defence, PL130186.

157 National Research Council of Canada, Record Identifier 5b5d5920-29fe-45c0-b096-843ca5e8d932.

158 Department of National Defence, Master Corporal Pat Blanchard, IS03-2016-0036-004. Department of National Defence, cf-school-of-search-and-rescue-600.

159 Department of National Defence, 4 Wing Imaging, Corporal Bob Mellin, CK2006-0152-04.

160 Photo courtesy of Derek Mickeloff.

161 Department of National Defence, COSPAS-SARSAT logo v2 3D. Department of National Defence, Sergeant Blair Mehan, ET2007-0233-25.

162 Department of National Defence, Master Corporal Johanie Maheu, 14 Wing Imaging Greenwood, GD2016-0075-31.

163 Department of National Defence, Corporal Rod Doucet, 8 Wing Imaging, TN05-2016-0270-002.

164 Department of National Defence, April 30, 2023, https://forces.ca/en/careers. Department of National Defence, Corporal Penney,

REC00-146-3A.

165 Department of National Defence, Sergeant Paz Quillé, FA02-2016-0015-24.

166 Department of National Defence, 442 Squadron. Department of National Defence, Corporal Parker Salustro, 20211115CXB0303D005.

167 Department of National Defence, Corporal Parker Salustro, 20211115CXB0303D021. Department of National Defence, Corporal Parker Salustro, 20211115CXB0303D033. Department of National Defence, April 30, 2023, https://forces.ca/en/careers.

168 Department of National Defence, MDA Sapphire 2.

170 Department of National Defence, Corporal Pierre Habib, 3 Wing Bagotville, BN2011-0028-30.

172 Rideau Hall, Sergeant Johanie Maheu, GG05-2017-0309-016.

173 Department of National Defence, Royal Canadian Air Force.

174 Photo courtesy of Captain Chris Swartz.

175 Department of National Defence, April 30, 2023, https://forces.ca/en/careers. Photo of Chris Swartz. Courtesy of the Naval Aviation Warfighting Development Center.

176 Lockheed Martin, Angel

DelCueto, FP20-12486-0184_PR.

177 Department of National Defence, Corporal Danielle Bernier, 4 Wing Cold Lake, ckd99-2034-05.

178 Department of National Defence, CF67-167-7. Department of National Defence, Master Corporal Robert Bottrill, April 23, 2009, IS2009-0395.

179 Department of National Defence via James Craik, Sky Lancers, 1955. Department of National Defence, Spellmeier, WG 67-104-3.

180 Department of National Defence, DGPA/J5PA Sergeant Dennis J. Mah, IS2002-6413a-431. Department of National Defence, Tutor-26050, Kaehler, April 24, 2018.

181 Department of National Defence, Master Seaman Roxanne Wood, CX04-2017-0135-078.

182 Joint Base Elmendorf Richards, 201016-F-XX000-1001.

183 Department of National Defence, April 30, 2023, https://forces.ca/en/careers. Department of National Defence, Corporal Bryan Carter, 4 Wing Imaging, CK04-2018-0922-105.

184 Department of National Defence, April 30, 2023, https://forces.ca/en/careers. Department of National Defence, Corporal Elena

Vlassova, 4 Wing Imaging Services, CK2014-1279-C002.

185 Department of National Defence, REC70-789.

186 Department of National Defence, Corporal Braden Trudeau, 20220409RPAO0200D001. Department of National Defence, Master Seaman Dan Bard, IS14-2019-0002-168.

187 Department of National Defence, Corporal Braden Trudeau, 20220404RPAO0200D011.

188 NASA/CSA, Robert Markowitz, NASA Johnson Space Center.

189 Canadian Space Agency. NASA. NASA/Chris Hadfield.

190 Department of National Defence, 3 Canadian Space Division logo. Department of National Defence, Sailor First Class Alexandra Proulx, 3 Canadian Space Division.

191 NASA, Josh Valcarcel, March 30, 2023, Artemis II Crew.

192 Department of National Defence, via Brian Rainville. Canadian War Museum 20080098-009.

193 Department of National Defence, Corporal Jean-Roch Chabot, RE03-2017-0230-017.

194 Department of National Defence.

195 Department of National Defence, 440 Squadron. Department of National Defence, April 30, 2023,

https://forces.ca/en/careers. Department of National Defence, Master Corporal Charles A. Stephen, 20200422YKA0021D001.

196 Russell Lockheed Martin, Darin Russell, April 1, 2016, 16J00158_10.

199 Department of National Defence, PL-523.

200 Department of National Defence, via James Craik, PL-15055.
Department of National Defence, PC-81-adj.

201 Department of National Defence, Corporal David Hardwick, TN2007-0745-02.

202 Department of National Defence, Corporal Manuela Berger, 4 Wing Imaging, ck01-2016-0428-031.
Department of National Defence, Master Corporal Gabrielle DesRochers, Canadian Forces Combat Camera, July 18, 2017, is09-2017-0014-037.

203 NASA, April 10, 2016.
Department of National Defence, Seargent Paz Quillé, FA2013-3000-05.

204 Photo courtesy of Michael Hood.

205 Department of National Defence, PL-122793.

206 Department of National Defence, SU14-2018-1330-001. Via RCAF Foundation.

207 Photo courtesy of Richard Rohmer.
Beata May, February 2, 2012.

This work is licensed under the CC BY-SA 3.0 Licence.

208 Department of National Defence, PL-129446.
Photo courtesy of Salina Larocque, Cultural Development Coordinator, City of Windsor.

209 Department of National Defence, Sergeant Kev Parle, BM2010-2022-50.
Colin Cameron, Edinburgh, Scotland, September 22, 2008, Floriana War Memorial.

210 Royal Canadian Legion Branch 447, Warrant Officer II Pilot Leslie Gordon Sutherland.

211 Department of National Defence, Master Corporal Desiree Bourdon, January 31, 2023, 20230130ISF0001D011.

212 Department of National Defence, Corporal Ken Beliwicz, August 25, 2018, TM01-2018-0057-076.

216 Department of National Defence, PL-995.
Department of National Defence, PL-911.

217 Nelson Museum, Nelson, British Columbia, RHG 1.
Department of National Defence, PL-996.
Department of National Defence, PL 30823.

218 Department of National Defence, September 7, 1945, PL-37038.
Department of National Defence, October 30, 1946, PL-38261.

226 Department of National

Defence, Corporal Braden Trudeau, 20220213RPAO0200D032.

232 Department of National Defence, Corporal David Veldman, Formation Imaging Services, September 11, 2019, HS33-2019-0679-104.

240 Department of National Defence, Leading Seaman Erica Seymour, 4 Wing Imaging, November 7, 2019, RP26-2019-0024-013.

INDEX

34–35, 36, 38, 42; Supermarine Stranraer, 53; Spitfire, 25, 49; Syd "Cyclops" Burrows, 64; Willard John Bolduc, 50

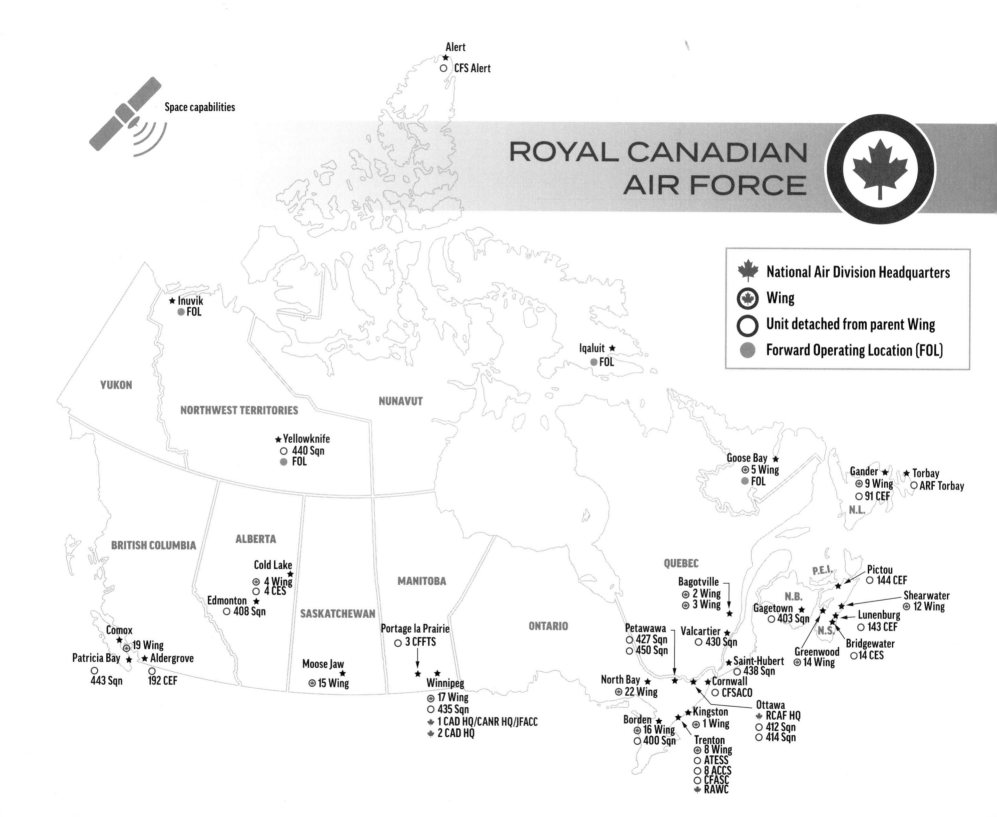

Space capabilities

ROYAL CANADIAN AIR FORCE

Alert
○ CFS Alert

National Air Division Headquarters

Wing

Unit detached from parent Wing

Forward Operating Location (FOL)

★ Inuvik
● FOL

YUKON

NORTHWEST TERRITORIES

NUNAVUT

★ Iqaluit
● FOL

★ Yellowknife
○ 440 Sqn
● FOL

Goose Bay ★
⊕ 5 Wing
● FOL

Gander ★   ★ Torbay
⊕ 9 Wing   ○ ARF Torbay
○ 91 CEF

N.L.

BRITISH COLUMBIA

ALBERTA

Cold Lake ★
⊕ 4 Wing
○ 4 CES

Edmonton ★
○ 408 Sqn

SASKATCHEWAN

MANITOBA

Portage la Prairie ★
○ 3 CFFTS

ONTARIO

QUEBEC

P.E.I.   Pictou ★
○ 144 CEF

Bagotville ★
⊕ 2 Wing
⊕ 3 Wing ★

N.B.   ★ Shearwater
Gagetown ★   ⊕ 12 Wing
○ 403 Sqn   ★ Lunenburg
N.S.   ○ 143 CEF
Greenwood ★ Bridgewater ★
⊕ 14 Wing   ○ 14 CES

Comox ★
⊕ 19 Wing
Patricia Bay ★ ★ Aldergrove
○   ○
443 Sqn   192 CEF

Moose Jaw ★
⊕ 15 Wing

Winnipeg ★ ★
⊕ 17 Wing
○ 435 Sqn
✿ 1 CAD HQ/CANR HQ/JFACC
✿ 2 CAD HQ

Petawawa ★
○ 427 Sqn
○ 450 Sqn

Valcartier ★
○ 430 Sqn

Saint-Hubert ★
○ 438 Sqn

North Bay ★
⊕ 22 Wing   Cornwall ★
○ CFSACO

Kingston ★   Ottawa
✿ 1 Wing   ✿ RCAF HQ
                ○ 412 Sqn
Borden ★   ○ 414 Sqn
⊕ 16 Wing
○ 400 Sqn   Trenton ★
            ⊕ 8 Wing
            ○ ATESS
            ○ 8 ACCS
            ○ CFASC
            ✿ RAWC